ॐ

LORD GANESHA

by
Sadguru Sant Keshavadas

To Karlene,
Thought you'd like to know more about this special friend.
B.

© 1988 by Sadguru Sant Keshavadas

All rights reserved.
No part of this book may be
used or reproduced
in any manner whatsoever
without the written
permission of the author.

Published by

VISHWA DHARMA PUBLICATIONS
174 Santa Clara Avenue
Oakland, California 94610 USA

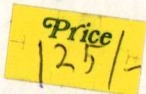

Printed in India
Sri Sudhindra Printing Press
Bangalore 560 003

Sadguru Sant Keshavadas is a prophet of divine love and universal peace. His name means "saint who is the servant of the Lord."

Sri Sadguru was born in 1934 in Bhadragiri, a small South Indian village near Bangalore in Karnataka State. He earned a B.A. degree from Mahatma Gandhi College and an LL. B. degree from Udipi Law College. He is a gifted composer, musician, lecturer, author and teacher of yoga.

Through the ancient wisdom of the Himalayas, he tries to unite all the world religions into Vishwa Dharma, or Cosmic Religion. In his mission to show the essential unity of all world religions, Sant Keshavadas has made twenty-eight global tours. His devoted wife, Srimathi Rama Mata, and their three children assist in this mission.

In 1961, Sant Keshavadas established Dasashram International Center in Bangalore, South India. In 1976, he established Keshavashrama in Uttarakashi, Himalayas, in 1982 Vishwa Shanti Ashram near Bangalore and has established many other ashrams, meditation centers and Temples of Cosmic Religion around the world.

Truth is one, many are the names

— Sadguru Sant Keshavadas

Dedication

I offer my prayers to Lord Ganesha to shower the choicest cup of blessings upon the donors for the printing of this holy book, **Smt. Indira Dayabhai Champaneri,** who offered this *seva* in memory of her late husband.

Sri Dayabhai Kalyanbhai Champaneri

LORD GANESHA

Meditation on Lord Ganesha

I meditate on Lord Ganesha, whose body is of the color of vermilion, who has a large stomach and three eyes, displaying in His four hands a noose and goad, the conch, and the gesture of benediction.

I meditate on the great trunk of Ganesha, symbolizing the mystical syllable "OM," which is holding a bowl containing food, the symbol of plenty. His forehead shines with the crescent moon. The elephant-headed god is adorned with serpents. His cheeks are red; His dress is red and His celestial body is smeared with sandalwood paste and other perfumes.

MUSHIKAVAAHANA MODAKA
CHAAMARA KARNA VILAMBITA SUTRA
VAAMANA RUPA MAHESHWARA PUTRA
VIGHNA VINAAYAKA PAADA NAMASTAE

O remover of obstacles, Almighty Lord Vinaayaka! Riding on a mouse, holding sweet pudding in Your hand, with wide, fanning ears and huge elephant trunk, You are short in stature and shine brightly. O son of Lord Shiva, salutations unto Thee!

Foreword

Ganesha, philosophically, means the word OM. OM is the omnipotent, omnipresent, omniscient Lord. Ganesha, the symbol of OM, is the god of wisdom and prudence. His elephant head is an emblem of sagacity. His vehicle, the mouse, is the symbol of the tamed, or sattwic ego, the power of which is knowledge and foresight.

At the outset of any endeavor, He is to be worshipped first for the removal of all obstacles and for protection. The Upanishads emphasize the significance of the mantra, OM GAM GANAPATAYAE NAMAHA to ward off all evil. Prosperity, and the attainment of supernatural and healing powers are only some of the blessings bestowed by Lord Ganesha. Among Hindus in India and around the world, there is no home, shop, temple, village, or place where He is not addressed and worshipped. His festivals are unequalled and universal throughout India and wherever Indians dwell. The images of Ganesha of varying kinds are seen in Bangkok, Cambodia, Tibet, Nepal, Sri Lanka, West Indies, and in several American museums. The Western people understand that Ganesha brings them good luck. Ganapati Atharva-Sheersha, the famous hymn on Ganesha, is read by the wise almost every day in India and elsewhere.

Among the limitless stories and hymns of Lord Ganesha, I was able to present only an infinitesimal part in this book which is really a holy book or scripture. If one reads it being duly purified through bathing and meditation, one will get the benefit of Ganesha realization which is cosmic consciousness. The devotee will attain the unattainable and all his works will be crowned with success.

I offer my special prayers to God to bless our dear Sister Vandana who worked tirelessly in completing and editing this holy manuscript. I say the blessings to my dear wife Rama Mata for assisting in my work. My special blessings to Srinivasa and Veena (Ed and Elisabeth Seabrook) for inspiring me to write this book by helping me in every way.

May Lord Ganesha bless all of you.

OM and Prem,
Sant Keshavadas

LORD GANESHA

Death separates the soul from the body, but if the ego and desires are not erased completely before that separation, then the soul revolves again in the whirligig of *samsara* (the round of rebirth). Just as a burnt seed will not sprout again, when the seeds of ignorance and karma are burnt by the fire of wisdom, the soul will not take birth again in this world. It attains *mukti* (liberation).

It is attachment to the body, property, wealth, spouse, children, fame and name which makes everyone restless and peaceless. We eat for strength to work; we work to get the food—a vicious circle. Like a worm that is swept away by a current, tries to escape from it, but is taken away by another wave in the ocean, similarly our ego, caught in the currents of desire, is swept away by many more desires.

Self-inquiry is the most important discipline to get rid of the ego and selfish desires. Question thus: "Who am I? Am I this body that constantly changes and undergoes pain, hunger, thirst, sickness and finally, death? Am I this mind that constantly changes and is confused? Am I this ego that creates conflict, duality and is very possessive? Why am I here? Should I go through all this? Is there a way out of this through which prophets and saints have reached the Truth?"

If you analyze the pain of life, sickness, old age, fear, jealousy, birth/death cycle and the untold agonies of death, the torments of hell and the astral worlds, etc., you would immediately declare, "I must find the way and attain the Truth in this very life!" With the aid of saints and the grace of God, you begin your self-inquiry, a serious search—a deep meditation—dissolving the ego in *Atman* or the great Self. Then one attains "Self-realization."

Sometimes, we forget we are *Atman*, the great Self, and by the power of the old habits of the ego, we again and again fall into illusions of *maya*. Then the Guru reminds us that we are "Atman" and by repeated strong suggestions and meditation on OM, we eventually get settled in Truth and realize the great Self.

For even as the butter is hidden in the milk and through proper processing of the milk you get butter, likewise, the Truth is hidden in your soul. Through the disciplines of initiation, listening, reflecting and meditating on the Truth with the help of the Guru, you are able to attain Self-realization and enjoy eternal peace and immortal bliss. At that very moment, the bondage of karma gets destroyed and the soul attains *jeevan mukti* (liberated state while living in the body).

Even as one light kindles millions of candles, similarly the Light of Guru kindles millions of minds. If all those who have the light kindle the light in the minds of the rest of humanity, there will be no darkness of ignorance. There will be only THE LIGHT. This Light of Wisdom brings freedom and knowledge of God—the panacea for all grief. It is only then that the entire world will be filled with peace.

Preface

It is an honor to say a few words on behalf of Sant Keshavadas and about his new book on Lord Ganesha. We all know the joy that Sant Keshavadas brings to the world through his skill at the unique Hindu art of katha-kirtana. His spirit of love and selfless service uplifts and brings a positive spiritual influence upon the youth of our day, the future leaders of this planet.

Within the family of religions which we call Hinduism, Sant Keshavadas stands as an exemplar of the Madhva Vaishnava Sampradaya having personally chosen Lord Vishnu as his Ishta Devata. This work on Lord Ganesha is a valuable contribution to the contemporary literature of the Smartas, Vaishnavas, Shaaktas, Shaivites and Gaanapatyas—in general, all Hindus—and will be especially useful to followers of Smarta tradition. The Smarta Sampradaya has been propagated outside of India primarily through its philosophy of Advaita Vedanta. This work serves to also introduce English-reading non-Hindus to the religious perspective, mythology and puranic theism of this sect of Hinduism.

Especially valuable in this work is the section on Ganesha puja. In ancient times, the Smartas adopted the Agamic puja as their pattern of worship. The Agamic puja is the heart of ritual life and a preeminent well-spring of spiritual inspiration for all Hindus. But it has not been well understood in the western world. Sant Keshavadas carefully delineates a Vaishnavite Ganesha puja, with translation of the mantras into English and a description of all the kriyas (actions) of the ritual. Readers will imbibe a fine feeling of the meaning behind puja. Smartas and Vaishnavas who wish to perform Ganesha puja will be able to use this section as an actual manual for performance.

It is a joy to see our beloved Lord Ganesha brought to the foreground. This great inner plane being, invoked first by Hindus of all sects before beginning any worship or task, to Him we pray for protection, opening of doors, and wisdom. May He send His blessings to all who read this work. Jai Ganesha!

His Holiness Sivaya Subramuniyaswami

LORD GANESHA

Table of Contents

Introduction 1

Part I—Philosophy 8

Part II—Mysticism 24

Part III—Mythology 39

Sri Ganesha Puja 91

Sri Ganesha Sahasranaamavali 133

Introduction

OM GAM GANAPATAYAE NAMAHA

With this prayer, may all your works be attended with victory and success.

Lord Ganesha is the most fascinating, widely known aspect of God. Ganesha is the "Son of God," or that which you call Christ in another story. He is the ocean of wisdom (*vidya vaaridhi*). He blesses us with illumined intellect (*buddhi*). He is the bestower of supernatural powers (*siddhi*). He is the embodiment of all sacred blessings (*mangala murthi*). He is all-pervading spirit, all-powerful and radiant like millions of suns. Children worship Ganesha for success in their education. People pray to Lord Ganesha for the blessings of creative intelligence, success in their business and in their lives.

In all world religions, the Trinity is represented through A-U-M. AH-OO-MM, or OM. It is the beginning, middle and end of all languages. That OM is Ganesha. He is the son of Shiva, one among the Hindu Trinity of Vishnu, Brahma and Shiva, or the Father, the Son, and the Spirit.

Because the Self is invisible and cannot be seen by the two fleshy eyes, we require our third eye (located at a point between the eyebrows) to see Him. During *samadhi* (an experience of transcendental consciousness), the third eye (*ajna c'hakra*), opens, and in a mystic vision sees the Atman. Thus, it is through seeing a reflection of your Self that the Truth is realized. There are only four 'mirrors' (*darpana*) which are capable of reflecting that Truth. Guru (*Gurudarpana*) is one of them, and is a 'living mirror.' *Murtis*, or the symbols of God, are another 'mirror' (*murtidarpana*). The universe (*vishwadarpana*) is the third mirror. Finally, discrimination (*vivekadarpana*) is the fourth mirror.

The erroneous idea of 'idol worship' comes from the use of many symbols. It may confuse you that Ganesha (the symbol of the Word of God) is God, that Tara (cosmic energy) is God, that Guru (the symbol of the light of God) is God, or that Panduranga (Vishnu) is God. All are different names of the same God giving you several mirrors in which your Self is reflected. This is similar to keeping mirrors on both sides and behind you so that you can see from the back, front, sides and everywhere; the reflection will be *ad infinitum*. But all of them are for the same purpose and that is to reflect the Self. *Viveka*, the mirror of the light of discrimination, is the best of the four mirrors. That is what, in an initiation, the guru gives you by transmitting the energy—a mirror which will always be with you.

Though we try to use lesser tools like the lower mind and the egotistic, extroverted intellect to realize the Self, the data collected through those instruments is always confusing. Let me say plainly to you, you cannot realize God through the extroverted mind or intellect. But there is another faculty given to man by God—intuition—which alone enables you to see or realize the Reality.

The moment the mind or the intellect goes inward through meditation, all external noise, duality, negativity and sounds are stilled. During the inward journey, the intellect gets introverted. It is through this introspection or contemplation that the intuitive light of the Self (*Atman*) reveals the Truth within. Just like the sun is revealed in sunlight, the great Self or God

LORD GANESHA

within you is revealed in His own Light. You cannot borrow any other light to see that. God Himself is the Light of all the lights.

The purpose of prayer, *puja* (worship services), *satsang* (company of the Masters), *yoga*, breathing exercises, and mainly *mantra japa* (repetition of the Holy Names of God) is to still the mind and make it sojourn inward. You are most successful on this journey in meditations guided by realized Teachers. Then easily, effortlessly, joyfully, your mind spontaneously soars high.

In Sanskrit language, "*man*" means mind; "*tra*" means that which takes you beyond the mind. The vibration of the mantra removes all worries from the mind and gives you peace. It has the power to calm your emotions. It has the power, mystically, to heal within and without. Mantra reveals to you the will of God. It is the Holy Name of God, the Word of God—Ganesha. When the introverted intellect is made transparent by stilling the thoughts in meditation with the aid of mantra, the light of the *Atman*, the Self, the Truth, is revealed to you.

That most mysterious truth, which is in every one of us, also takes form. As an illustration, electricity has no color or form but it has the potential for both. When it manifests through the colored bulb, it assumes the form of colored light. Similarly, the coloring of our mind which occurs by repeating mantra gives us the experience of several kinds of angels and archangels; the coloring of our mind which occurs by repeating negative thoughts appears as devils, *rakshasas*, *asuras* (various types of demons) and the dark powers of Satan.

Man's mind is a bundle of thoughts, a complex mixture of three *gunas* (qualities of Nature). When the mind is predominantly influenced by *tamo guna*, then you become inactive and lazy or actively sinful. When it is predominantly influenced by *rajo guna*, you are passionately active. When, by the power of mantra, your mind is rid of *tamas* and *rajas*, the darkness and the duality, you have the poise and serenity of *sattva guna* (poise or quiescence). In that state, the highest truth will reveal itself to you. And as long as you are in *sattva guna*, you are definitely very near to Truth.

All of you should feel that you are the sparks of the Divine because you know that you have come from God. The Divine is in everyone, so each soul is potentially divine. There is no way that you could be so bad as to be damned in hell forever. You can do bad only up to your limit, your capacity. Reaching that, you will have to do good because there is no more bad to do. And that is why, finally, you have to come back to the path. Swami Vivekananda used to encourage people by saying, 'If you cannot do good, at least do something bad. Because when you do bad, you'll get pricks and kicks by the laws of karma which will make you behave. And then you'll come back on the straight road.'

Our ego is like a big pig which wants to wallow constantly in the mire. It wants to wallow in gratification of itself, in what is called 'creature comforts.' That tendency is in every one of us. We have flesh, we have ego, and we also have a beautiful transcendental heaven inside us. The struggle or the fight between the flesh and the spirit is life. The more you lead your life in ego, the more miserable you will be. The more you lead the life in spirit, the happier you will be. Everyone wants to be happy because it is their birthright. But no one is happy until he dwells in the true Self. At all other times, there is the misery and pain of duality.

Introduction

We learn our lessons slowly. Nature is like a book and each life which is given to us is just like a page. Once you took a Hindu body, and then you turned a page and took a Christian or a Jewish body, and then you turned another page and took a Muslim or a Sikh body. Finally you realize that you are holding the same book and merely turning pages. Every day is also like that, a turning of a page. Every day again there is hope. Is it not good news? No matter how much sin you do, no matter how much karma you do, your soul, eventually, cannot become anything else other than God-conscious. Because it has come from God, it has to return to God. Some will go by walking, perhaps, and some by bullock cart, some by cars, and some by plane as per their capacity—eventually all will reach God.

God is not in a hurry. You can go by whichever path you want—the choice is yours. The law of karma is definitely going to teach all of us. Still, there is no way that we can escape God because we are all inside His belly. Even with all of our airplanes, armaments and fights, we are still like the teeny, little worms inside the fruits of the banyan tree. Compared to the greatness and all-pervasive Truth of God, our bodies and our movements are like those little creatures. But soul shall some day arise by the word of the Guru, or mantra initiation.

That is what is known as 'born in spirit.' The rebirth takes place right here. Again we might make mistakes, but again there is a possibility of getting up. A parable will make the point clearer. Once a upon a time, Indra, the head of the angels, wondered about human birth. He couldn't understand why people are unhappy when they have been given the human body to realize God. Even *devas* (gods) wish to have a human body through which they can attain *moksha* (liberation).

Indra thought, "Why don't human beings, though in an animal body, meditate, realize the truth and become happy forever? And how shall I know the reason unless I, myself, become a creature on this planet earth?" So he told his secretary, "Look! I see a dead pig body. My spirit is going to enter into that. I want to experience why, in an animal body, they are not able to realize the truth. But I want you to promise me something. Suppose I forget that I am head of the angels while I'm in that animal body. I request you to hold a weapon and kill me so that I leave the pig body and realize who I was."

Indra's secretary promised to do that. Immediately, Indra left his divine body and entered into the body of that animal. The moment he entered it, he completely forgot that he was Indra, the head of the angels. He became one with the idea that 'I am a pig.' He took a mate and had lots of kids. With his big family he was very, very happy rolling and wallowing in the mire and filth which is heaven for a pig!

Indra's secretary came with his weapon, as promised, and said, "I am going to kill you and release you from this. You are Indra!"

The pig said, "Sheer nonsense! I am not Indra! Get out of here!"

The secretary reminded him, "Look, you are the head of the first heaven!"

But the pig, instead of quitting the mudhole, extended an invitation to the secretary. "Come and wallow here. Then you will know what is heaven and what is not. This is heaven! This is wonderful. Look! See how my kids and my mate and myself enjoy!" No matter how much the secretary tried, he couldn't convince the pig of his true identity.

LORD GANESHA

This is a great story. It has so much meaning in our own lives as well as the entire creation—why we have forgotten and why we think that this is everything.

Well, fortunately, the secretary released Indra from that pig body. Fortunately, because as long as he was there, true awareness was not coming to him. It is only by killing that pig, which means our ego, that awareness comes. When Indra was released, he asked his secretary, "While I was in that body of the pig, tell me, what did I do?" When he heard the news, he was miserable. Now he understood why the spirit in human beings in an animal body—until their ego is destroyed by the guru with the weapon of mantra—is not released to realize its beauty, absolute existence, peace and bliss.

All mantras are like weapons. Mantras will humble the ego and destroy the tamasic and rajasic *gunas*. Just a tamed, tranquil, sattvic ego for the maintenance of the world order will be with you. With that, you are able to reflect your Self in a tranquil mind. So the purpose of *pujas* and mantras are all to achieve that tranquility, equanimity and purification.

If the mind is all right, everything will be all right. Mind is the cause of bondage, and mind is the cause of freedom, as well. Mind, when it is filled with ego . . . oh! You need not go to another hell. It is right here! And mind, when it is filled with the delight of that sattvic tranquility . . . oh! You need not go to another heaven or kingdom, it is heaven here! That is, the selfish mind, filled with ego, is the cause of bondage and the birth-death cycle. And the mind that is free from selfishness is *moksha* (freedom) or heaven, right here. Everything—hell and heaven—are inside you. And when you depart from this body, whatever is inside in your mind is what you take elsewhere.

So, to tame the mind is all about *yoga* and to silence the mind is all about meditation. The truth always shines. It is the selfish mind which is the cloud. To purify the mind, bathe the mind during meditation. Inhale OM, hold OM, exhale OM. Then the Word alone will manifest for you everywhere. You will not need to search for words for the Word will speak through you and sing through you. Everything is possible to the Word because the Word of God is the highest miracle. The word of God is OM and OM is Lord Ganesha.

The limitless powers of that Truth within you, when they are deified, are called the three hundred thirty million gods, angels, and archangels. But do not forget the fundamental philosophy in all religions and experience is that there is only one God. In the same manner that one electricity manifests through all the different kinds and colors of bulbs as per necessity, there is only one God manifesting through all the various forms we see. Therefore, when we speak of God, or the Son of God, or the Holy Spirit, it still doesn't mean three offices. Gabriel and the archangels and the various names and descriptions which you find in the Hindu, Christian, Moslem, and Buddhist scriptures, etc., are not referring to a different God. That Self, the Truth, is explained in every religion through various myths and symbols. But the foundation is that Truth is One, no matter how many Names by which it is called.

There is no one in the whole world who has not heard of the word OM because when you open your mouth, it is "AH"; when you modify it, it is "OO"; when you lock your lips, it is "MM." In every breath, it is going on. Every child comes with the cry of OM. All languages of this world and the other are included in that monosyllabic OM which is written in Sanskrit like number '3' in English.

Introduction

That number 3 is all three dimensions—the nether (*patala*), the middle (*martya*), and the above (*swarga*). It is also the physical, the astral (subtle), and the causal bodies. (Beyond the astral is the causal body, the cause of birth and death where the latencies called the *vasanas* are stored. When the causal body disappears by the knowledge of Truth, then you will have no more births or deaths.) The 3 represents the wakeful, the dream, the deep sleep states of consciousness and beyond. Everything that is triad—Vishnu, Brahma, Shiva, the Father, the Son, and the Spirit—everything that is triune is included in that three. The nasal sound which continues after singing OM—the MMMMM—is represented by the tail. Beyond the physical, subtle and causal, beyond the nether, middle and the above, beyond the wakeful, dream and the deep sleep states, is the transcendental sound called the *nada*.

Also in that symbol, there is the crescent moon-like mark representing the *kala*, the aura. As much light as you are able to reflect in the transparent mind, so much will be the divine aura surrounding you. All those blessings of forgiveness, kindness, compassion, healing powers, creativity, writing capacities, and singing capacities are *kala*. When you speak it is wisdom; you are at peace in the midst of intense activity—all that and more are called *kala*. *Kalaas* are just like the digits of the crescent moon expanding into full moon.

Lord Shiva wears the crescent moon in the forehead. All of us have a moon *chakra* in the forehead. During singing or listening to the stories of God, the sixteen-petalled lotus called the *soma chakra* blossoms causing nectar to drip in our saliva. At those times, we feel very happy in the temple of God, the church of God, or in *satsanga*, or the yoga center or wherever saints dwell and the divine discussion takes place. Then a separate kind of taste is there.

During that time, the alpha and the theta waves manifest in a clockwise circuit in the brain. When the union of Shakti and Shiva in the crown *chakra* takes place, the result is *sat* (the existence or truth) and *chit*, (the consciousness) coming together. The result is the birth of Christ, the birth of Rama, the birth of Buddha consciousness, the birth of *ananda* (bliss). That really happens in our body daily while attending *satsanga*, listening to or reading the Holy Bible, Bhagavad Gita, Koran, Ramayana, or whatever divine scriptures are appropriate as per the background to which you belong. Any holy word of God in any language, in any country, produces the same result. People drink and taste the divine nectar. It is an immediate experience. As you sit and sing the Holy Name, it comes to you. Your physical, mental, and spiritual health improves. Intuitive powers manifest in you.

The final dot, the point in OM as written in Sanskrit, represents the source from which everything comes and that point is called *bindu*..

So what is OM? OM is the Word of God. As the Bible teaches, "In the beginning was the Word, and the Word was with God, and the Word was God" (John 1:1). OM is God, the Word, unmanifested. When He manifests, He is OM GAM, the manifested Word. In Sanskrit, God the manifested Word is called Ganesha which is a combination of two words, '*gana*' and '*esha*.' *Gana* means groups or entities, i.e., species—human species, divine species, animal species, every kind of *gana* not only on this planet earth, but in every *loka* (dimension, sphere, region). *Esha* means the Lord. So Ganesha means the word of God, OM, is Lord of all universes and species.

In OM, everything is. Everything is OM. Therefore, everything is the Word of God; everything is Ganesha. All of us are *ganas*. We are *janaganas*, which means human beings.

LORD GANESHA

There are *devaganas*, the divine beings. There are *Shivaganas*, the attendants on Lord Shiva. There are *pitraganas*, the ancestral *ganas* or species.

For all these species, there is one Lord Ganesha. He gives three important powers for daily activity—*vidya*, *buddhi* and *siddhi*. *Vidya* is also called *riddhi*, which is eternal wisdom. *Buddhi* is that illumined intellect whereby your mind is so alert that in your work you are able to see everything by the power of that illumination. And *siddhi* is the attainment not only of supernatural powers but also spiritual fulfillment.

Do you know what the highest *siddhi* is? It is when you are able to conquer your anger. It is when you are able to control your tongue and senses. *Siddhi* is not just being able to materialize a wristwatch, although that is possible. Materializing anything you can purchase is not the proper use of *siddhi*. *Siddhi* is when speaking one word, men and women of temper give up or become very slow to anger, understanding the inherent dangers. That is *siddhi*. Anything which you have not attained, when the Guru says a blessing, and you get it, that is *siddhi*. Everything above and below, that which is inexplicable, that which is not available in any book, is visible to the third eye of the teacher. When, by his words, he brings and connects to your soul the remembrance of all those *lokas* in which you were before—as if they were an apple in your hand—that is called *vak siddhi*.

But you can get *siddhi* in any endeavor. For instance, driving your car, you'll be playing the cassette, rocking and rolling, yet the brakes are under control and everything is automatic. You have driving *siddhi*. A man can dig deep in the earth and sit for forty-eight days without breathing, eating or drinking. These are great psychic powers, of course—physical control of the breath, etc.—but still, these are not spiritual attainments. The highest attainment is when you do not have desire for anything other than the Truth. That is the highest of all the *siddhis*. Then all the *siddhis* roll at your feet. When you go beyond them, all powers will follow you automatically.

When Satan was tempting Jesus to exhibit the *siddhis*, Christ said, ". . . thou shalt not tempt the Lord thy God . . . . Get thee hence, Satan: for it is written, thou shalt worship the Lord thy God, and Him only shalt thou serve" (Matthew 4:7, 10). Though Jesus and many Masters have used the *siddhis* for the service of mankind, it was not for a demonstration, nor for fame and name, but for a gentle healing to someone, or to protect someone. It is then that the *siddhis* properly are and should be used.

In short, if you know OM, you know everything. If you know the Word of God, you will know the will of God. Then you become one with Him. When Christ came, he said, 'I want to make all of you the sons and daughters of God.' That sonship is waiting for us the moment we recognize the Father in us. And in the final stage, the Son becomes the Father, soul becomes God. That is the meaning of telling the Son and the Father are one and the same. The Word and God are one and the same.

The simplest technique for Self-realization is to engage your body, mind, heart and soul in a forty-day (ten to fifteen minutes each day) *sadhana* (spiritual discipline) of inhaling OM, holding OM, and exhaling OM. Then the noise of a car, the noise of an airplane and everything else will be one sonorous sound of OM all over. You will experience that. Along with that, you will experience new creativity, divine poetry and dance. You will feel so light, and such delight

Introduction

will manifest in you. You will know and remember your Self. Forgetfulness is *maya* (delusive ignorance) and remembrance is knowledge. That is awareness. Such awareness is possible by the power of the mantra.

Part I– Philosophy

God, the One without a second, is called *Ekam Evam Advidyam Brahma* (there is nothing else besides the Truth or God). The same thing is said in the Bible, the *Vedas*, the Koran and every major scripture. There is no God besides God. When it came to the human level, though, people couldn't understand God unless they named Him. So they named Him, then began quarreling over it, a practice which continues to this day. My name for God is 'Allah,' your name is 'Rama,' her name is 'Christ,' fourth's is 'Heavenly Father.' It is all human language; each group gave a name to God because it couldn't understand without affixing a name and giving 'Him' a form.

In the *Vedas*, that all-pervading Truth is called Vishnu. Vishnu is not the name of a person; it is the name representing a principle—"all-pervading." When Jesus said 'my Heavenly Father,' he didn't mean a bearded big Daddy sitting there with gold in one hand and a rod in the other, so that whoever meditates on Him receives gold and whoever doesn't care to meditate receives a blow on his head. It is not that way. That is how people in all religions depict God. The donkey can only think that God is a big donkey. Human beings think that God is a big granddaddy; but He is, She is; He is She, and She is He. Even the use of the pronouns 'He' and 'She' are used because we can't understand without differentiating. It is the nature of the mind to classify. Therefore, humans have given God names such as Father, Mother or whatever. Still, God is Father, Mother, Guru, everything.

God is your own great Self. God is immanent, transcendent, and also incarnate. All this is God, there is nothing else but God. You and I are a myth. It is a dream. In the awakened state, everything looks like Vishnu, which means the all-pervading Truth, the reality.

The human mind will not understand this. Only when the mind is not there is it possible to become one with the reality and experience that. As long as 'I' is there, the reality—that I AM THAT I AM—is not realized. When the 'I,' the ego, quits, that is when the Self is revealed. The Bible states this truth, which is also a definition of meditation: "Be still and know that I am God."

Towards that is all *sadhana* (spiritual disciplines). Those who have realized the Self, the Masters, have made the journey themselves. Out of compassion, they returned and brought us a map to that kingdom. They have spoken about the roads (the *yogas*, the pathways) and which is better suited to us. For instance, the temperament of an individual who is emotional is better suited to the path of devotion called *bhakti yoga*; he who is intellectually oriented is better suited to the path of knowledge called *jnana yoga*; and he whose temperament is inclined toward selfless service is suited to the path of *karma yoga*. But no matter which *yoga* you take, as per your temperament, still finally, all these will be leading towards the same goal. Like 'all roads lead to Rome,' all *yogas* lead to OM!

God, the Supreme, is called *Paramatma* (Supreme Soul) or Purushottama. When He wants to express His joy, His *shakti* (the energy of creation) emerges. That *shakti*, in relationship to the name Vishnu, is Lakshmi; in relationship to Shiva, She's called Parvati or Durga; in relationship to Brahma, She's called Sarasvati or Sharada. *Shakti*, in Sankhya philosophy, is called *prakriti*. From *prakriti* comes the English word 'procreation.'

Philosophy

When *prakriti* manifests, it has three *gunas* (qualities): *sattva, rajas, and tamas. Sattva guna* means poise and white light; *rajo guna* means activity and red light; *tamo guna* means inactivity and darkness. In the jargon of modern science, *prakriti* manifests as the negative electron (tamasic); the positive proton (rajasic); and the neutralizing neutron (sattvic). These qualities are found in everything—in the whole of nature, in our mind, in our food, in our activities, in our body. In everything which is created by God, these three *gunas* operate.

The Manifestation of OM

The coming together of *prakriti* and Purushottama, which is also called *shakti* and Shiva, produces a cosmic intelligence called *mahat*. From that *mahat tattva*, the Word of God (OM, Ganesha, the Son of God) came. The manifestations of OM continue from the subtle to the gross, each one having the preceding qualities or attributes in addition to its own.

The first manifestation from OM is KHUM (*akasha*, ethereal space). The ethereal space is the support for the entire creation. The all-pervading sky, the all-pervading space in which all the galaxies and endless universes abide is *akasha*. In our bodies, which is a miniature replica of the universe, the *akasha chakra*, the throat center, is made up of the KHUM principle. The quality inherent in space is *shabda* (sound). What is the sound in *akasha*? It is OM OM OM.

Out of the ethereal space came another principle, air. Its quality is touch along with sound. You can feel and hear the air.

Out of the air, the third element, called fire, came. Fire has three qualities—sound, touch and form. In addition to hearing and feeling, you can see the fire.

From the fire comes water. Whenever there is combustion, as in the burning of fuel or the digesting of food, water is released. It has four qualities: sound, touch, form and taste.

From these four came the fifth, earth, with its quality—odor. Rainwater has no odor until it touches the earth. If it goes through a flower, then it has that fragrance. If it goes through the gutter, then it has a bad smell.

Thus, the *mahapanchabhutas*, the five cosmic elements—ether, air, fire, water and earth—and their *tanmatras* (the corresponding subtle properties of sound, touch, form, taste and smell), are the belly, the manifestation of OM, Ganesha. These elements and their properties are right here above your neck, all over the body and in your own senses of perception, as well.

What is *akasha* in your head? It is the ear which is made up of space. Sound is the result. You cannot plug your ear completely and hope to use another hole in the body to hear music. Touch, the air principle, is all over your body as long as you have good health. Even though fire also is throughout your body, it is your eyes alone which are able to see forms. Therefore, the fire is in your eyes. The water principle with its corresponding *tanmatra* of taste is located in your tongue. The earth principle and its quality of smell is in your nose. Unfortunately, you cannot transfer the portfolios. Over a million years, man may try to give the job of the nose to the ear, but no matter what he does, still it will not be perfect.

In between these two—God (Purushottama) and His energy (*shakti* or *prakriti*)—there is a third manifestation, the spark of the divine called the individual soul, *jivatma* or *purusha*. *Purusha* means 'one who is dwelling in the city' (the body). *Pura*, in Sanskrit, means the city.

LORD GANESHA

One who is dwelling in this city, the light in this body, is called *purusha*. Though everything has soul, *prakriti*, the creative energy, prepares bodies for these individual souls as per the divine plan—either a frog body or a monkey body or all the other different kinds of animals—birds, fish, and even plants.

In the human body, the *purusha* dwells in a 'city' which has nine gates or doors (the openings in the body). The purpose of life is to open the tenth gate at the crown of the head, the *Brahmarandhra*, also called *surya mandala*. *Brahmarandhra*, the niche of Brahman, is the spot through which the individual soul entered into the body. (That is the 'soft spot' on the top of a baby's head.) It is the one, continuous effort of the yogis to make the soul depart from there because the hole or door through which the soul escapes at death declares what type of life we have led and which *loka* (sphere of consciousness) we are going to attain. Therefore, with the third eye laser beam treatment, yogis endeavor to penetrate that spot in order to make the *brahmarandhra* open for the final departure.

Purusha, the soul, is of atomic size in the sense that it is invisible, but its manifestation is visible. Just as wherever you see smoke, you feel there is fire, like that, through your eyes you see, through your ears you hear, through your mouth, you speak and taste. All these things show that light is dwelling in you and that the body is living. But the light departs from the body after its karma (the results of the law of cause and effect) with this body is over. Then another body will be given to us as a result of our good or bad karma. This donning and shedding of bodies continues until you, the soul, no longer require them.

Until that time comes, you'll be discriminating between good and bad. Hearing good music, you say 'ah'; hearing something which you feel is not music, you say, 'Oh, I don't want to be here, it's just noise.' Something which is very comfortable to look at, you want to see again and again. If something has smallpox or dirt on it, though, you say, 'ugh, ugly'. And sometimes, even though something is beautiful, if you don't like it, you'll say, 'I don't want to see it.' All of the holes in our body, especially the five senses of perception, are conditioned by these positive-negative aspects. Definitely, as long as there are likes and dislikes there is ego, but when ego is transcended, you go beyond both and treat everything as Truth.

The snake that is coiled and sleeping in a basket, when aroused by your clap, raises its hood with anger. Immediately, how does the charmer hold him captive? By playing a certain melody, the snake forgets its anger and begins dancing on its tail. This is the allegory for the *shakti* which is coiled like a serpent—with its poison of lust, anger, greediness and jealousy—at the base of the spine. When you awaken, Guru is like a snake charmer. Each one of our bodies is like a basket carrying several snakes in us. All those snakes are coiled energies. The snake is evil in the Bible because the outward manifestation of energy in the form of anger and arrogance, etc. is evil. But the same energy, when it is transformed, becomes good. When the serpent is rid of its poison, you can play with it. When you remove the fangs, it has no more power to harm.

Like that, our mind, free from these negativities, is a very good place to dwell for there the nectar dwells. That sleeping serpent is awakened through OM HUM. After that, all the different mantras are used to make you sattvic. Sometimes, for whole lifetimes even, if you do not meet the Guru, or you do not have an initiation or contact with the other world, then that *shakti* never awakens. It's just there with food and sex. Nothing more than that. When we have the intuitive power to reach the other layers of our consciousness, that is when you is get the snake charmer. Otherwise, this hissing sound, anger, will manifest, as it is in the tamasic world outside, where constantly there is fighting and war and struggle and killing without realizing the spirit. But rid of tamasic and rajasic energies (which means passionate, egotistic activities), your *shakti* will awaken into a poise called *sattva guna*. It is when your mind is in *sattva guna* that you understand the higher values of life. Then you feel, 'why should I worry constantly that I don't have this, I don't have that?

'What is the cause of this worry? What have I brought with me other than the latencies (good or bad karma) from the past life? What am going to carry with me when I leave? Certainly not this body upon which I have spent my money all these days.' Even that is left here in an instant. We have to analyze this and relax. Money is not everything. The greatest wealth is wisdom.

If you must worry, worry about the Truth. When you worry about the Truth, it is called meditation. You have a great treasure inside, attaining which you'll be immortal while living in this body, a state called *jivanmukti*. Again and again we have to think, how long I have been living as a tenant in this home called the body? Before I go to another home (another birth), is it important to me to avoid that birth and attain the immortal bliss and peace right here? How shall I do it? By constant self-inquiry, seek and find the answers. Who am I? Who am I? Questioning thus will lead to answers through *jnana yoga*.

Ramanamaharshi, a great master from India in the 1950's, used to teach a simpler technique. Sing OM, then send your mind all the way to the source of the sound. When the mind reaches the source of that sound, the mind becomes fascinated and merges in that sound. That state is called *samadhi*. All of us speak, all of us sing OM. Thereafter, meditate and investigate from where this sound emerges.

Lokas

If you send your mind to the source of the sound called *para* (the inexpressible Word) at the base of the spine, and enter the *sushumna* (passageway for *shakti* in the astral or subtle body), then sound becomes visible (*pashyanti*) at several points along the spine (the *chakras*). Each *chakra*, which are of different rates or degrees of consciousness, represents a different *loka*. The maxim, 'as above, so below' is relevant here. That which is in the macrocosm, i.e., the whole universe, is in the microcosm—the human body which contains the essence of evolution.

The *Vedas* teach that there are many other planes (*lokas*) above and below our planet earth. The universe is broadly divided into fourteen main ones. The Gayatri mantra includes all the seven luminous upper spheres. OM Bhu is the earth planet. OM Bhuva is the atmospheric region. OM Swaha is the first heaven or celestial kingdom. OM Maha is the sphere of the cosmic intelligent beings, *mahatattva*. OM Janaha is the region of the progenitors like Daksha and others who prepare a spiritual body for the soul. OM Tapaha is the *mandala* (circle) of the seven great sages, the mind-born sons of the Creator, the shining beings who guide and guard our third eye when the Guru gives the initiation. OM Satyam is the *loka* of Truth.

These *lokas* correspond to the *chakras* in our body up to the crown *chakra*. Those which are beyond even the crown *chakra* are the Kaivalya and Vaikunta *lokas*.

LORD GANESHA

Similarly, below the groin all the way down to the soles of the feet, the seven lower *chakras* are represented. Below Mother Earth are the seven *talas*. *Tala* means subterranean or nether regions. There is no sun or moon there, but there are *nagas*, the serpent gods (symbolic). Manikya, the shining gems of the lady serpents, is the light there. The names of those *naga lokas* are: Atala, Vitala, Sutala, Talatala, Rasatala, Mahatala, and Patala. They are all filled not only with darkness but also with extraordinary enjoyments and millions of different kinds of 'wines.' All *rakshasas* and *asuras* (various kinds of demons) dwell there.

In our own soul, also, we feel that this earth planet is not everything. It is only a small speck that, even according to modern science, is floating in the vastness of space. Compared to the cosmos, all our fighting, armaments, guns and airplanes are so insignificant, merely little kites with which the babies play. Materially, we are nothing compared to the universe.

Spiritually, we are everything, because the Truth is full in everything and everyone, always. To realize that Truth, we assume different birthday coats, sometimes white, sometimes brown, sometimes black—different bodies in different lives. But in between the birth and the death, you should know that you were in some of these *lokas*. Either in the astral or in the celestial world, you were dwelling for some time as per the good or bad karma which you performed here.

The higher *lokas* dwell in your feelings; they dwell in your heart. They dwell in your finest emotion called love. Do not neglect that part with the facts and figures of the modern scientific world, because one fine morning we will leave all these things with a heart attack or something. Then what? Have we reserved our seat in the higher *chakras*? While we are living in this body, is the tummy everything? Or is there something above the tummy called the heart? Reflect and you will know that in your own family, in your own neighborhood, in your own kith and kin, you have seen the pain, the death, the change. It is an inscrutable law which will come to my body and your body. It has come before to our other bodies.

Death to the body or anything that is born is a tremendous fact. I cannot say it is Truth, but it is a fact. I don't think sometime fact is Truth because many a time, fact is *maya* (illusion). It is a thing to be discussed in your own mind as food for thought. For the third eye, fact is an illusion and the history of the whole cosmos and the *lokas* is known to it.

In this endless universe of the Lord, His different sparks have their own *lokas*. The manifestations of God—those who have brought a new inspiration to humanity at different times—were sent by the same God, and each one of them are given different kingdoms where they dwell in the vastness of the sphere and beyond. So there is Christ *loka*, there is Brahma *loka*, there is Vishnu *loka*, there is Shiva *loka*, there is Indra *loka* and so on. And after death, each soul, as per its good or bad karma, goes in these mixed planes for some time here, some time there. Then, because of their deep attachment, again they come back on earth and that is rebirth or reincarnation.

We carry our strong habits for good or bad into the next or succeeding lives. As an example of this tendency, the following true story is told. A dog near Uttarkashi would not eat on Ekadashi (a fasting day to propitiate Lord Panduranga Vishnu, the Heavenly Father). That day the dog would not touch even water. It fasted. Even the dog's master was reminded without seeing the Hindu almanac that it was a fasting day, for when he took food to the dog in the morning, that day the dog would not touch it. When forced by the owner to eat, the dog, being

Philosophy

obedient, would lift the food to its mouth, go hide it in the bushes and come back licking the corners of its mouth. Not until the next day would it actually consume the food.

So the Masters observed this and explained that a great Vaishnava (worshipper of Vishnu) who had been observing this tremendous discipline of fasting did a great sin or great wrong knowingly. Then, in accordance with the law of metampsychosis, which means a reverse process called regression, he was pushed back or degenerated to a dog level, a dog body. But he never forgot his discipline of fasting on Ekadashi. And when he gave up the dog body, he was restored to the same Vaishnava position he held before to continue his *sadhana*.

All over the world you will hear similar stories. Observe the dog, observe the cat, observe your own children and what they are saying at two, three, and four years of age. The four-year old daughter of an American Jain woman suddenly burst out saying, "I hate you! I hate you because you are ill-treating my three children!" What did it mean? A man had married the older of two sisters. His wife suffered throat cancer and before she died, she offered her three daughters to the younger sister, whom her husband married. The three children were ill-treated by the younger sister. Then the man and his new wife conceived a child. Who was the new baby? The older sister herself had come as her baby and told her, "I hate you! You are ill-treating my children!"

These are not mere stories. Because we have come from different *lokas*, we feel that we were all angels, we were all *devataas* before and we want to be restored to that heaven again. That tremendous feeling remains. At times, when our minds are tranquil and pure, we feel we are in contact with those *lokas*. Jesus said, "My Father's house has many mansions." That house is the Kingdom of Heaven, Vaikunta. The many mansions are many *lokas*. Buddha said, "I am taking you to my *loka* called Brahmavihara," a place of that light of Truth. That is the Vaikunta of Sriman Narayana, Satyanarayana, Panduranga. (The recent name of that living Lord is Panduranga. Just like you say, 'God of David,' 'God of Jacob,' whoever propitiates and realizes God, then for him, God becomes a living God. Like that, the living God of Kaliyuga, the current age, is Panduranga. He is the same Mahavishnu of Vaikunta). So there is Christ *loka*, and there is the *loka* of each prophet or the ray, the higher manifestation of God. Each has promised, "I will prepare a seat for you at the feet of the Lord." They are all sparks of the same Divinity. And that is Truth.

Ganesha *loka*, the source of OM, is in your *muladhara chakra* at the base of the spine.(For each *chakra*, there are different names of the deity, but they are of the same Truth, the same energy called by different names.) Then you see that sound in your navel center. You hear that sound in your cardiac center and it becomes the uttered speech of wisdom or song, and more, you realize the source of the sound. Then invariably, when you speak, it brings realization to the hearers.

Tuned in to the *nada* (sound) of OM in you, you will realize that every 21,600 times you breathe, in every inhalation and exhalation, is this SO HAM or HAM SO, which is another expression of the OM, or the I AM THAT I AM. If you go to the source of I AM, then within a few moments, in unutterable speech, an inexplicable emotion and indescribable peace will possess you, and you are able to become one with that. There you are speechless and mind is stilled. When you come out of that, this whole universe changes its color. It stands in its true color. When it stands in its true color, that is the cosmic form of God, the cosmic form which

Krishna showed to Arjuna in the 11th chapter of the Bhagavad Gita. It is that transfiguration which Jesus showed to Peter, John and other apostles.

You are transformed and everything is transfigured. In the heart of everything, you are able to see that OM, that light, that sound. You are able to constantly dwell in this world without being attached.

A stillness comes into you and worries subside. The water of your mind becomes transparent and in that rippleless, transparent water, the Truth is reflected. You become so happy and so peaceful. You taste it and that peace and happiness is abiding. It is not fleeting. It is permanent. You relish that taste and want to go again and again to that realm to know the will of God and the secret of the other kingdoms above until you reach the highest kingdom of heaven. All this is within. The kingdom of heaven, or Parabrahma, *Paramatma*, is within, as Christ teaches. It is within every one of us.

The same energy which brings us ill health through worries and anxieties is the same energy which, when you worry about the Truth, becomes concentration. Concentration leads to meditation and meditation leads to *saguna samadhi* (transcendental consciousness where the devotee is face to face with God). *Saguna samadhi* leads into *nirvikalpa samadhi*, where the knower, the known and the knowledge—the lover, beloved and the love—become one and the same.

When you return from that, you are able to bring peace on this earth. When you return from that non-dual Oneness, then you cannot distinguish between Christian, Moslem, or Hindu, or even animals, birds, or plant kingdom, for all are filled with that Krishna, that Christ, that Panduranga, that Buddha—whichever name you understand. In an ant, in an elephant, in a cow, in a dog, in an untouchable, you will see and feel that everything is filled with the divine, with the pure consciousness called *chinmaya*. The whole world is filled with that, *jaganmaya*. Everything becomes Ramamaya or that OM which is the Word of God.

Inhale OM. Mentally saying OM, inhale that highest thought. Fill your heart with that wonderful purple, blue, yellow consciousness. Now, as you sing OM, let your entire breath course through that *pranava*. During the pause between the inhalation and the exhalation, meditate on that OM. Inhale again, the Ganesha, the OM, mentally. While holding the breath, heal the entire body, the physical, astral, and causal. Feel that you are the universe and that the Word of God is emerging out of you with light.

Chant OM. Inhale the OM and hold in *kumbhaka* (retained breath). While you are holding that *prana* (lifebreath), vibrate throughout the body that divine *shakti* of the Word of God. Course the *prana* through again, healing the lungs, the chest, the throat and everything as the Word emerges out of your mouth. Feel the holiness and the healing which happens. The *prana* course is continuous and the more and more you practice this simple but powerful practical meditation, you will definitely be led to an experience of the inner sound, of the inner music.

Sometimes it could be like the drum of Shiva, or the mellifluous sweetness of the flute of Krishna or the Sermon on the Mount or angels jointly singing or the roar of the Lion or the chime of a distant church bell. Or, sometimes, you feel as if you are experiencing the movement of fireflies all over your body. Or the sun, moon and the fire appear simultaneously. Or perhaps your astral body will project into different *lokas* or you are able to reach *bhava loka* (the *loka* of

Philosophy

feeling), where ancestors, *devataas*, archangels, and even God are contacted by the power of your heart's love.

That heart's love, that devotion, is the result of all this *yoga*. Practice until you realize that love is God. Nothing is impossible to that love, in front of which the entire universe obeys, bringing the soothing effect of peace upon everyone. Therefore, practice this *nada* everyday for at least ten to fifteen minutes. Whenever your work is done, either early morning or evening or just before you sleep—with a commitment to God to experience the Truth—inhale the Word, hold the Word, exhale the Word. As you practice this, within a few days you will be able to listen to the cosmic sounds, the cosmic chants and the music of the angels.

As a result, you become a calm and quiet person. All restlessness stops, and you know that whatever is written by the Lord is going to happen. More and more, you surrender your egotistic will to the pure will, the supreme will of God. All the activities which you do will then reflect only the divine and you become a yogi. Then you are the Light. Wherever you go, people are able to see this Light in you, bathe in that Light, bask in that sunshine and become healed. That is the highest healing of all, to give the *ashirvada*, the benediction, the blessing.

By practicing the great mantras, you will come across certain tremendous powers called the *siddhis*. They invariably come to you. (The other, higher meaning of *siddhi* is perfection or attainment.) It is very important to know about the *siddhis* because sometimes you can become so flooded with the spiritual energy that you will be at a loss to know what to do with it. Just as a man who obtains but doesn't know how to operate a gun can be a source of danger to himself and those around him, a person who has attained the *siddhis* without a corresponding wisdom in their use can be equally dangerous. This has been true in the lives of many Masters in the past and in the lives of many gurus in the present.

Not only in the spiritual realm but also in the political, religious, social, historical, and scientific levels, when man gets power, that power corrupts unless he has the humility to receive the blessing and use it for the the service of mankind in the service of God. That is why the Masters always encourage us to go beyond the *siddhis* and dwell in nectar. Power used selfishly will kill you or drive you crazy unless you use it for service.

Though there are many *siddhis*, such as clairvoyance (supernormal vision), clairaudience (supernormal hearing), extrasensory perception, psychometry (matter moving by the power of the mind), and many others, eight important ones are described below:

Anima means you know the subtlest of things around you and just by mere will, you can make yourself appear very small to everyone. Or you can become so subtle that you can enter into the dreams of people and guide them or if you misuse the power, you can misguide them, which is dangerous. Or even though all the doors to a room are locked and the walls are solid, by assuming a subtle form, you are able to penetrate those walls and doors. So *anima* means very subtle, to be atomic in size or to assume the minutest form with which you could go anywhere you like.

Garima is to be able to assume a mountainous size which means your form appears colossal, mountainous or cosmic.

LORD GANESHA

Laghima means to be very light. By practice of the mantra, no matter how weighty you are, you have the power to make your entire system very light, like cotton or flower petals. That is the secret of levitation and reaching anywhere.

Mahima means to be very, very, very heavy. These are only the surface meanings. There are so many other celestial meanings to these most practical powers which come to you.

Prapti means that whatever you wish for, either for yourself or for others, immediately you obtain the same.

Prakamya means, among other things, that if a soul is not resurrected, that is, it is caught somewhere in the astral worlds, it is visible to you, and you can use that *prakamya* power to send that soul to a higher dimension. Or if someone is asking for help in conquering the *prarabdha karma*, the incurable karma, and he remembers the guru, the guru is able to cure that karma and see that the person is healed, restored to his health or pristine purity or lifted from any fall and raised to a higher height. With *prakamya*, you even have the power to create new dimensions or to ask a special favor from God for certain souls for their enlightenment. This applies not only for individual wishes, but for the collective wishes of mankind.

Ishitva means lordship. You are the lord of your senses, the lord of your mind. It means you conquer and wherever you go, that lordship is there. That is why you call Jesus 'Lord Jesus,' or Krishna 'Lord Krishna.' Often these powers come to a social, political or religious leader and all too often, we see how this power is misused. You have to develop humility and remember that God alone is Lord. If you allow the ego to operate this *siddhi*, then definitely there will be brainwashing and the killing of the spirit of others. You must be very careful to remain humble. All great Masters fall on their knees when this *siddhi* manifests and pray again to the Almighty to bless them with humility. "Blessed are the poor in spirit . . . " it is said, "for theirs is the kingdom of heaven." Otherwise, you will get lordship over certain things, such as continents, or wealth, etc., but you'll lose the Kingdom.

The eighth power, with almost the same connotation, is called *vashitva*. It means attraction. Wherever you go, you are the magnet, the center of attraction. You attract everything—all the angels, all the human beings, all the species—towards you.

In the 1950's, a cow called Lakshmi would part thousands of people gathered around Ramanamaharshi to go to the guru every day for a blessing. He would not eat until he had personally fed that cow. All animals, all creatures are attracted toward such Masters. You have heard in many stories how the cat and the rat, the tiger and the deer, the snake and the mongoose will forget their enmity in the presence of such a saint and play together. *Vashitva* means that. Everything is attracted towards you, but you are not attracted towards them because you keep God as your central attraction. You look to God and they look to you. Then you are safe.

If you are attracted by the things which are attracted to you, then very soon the power will be gone, for it is that God which dwells in you which is the source of attraction for the whole humanity. Bless them, make them stand on their own two feet and give them the Light so that they may walk in the Light and not in darkness. But at the same time, tell them that these blessings come from God and not from you.

Philosophy

If you take the credit, you'll have a large following for a few years before that very following becomes the instrument of your downfall. History proves that. Be careful in acknowledging that the blessings are from God. Somebody said to Jesus, "How good you are!" Immediately he said, "Why do you call me good? There is only one who is good and that is my Father in heaven!" This form of humility should be there constantly. You may not have a large following and you should not be attracted towards that either. It comes to you when you don't want it.

Everything comes to you when you transcend the desire for it. This is the one lesson which you and I have to learn eventually. It is very tricky for it teaches 'if you want a desire to be fulfilled, just conquer that desire.' At that very moment, the desire is fulfilled. That is food for thought. Think about it. Anything you want to have, go beyond that want, and then it will be there at your feet.

It is taught that we should strive to go beyond all desires other than the desire to attain enlightenment. That desire is not included in the baser, lower, egotistic selfish desires for that is an aspiration. Like the lotus blossoming by seeing the sun, like the river dancing down into the ocean, similarly, the soul has to reach God from where it has come. It is that aspiration—I won't call it a desire—it is that longing alone which will make you reach the Truth.

In the meantime, by the practice of mantra, there might be several other forms of *siddhis* which will come to you, including the higher *siddhis* such as walking on water or going to any *loka*, or entering into another's body (*parakaya pravesha*), or blessing an individual.

A poor lady, when Shankaracharya came to beg for alms, had nothing except one fruit. Yet she brought that amalaka fruit and with tears in her eyes gave it to the guru in his begging bowl. Immediately, he uttered the *kanakadhara strotra*, which means invoking the supreme Lakshmi, and showered all kinds of wealth and riches on her. There are many more, such as restoring the dead, or enabling a childless couple to have a baby. All these blessings and more are possible by the proper use of *siddhis*. If you maintain humility, then you will use the *siddhis* for the service of humanity and in the eyes of the Kingdom, you will be considered as sons and daughters of the Heavenly Father.

So this is the knowledge and the warning about the powers which might come to you. Ganesha and Hanuman, especially, give the *siddhis* immediately. These two aspects are quick *siddhis*. But when the king wants to give you the kingdom, if you beg for a few cents (pray for the *siddhis*), that would be foolishness. That is what the *siddhis* are. Do you understand? A parable will clarify this point.

Once there was a king travelling in a golden chariot and he met a beggar who was on his way to ask the king to make him become superwealthy overnight. But before the beggar could beg of the king, to his wonderment, the king began begging of the beggar. Descending from his chariot, the king asked the beggar to give him something. At that, the beggar began pushing his knapsack behind him, saying, "I don't have anything, I don't have anything." He had seven or eight handfuls of rice in that sack but he said, "I don't have anything."

The king replied, "Well, whatever you have, give a little bit of that to me."

But the beggar was not willing. He said, "You are the king, I am the beggar and you are begging of me? Then both of us should go together as beggars!"

The king insisted, so the beggar, much against his will, put his hand into the knapsack and pulled out seven or eight grains of rice from the seven or eight handfuls which he had. And the king accepted that very gladly and in his golden chariot, returned to the palace.

The beggar was very unhappy thinking, "not only did the king not give me anything, but he took from me also! How unfortunate I am!" Thinking thus, the beggar with great agony came back to his mosquito-infested hut and emptied the sack. Lo! To his surprise, among the seven to eight handfuls of rice, there were seven to eight grains of rice which had been converted into gold. Now he began beating his forehead, lamenting, "how foolish, how dull-witted I am! Had I known what I gave to the king would return to me in pure gold, I would have given all seven to eight handfuls of rice. I would have emptied everything there so that I would have been filled here!"

We are all like beggars. We have something and we go to God to ask Him for more and more. Instead, God asks us to give what we have. But our ego says, "I don't have anything, I don't have anything!" We try to hide the knapsack behind us. God insists, but still we don't agree to give our time or our breath for meditation. God has given us our whole life to realize Him and we say, "We have no time, we have no energy. We are very busy, we have no money, we have no health, we don't have this, we don't have that." Yet God insists.

Still, when you do not behave, then God 'kicks,' 'throws bricks,' sends difficulties, problems, ill health, headaches, etc., to make us give something to Him so that we could be blessed. Then, much against our will, we give seven to eight minutes of meditation in twenty-four hours, or seven to eight hours in a month. Some people do not even give an hour in a whole lifetime. Then the time comes to empty the sack, to depart from this body, and you realize that those days, those minutes, those hours, those breaths which I spent with the Lord or in the company of saints—those moments alone are the golden moments of my life, like the seven or eight grains of rice converted into gold. At the time of death, you beat your forehead and cry with agony, "Had I known that this would be completely golden and I would be basking in that yellow, healing light and God Himself would come with His messengers to take me to the immortal kingdom of Truth, I would have dedicated all my breaths and all my time for God!"

But, by then, it is too late. You'll be reborn again. Still, with that as your last thought, when you are reborn, you'll come as a yogi to end your evolution. This parable is the greatest parable, related to every one of us. Life has value only relative to the time you have spent in realization of your great Self or doing any action with the spirit of God. All the rest is, compared to the immortal truth, worthless. The moments which we spend with God are golden moments which will be returned to us as golden moments. So make the whole life a golden moment. Get initiated into the truth and represent God in every work which you do. A little more kindness added to our work, a little more selflessness added to our work, is an expression of that love for God. That is what will make the earth the Kingdom of Heaven.

Do the *sadhana* (spiritual discipline). Never eat your breakfast without doing *sadhana*. Never go to sleep unless you pray and conduct your *sadhana* daily, without fail. Because that alone is life. That alone is divine. Morning prayer gives you energy throughout the day to work

Philosophy

with all alertness in healing and helping. All those who come to you will take with them that kindness and compassion which you manifest by the power of the prayer. Just as you take time for sleep, time for food, time for recreation, time for everything else, you must take, similarly, time for meditation until you make the meditation or prayer constant in the midst of all activities, and in every breath. Then you shall not be reborn, and if you do come back, you'll come back with compassion in order to help humanity reach that higher stage.

Each one of you, along with your other works, kindly bring this potential healing power in you to the surface and bless people around you who really require these great mantras and *ashirvada* (the benediction). Become the great healers of humanity. It is neither caste, creed, color, country nor anything else that counts nowadays, other than the power to heal, the power of love, the power of God to manifest in each and every one of you. It is potentially in you but hidden. The guru invokes it and brings it to the higher level. Do not allow it to go back. Instead, recite the mantra, get those powers and, with humility, heal humanity.

Diksha

Diksha (initiation) is a special gift of God and guru. To go within, you require help, a guiding light, a word, or a path that is shown to reach the destination. By giving the blessing called *diksha*—a word, a glance, or a touch which makes the disciple to sojourn within—you are shown the inner path.

No matter how much book knowledge we have, no matter how many pilgrimages or different things we have done, until the Light of the Guru is again lit, all that we do is only preparation. Like the candle that is a kindling light to other candles, the living light in the guru is given to the living *chela* (aspirant). Everything is a help, but the final and the most important of all is the guru to tell you what to do for the attainment of the highest truth.

There are different degrees of receiving, like different degrees of giving. You have heard how the reflection of the sunlight on a muddy wall is dim and yet the same sunlight on water reflects and is beautiful; with a mirror you can make the light go into a dark room and illuminate the interior; and when the sunlight is focused on a magnifying glass, you can concentrate the sunlight and burn cotton behind it.

The light of initiation, the light of mantra, shines the same on everyone. It is the recipient, as per his *tapasya* (fasting and prayer), his maintenance of holiness, his background and preparation for receiving the *diksha* which makes the difference. Some are like the muddy wall; some are like water; some are like mirrors; some are like the magnifying glass. That is where, for the same teacher, the different disciples will have, as per their temperament, different kinds of realizations.

There is no difference between the mantra and the Guru or mantra and God. God alone is the guru. Guru means the Light of all the lights—the Light of knowledge, the Light of truth. Guru is not a person. It is a principle within you. As you cannot see your Self sometimes, one who has seen it becomes a mirror and reflects that inner Light so you see your own Self. That is the true teaching. Therefore, *diksha* is given to inspire you in the invisible path to conquer the karma, humble the ego, melt and wash all the latencies completely from your psyche and purify the emotions to reach the culmination of all karma with illumination.

There are three important kinds of *dikshas*. The first, which serves as the foundation of the higher initiations, is called the *mantra diksha*. The second is called *shakti diksha*, well known as *shakti-pat*. The third, which is higher than that, is called the *shambhavi diksha*.

To be eligible for these higher *dikshas*, many preparations are required. Just like the revolver is filled with a cartridge and requires a spark to explode, similarly the preparation makes the difference during the initiation in bringing higher forms of mystical experiences.

Even the preparations are called initiations. The disciplines of getting up at a given time, bathing daily with the proper mantras and conducting the *bhuta shuddhi*, which means purifying the body, the senses, the mind, and the *nadis* (astral tubes through which the *prana* courses) through *pranayama* (rhythmic breathing) and other disciplines, are also not ordinary. It's not possible for people to do these disciplines daily unless the word of the Guru is settled in their mind.

When you want to be physically well, you go for rehabilitation. The doctor will say, 'do this, do that, do this, do that.' You do it, and you become well. Similarly, the teacher gives you a spiritual rehabilitation program. Even though you know the program, you need someone who can transmit that energy into you to do it. The guru does that, which means your own higher Self is speaking through the teacher.

There are very, very few highly evolved souls who did not need a guru to transmit that energy because they have gone through all those stages in a previous million lives. Therefore, they were born as gurus themselves. But even those born gurus—like Christ, Krishna, and Buddha—to show the way, the truth and the life, also went through an initiation by way of example.

Though John the Baptist said to Jesus, "You want me to initiate you? I initiate people through the water and you are initiated by the Holy Spirit. I need initiation from you, not you from me!" Jesus gets into the water, the river Jordan, and tells John the Baptist, "You are sent for this job. I am sent for another job. You do your job. I do mine. And both of us are sent by Him who knows His job." So John the Baptist had to initiate him.

Krishna, the Lord, never needed an initiation either, but He took initiation from a sage called Sandipani. Every day He brought fuel for the fire and flowers for the *puja* of His guru. Though there are very few who never needed a physical guru—being God or the greatest Jagadgurus and Sadgurus incarnate to spread the word of God—even they, again to show the way, the truth and the life, had to take someone as the Teacher.

So the preparatory initiations are also difficult, but very beautiful and one has to do them to prepare for the higher ones. The *Vedas* speak about five or six kinds of disciplinary initiations.

One is called *kriyavati*. This means *puja*, the worship which we do every day to purify. If you say *puja* is just a ritual, what is your brushing the teeth? What is your breakfast? Is it not a ritual? What is sex? What are children? What is daily life but ritual? What is going on outside? Look at the big candle, the sun that is shining. Look at the waves coming and dashing to the lotus feet of God. Look at the variegated hues of flowers. Are they not also engaged in ritual? It is the great *puja* going on in the cosmic temple. Don't be ignorant thinking that the greatest of the liturgy—the *yantra* (diagram), the mantra, the entire technique of operating your psyche—is an ordinary ritual. Liturgy is the most difficult of all the disciplines. You have to know the *mudras* (gestures), you have to know the *yantras*, you have to know the *tantra* and the science of invoking the presiding deities over the nine planets, etc.

Millions of people in this country practiced meditation—transcendental meditation, yogic meditation, every kind of meditation. Why did they fail in their marriages? Because they never knew the *puja*. Meditation only purified their minds. They soared very high but they couldn't balance their bodies with those of their wives or husbands or children. They never knew the art of living a family life. The reason? They never did that prayer and worship together.

Worship purifies your senses like meditation purifies your mind. Worship is meditation in action. You speak so many untruths, your tongue requires mantras to repeat. You hear so much gossip, your ears need purification. Through this body, we commit so many mistakes, so-called sins, that it requires purification. Worship— going three rounds and saluting, bathing, fasting—all these things are done for the purification of the senses.

Sometimes, even though mentally you have gone very high, unless the senses are purified, those very senses could devastate even a yogi. The Bhagavad Gita says, "just like a barge on the sea is carried away by a tornado, like that the tornado of the impure senses controlled by the ego can toss all your meditation in a trice." For this reason, *kriyavati* initiation called the *puja* should not be underestimated.

Unfortunately, people want the highest initiations without preparing themselves with the 'lower' ones. They have been trying, in every church, in every temple, to make the truth adjust to their ego. Truth will not adjust to our churches, our temples, our egos. Truth is God. Whether we vote for truth or not, it makes no difference. Truth is not dependent on our votes. Kings or billionaires may come, great rulers or Hitlers may come, but no matter who comes, truth is all-powerful. Truth speaks for itself and requires no proof. When the sun is shining, even the blind can feel the warmth. If truth requires proof, then how do you know the proof is true? If truth requires evidence, where is the evidence to prove the evidence is true? Truth is beyond proof. Truth is self-effulgent and truth is God. Thus, you must prepare your minds and bodies for it.

A second discipline is called *varanamayi*, which means the power of the word. Locating and feeling the expansion of consciousness in different parts of the body while repeating a mantra is called *nyasa*. It is to purify every *chakra* by touching and saying the mantra also. GAM GANAPATAYAE. OM PARABRAHMA. KLEEM KRISHNAAYA. DUM DURGAAYA. All these are *varana*, the powerful word of God. To establish within and make Rama mantra, for instance, vibrate all over your body, is that discipline called *varanamayi*.

The third initiation is *kalavati*. *Kalavati* has five *shaktis*. When you say OM during *kalavati* initiation, while standing, you feel from the soles of your feet the *shakti* pervading and healing all the way up to the knee joints. That is called the *nirvritti shakti*. The next is called *pratishta shakti*. You are healing the entire body and charging it by *prana* from the knees to the navel center. Healing from the navel center up to the throat is accomplished by *vidya shakti*, while from the throat to the forehead center it is called *shanti shakti*. From the forehead up to the crown of the head, the niche of Brahman, it is called *ananda shakti*. This initiation is to charge, by the power of *prana*, the whole body and all the *chakras*, even the seven *chakras* below which are not usually treated.

LORD GANESHA

There are *dikshas* called the *vedamayi diksha*, the *panchayatini diksha* and the *krama diksha*. The most important of all, in attaining the illumination through the *diksha*, is the preparation called *bhuta shuddhi*. *Bhuta shuddhi* itself is one of the greatest disciplines. Say a prayer as you are bathing. As you shower, feel that the Ganges and all the holy rivers are conjoining on your head. *Bhuta shuddhi* means you are cleansing the body born of five elements. Now you have purified your body. At the same time, your mind should not be thinking of other things. Think that "this water is the mercy of God flowing over my head. It washes not only my skin but also my sin." It is with this tremendous holy feeling that you bathe.

After bathing, purify the place where you are going to sit for meditation and worship. Remember that the moment you try to purify—at that very moment!—Satan with his entire military will be attending on you, trying to bring impurity and impediments. Always that is true. Therefore, invoke the guru and then say, OM GAM GANAPATAYAE NAMAHA. You should imagine that the mystic fire of God surrounds you. Look what an extraordinarily beautiful purification! This tremendous feeling of the fire around you is a complete protection for you. No fiends, goblins, Satan, his troupe, nor impure thoughts can penetrate that fire to disturb your body, mind or emotions from meditation.

The *bhutas*—in this context, the *bhutas* means not only the elements, but also many kinds of evil spirits, fiends and goblins—come to confuse when you try to meditate on God and invoke the light. That is what happened to Christ Jesus even after forty days of fasting and prayer. It happened to the Buddha. To Buddha, he came as Mara, the Tempter. To Jesus, he came as Satan, the Tempter. The moment you try to purify, the Tempter will be there bringing unnecessary, impure thoughts. He tries to undermine your efforts and make you feel that you will be defeated. If he succeeds, then right there, behind you, in some corner, Satan bursts into laughter. 'Look, I have won. He is again my slave. I possess his entire body and impurify him again.' Day after day, moment after moment, it happens in our lives. Therefore, this *bhuta shuddhi* is to definitely give a warning to Satan the Tempter: you cannot penetrate beyond that fire of Ganapati and guru.

After these preparatory initiations, a guru who is capable of giving the higher and highest kind of initiation will first give the *chela* a *mantra diksha*. *Mantra diksha* means asking you to chant or write at least one page of mantra such as OM SRI RAMA JAYA RAMA JAYA JAYA RAMA every day. If you are successful in that, then the Guru sees that your psyche and your body are purified. Sometimes, your faith itself could bring you the *darshan* (transcendental vision) of Rama, also. These initiations are wonderful, wonderful, extraordinarily wonderful blessings of the kingdom from the living guru to the living disciple, so that the truth or the light—the principle called Guru—never dies. He lives in his disciple and continues as a tradition.

Following *mantra diksha* is *shakti diksha* or *shakti-pat*, the second initiation, which is a medium kind of initiation, neither the lowest nor the highest. It requires a lot of preparation. Especially in the West, where people want even instant coffee, instant *shakti-pat* has brought many people to mental hospitals. After proper preparations including proper diet, proper *pranayama*, and chanting correctly a certain mantra for a number of days, months or years, the guru gives the *shakti-pat*. It is firm and brings you a tornado of light. Your body and mind must have been properly prepared to receive that. Otherwise, *shakti-pat* will be very dangerous to the

Philosophy

entire nervous system and to the mind. The long years of *seva* (selfless service) the devotee does in an *ashrama* (hermitage) is to humble his ego and get ready for that wonderful experience.

The highest initiation is called *shambhavi diksha*. In *shambhavi diksha*, as the disciple gets obedient to the truth in the guru and goes on doing the *seva* with trust, *bhakti* (devotion), and faith, then at the time appointed by God, all that the guru does is look into the eyes of the disciple at that very auspicious moment or just cast a smiling glance upon him or touch him—any one of which has the power to inspire the disciple to reach the highest realization and proclaim, "All this is God!"

Just the touch of Paramahamsa Ramakrishna made Vivekananda, his disciple, fly into the highest *advaita samadhi* (non-dual transcendental consciousness). Just a touch. Just a look of Ramanamaharshi into the eyes of the American Paul Brunton in the 1950's answered all his questions once and for all, forever. One phrase, "be quiet!" from the guru, Siddharudha, spoken to his disciple who was restless all the time, made him quiet not only physically, but also silenced his mind forever. That is called *shambhavi diksha*, the highest of all. It is the complete grace of the guru given to a deserving disciple.

How worthy we should be to receive that! It is worth serving life after life to receive that blessing. That's why in the ancient Himalayan Upanishad methods which are still practiced, a twelve-year *brahmacharya* (celibate studenthood) and service of every kind—washing the laundry, washing the dishes, working in the garden, doing this, doing that—is done just to get that corridor glance of *kripa*, the graceful look, or blissful smile which transmits the highest energy of knowledge in *shambhavi diksha*.

There is a little story about three advanced students of Shankaracharya who were sitting for a class on Brahmasutra, the highest wisdom of the *Vedas*. A recently enrolled student, who had no knowledge of Sanskrit, had gone to the river a mile away to wash the cloth of his guru. The guru waited for him to return before beginning the class. The other students complained. "We have been studying for seven or more years here and you are waiting for a recently joined student who has no knowledge of Sanskrit? What would he understand? He's an ignorant fellow. We are advanced students. Why should you waste time for him?"

Shankaracharya lifted his hand to give the *shambhavi diksha* and said, "all the knowledge comes to you instantaneously as you wash my clothes." *Shambhavi diksha* transmitted into him and the disciple, just filled with the energy of guru and God, began seeing Brahman in every fiber of creation, every little cell revealing the truth before him. He burst into Sanskrit language in the highest meter called *totaka vrita*, and began composing songs on God and guru. With that wet cloth, he ran with one breath to the ashrama. All the advanced students paled before the immortal song which he burst into. "*Svarupam, shariram, navina, kalatram . . .*" (and more) he spoke the wisdom. "Mountainous wealth, an extraordinarily beautiful spouse and every kind of power—what is it for a God-realized, Guru-realized person? What is it to me before this Light?" That is how he burst into that great song due to the grace of his guru who gave him that initiation called *shambhavi diksha*.

Part II–Mysticism

OM SHREEM HREEM KLEEM GANESHVARAAYA
BRAHMAROOPAAYA CHAARAVAE
SARVA SIDDHI PRADAESHAAYA
VIGHNESHAAYA NAMO NAMAHA

Salutations to the supreme Lord Ganesha. Thou art Brahman. Thou art the bestower of all siddhis. O Vighnesha, remover of all obstacles, salutations again and again!

OM, the first manifested sound, is the sound of creation. OM is the Word of God. OM is God. The *Vedas* have declared with one voice that OM, Lord Ganesha, is the support of the whole universe, the foundation of existence. It is God Himself, one of whose Names is Ganesha or Ganapati, who is the Personification of OM. As OM is the first manifestation of God as Word, Ganesha is worshipped first, being the word OM itself.

In every world religion, the Truth within is represented outwardly by various myths and symbols. These figures and symbols are drawn according to the descriptions given by the *rishis* (sages) who saw the truth in their meditations. According to that, the paintings or medals are done. The worship of these concrete forms—so long as you remember that they are only representations—will lead you to the inner concepts. To build a building, you erect scaffolding and when the building is complete, you remove it. *Murtis* (idols), beads, medals, colors, stones, etc., are like scaffolding. You remove the scaffolding of these various images when you are able to see the truth with *chinmaya* (pure consciousness) in your own heart. Because some people in the West, especially, but the East also, can meditate on these different names and gods through the colors and forms, they are useful and make the journey inward a little easier.

The descriptions and Names of the eternal truth vary according to the different *yugas* (ages) in which the sages described their meditations. The *yugas* are broadly divided into four: the *Krita* (golden); the *Treta* (silver); the *Dvapara* (copper) and the current one, *Kali* (iron) ages. Ganesha manifested in *Krita yuga* as Vinaayaka; His color was gold. He had ten arms (symbolizing the eight directions, and above and below) and He was mounted on a lion. All of us were very tall, very energetic, golden-colored and very near to God in *Krita yuga*. As the ages cycle, we become short-statured, short-sighted, short-memoried, short-lived and farther away from God.

In *Treta yuga*, the same Lord Ganesha manifested with six arms. (You can interpret it as extra-sensory perception, etc.) He was white and mounted on a peacock (*Mayura*). So He was called Mayureshvara.

In *Dvapara yuga*, the age before this *Kali yuga*, He manifested with four arms and was known as Gajaanana. '*Gaja*' means elephant. '*Anana*' means face. Gajaanana means 'elephant-faced one.'

Kali yuga, the present iron age, is the *yuga* of confusion, the *yuga* of terrorism. Ganesha's fourth manifestation, Dhumraketu (Halley's Comet), has yet to come. In Ganesha Puraana, it is said that Dhumraketu will come by the end of *Kali yuga* on a blue horse. (Blue symbolizes infinity.) He will come for the destruction of all terrorism, negativity and dark powers.

Mysticism

Lord Ganesha's body is of vermilion color; His head is that of an elephant, the symbol of OM or infinite consciousness. His elephant face has one tusk, the symbol of oneness, one-pointed mind or concentration with which one can attain perfection. The four arms of the Lord symbolize the four directions or His all-pervading nature. He is holding in his upper hands the *pasha* (noose) and *ankusha* (goad). In His lower hands, He is showing the *abhaya* (fear-not) and *varada* (bestowing blessings) *mudras* (gestures).

The elephant has a majestic body, the symbol of macrocosm (*brahmanda*) and the human body is an involved cosmos or microcosm (*pindanda*). Truly macrocosm is in microcosm and vice versa. When you realize this, you have found the 'unity' of both of you. That is what Ganesha represents—a human trunk with an elephant head.

Lord Ganesha has a big belly, the symbol of plenty. The whole universe is in His belly for the whole universe is like the body of God. As He projects the universe out of Himself, He is known as the source of creation. His big belly is the symbol of holding all worlds within Himself. There are three marks on His forehead—the symbol of the third eye; the three dimensions—nether, middle (earth), and heaven; and the three *guna*s or modes of nature—*sattva* (poise), *rajas* (passion), and *tamas* (inactivity).

The elephant head has small eyes. The symbology here is that we should have the penetrating eyes (the inner eyes) to see the spirit of God in everyone. Then you will not see duality and negativity; instead, you will see unity in diversity. Ganesha represents that consciousness of unity.

The elephant head has two marvelous big ears which he is constantly fanning. The meaning behind this is that the world is constantly bombarding us with news—mostly bad and confusing news. 'Fanning the ears' is to ignore all that, to refuse to take in all those negative thoughts. Take in only that which expands your consciousness and let the rest be fanned away! Listen only to that which is good and meditate on that.

Mahatma Gandhi kept three gurus in the form of three monkeys—one with hands over his eyes, one with hands over his ears, one with hands over his mouth. Meaning speak not to create or add confusion to the world; if you speak, speak the truth sweetly. Many people speak the truth, but very arrogantly. Do not hear that which is against dharma and truth. Do not see evil or duality or insult anyone. See the truth, the divine or God in everybody.

Ganesha's vehicle is the mouse. The symbology behind this is that the mouse is our own ego. Just as the mouse moves in darkness and steals things from the kitchen and pantry, similarly, the ego moves in the darkness of ignorance and interferes in other people's business, always creating trouble. Lord Ganesha, with the noose and goad, curbs the ego, makes the ego behave and walk in the path of light. Thus, Lord Ganesha makes our tamed ego (the mouse) His vehicle.

In the beginning, that mouse was so big, and Ganesha was such a small boy. The mouse said "mount on me" because it wanted to kidnap Ganesha. The ego said, "what is this little OM? I can chant it!" But when the OM sat on the ego, it became so heavy that the ego could not hold it anymore. The mouse vomited all the arrogance, lust, anger, greediness, infatuation and attachment when Ganesha sat. "Why, I thought this was a small little boy," thinks the ego "How big He becomes with endless galaxies and countless constellations!"

LORD GANESHA

The Manifestations of Ganesha

'Truth is One, Names are many' is a great statement from the *Rigveda*. Even though Lord Ganesha as the support of the universe is One, His colors, forms, names, hands, weapons and powers differ due to His different *avataras* (incarnations) and manifestations. At least 32 such manifestations are described in a book called *Tattva Nidhi*. The descriptions are as follows:

Manifestation	Color	Number of arms
1. Baala Ganapati (child)	Blood	4
2. Taruna Ganapati (youth)	Vermilion	8
3. Bhakta Ganapati (loving)	White	4
4. Veera Ganapati (powerful)	Blood	10
5. Shakti Ganapati (energy)	Red sandalwood paste	4
6. Dwija Ganapati (twice-born)	Pure white	4
7. Siddha Ganapati (perfect)	Brown	4
8. Ucchhista Ganapati (sanctified food)	Blue	4
9. Vighna Ganapati (remover of impediments)	Gold	10
10. Kshipra Ganapati (quick manifestation)	Red blood	4
11. Heramba Ganapati (first to be worshipped; this has five elephant faces with a lion as His vehicle)	White Light	8
12. Lakshmi Ganapati (wealth)	White	10
13. Maha Ganapati (the greatest)	Red blood	10 and 3 eyes
14. Vijaya Ganapati (victory)	Red	4
15. Nritya Ganapati (dancing)	Yellow	4
16. Urdhva Ganapati (uplifter)	Golden	6
17. Ekaakshara Ganapati (one-lettered)	Red Blood	4
18. Varada Ganapati (bestower of boons)	Red	4
19. Trayakshara Ganapati (three-lettered)	Golden	4
20. Kshipra Prasada Ganapati (quick blessings)	Red sandalwood paste	6
21. Haridraa Ganapati (tumeric-colored)	Tumeric	4
22. Aekadanta Ganapati (one-tusked)	blue	4
23. Sristi Ganapati (creative)	Vermilion	4
24. Uddanda Ganapati (most powerful)	Red	12

Mysticism

Manifestation	Color	Number of arms
25. Reena Mochana Ganapati (remover of debts)	Red	12
26. Dundi Ganapati (short-statured)	Vermilion	4
27. Dvimukha Ganapati (two-faced)	Tumeric	4
28. Trimukha Ganapati (three-faced)	Vermilion	6
29. Simha Ganapati (lion)	White	8
30. Yoga Ganapati (meditative)	Vermilion	4
31. Durga Ganapati (creative energy)	Golden	8
32. Sankastahara Ganapati (remover of obstacles)	Vermilion	4

A very special aspect of Ganesha, having the body of an elephant but with a lion's face is called Simha Ganapati. This aspect of Ganesha is seen by the sages as playing *veena*, the lute. The meditation is described like this:

"He has eight arms. With His four right arms, He is playing the lute, holding *kalpalata* (a mystical creeper containing all supernatural powers), the chakra, the discus; and a hand bestowing boons or gifts to the devotees. In His left hands, He is holding a lotus, a golden vessel, a gold plate, and the fear-not gesture. His lion face is shining, and He has the body of an elephant. He is as white as the moon and the conch. His clothes are shining like gems. May that auspicious form of Ganesha protect us from all dangers. Tatastu, so be it."

The Significance of Different Colors

When a certain person is trying to harm you, a man who is an adept in the science of mantra can stop him from doing any harm by meditations on the tumeric-colored form of Ganesha with the mantra OM HARIDRAA GANAPATAYAE NAMAHA (108 times), sending that energy on that person to stop him from doing any harm.

When you want to attract people towards you or your work with good motive and for a noble purpose—without trying to take advantage of the person—then you could meditate on the dawn or crimson-colored Ganapati, saying OM VIJAYA GANAPATAYAE NAMAHA and send that radiant energy towards that person. This power should not be misused. If it is misused, great harm will come to the user.

Dark-colored Ganesha is meditated upon whenever you want to destroy negativity, hatred, demoniac ego, inner or outer enemies. The mantra is OM UCCHHISTA GANAPATAYAE NAMAHA.

To cast away the devils or evil spirits from a haunted home or from the body or mind of a person, you meditate on the brown color of Ganesha. The mantra is OM SHAKTI GANAPATAYAE NAMAHA.

LORD GANESHA

To attract a person or people towards you for your job, marriage, or in bringing harmony in your family, you meditate on red-colored Ganesha with the mantra OM VARADA GANAPATAYAE NAMAHA.

Those who want wealth and prosperity, meditate on the golden-colored Ganesha and say this prayer, OM LAKSHMI GANAPATAYAE NAMAHA.

Those who want enlightenment and *moksha* (liberation) meditate on pure white-colored Ganesha with this mantra, OM BHAKTA GANAPATAYAE NAMAHA.

Ganesha Loka

Ganesha's *loka* (abode) is known as *Svaananda Dhama* (Abode of Bliss) and is created by a special creative energy of Ganesha called *kaamadaayini yoga shakti*. He is manifest there both as God with form and as formless God. Both aspects are auspicious, meditating on which the devotee attains the supreme peace.

Even though He is all-pervading with His distinct transcendental personality, He dwells in His abode, protects all the *lokas* and gives attention to His devotees bringing them security and success. Filled with bliss and peace and free from all sickness, old age, hunger, thirst, etc., highly blessed souls dwell there to carry out the behests of the Lord.

Swaananda Dhama has four gates. Each gate is guarded by two special attendants of Ganesha called the *Paarshadaas*. Thus there are eight *paarshadaas* or attendants of Lord Ganesha guarding the gates. Their names are as follows: Avighna and Vighnaraaja; Swaktra and Balaraam; Gajakarna and Gokarna; Susaumya and Shubhadaayaka. All of them are short-statured and compassionate, but very powerful. All of them have four arms. They are holding different weapons in their two hands but in the other two hands all of them are holding a stick and the *tajani mudra* where the tip of the index finger touches the thumb—the symbol of the soul's unity with God. They are all beautiful and they bless the devotees of Lord Ganesha with protection.

Among them, those who guard the eastern gate are Avighna and Vighnaraja. They are holding a hatchet and lotus in their two hands. The southern gate is guarded by Swaktra and Balaraam. They are holding the sword and shield in their two hands. The western gate is guarded by Gajakarna and Gokarna who are holding the bow and arrows in their two hands. Finally, Susaumya and Shubhadaayaka are guarding the northern gate. They are holding a lotus and goad in their two hands. There are also two great shaktis who guard the abode of Lord Ganesha. They are called Tejovati and Jwaalini. They are the *shaktis* or powers of Ganesha.

Just as *Svaananda Dhama* is the name of His abode, *Chintaamani Dwipa*, the Wish-Jewel Island, is the name of the celestial kingdom of Ganesha. He constantly wanders in His magnificent garden in front of His abode called *Kalpa Upavana* (Garden of Wish-fulfilling Trees).

In the great book, *Sharada Tilaka*, while discussing the meditations on Lord Ganesha, the description of the Chintamani Island of Ganesha appears as follows:

"Among the seven oceans there is an ocean called *Ikshuraasa Sagara* (the Ocean of Sugarcane Juice). An extraordinarily beautiful island called the *Chintamani Dwipa* (Wish-Jewel

Mysticism

Island) rises from the Ocean of Sugarcane Juice which surrounds the island and whose waves constantly offer their salutations to Lord Ganesha dwelling there in His transcendental abode called *Svaananda Dhama*.

"All the celestial trees like *mandaara*, *parijaataa* and other wish-fulfilling trees are there in His garden called the *Kalpa Druma Upavana*. The mystic fragrance of the flowers is blissful. Every stone, flower, plant, bird and other things on that island have consciousness and constantly sing the glory of Lord Ganesha. Always the land looks like the color crimson.

"In the midst of this island, there is a celestial tree called *paarijaata* which is full of consciousness. Its leaves and flowers sing and chant the glory of Ganesha in all seasons. At the foot of that tree there is a *mahapeeta*, the great altar. In that altar there is a great lotus. In the midst of the lotus there is a six-pointed star (*shatkona*). Inside this there is a triangle (*trikuna*). The supreme power of Lord Ganesha is established in the midst of that triangle. Ganesha is seated there. Thus one should meditate on Ganesha *loka*, His abode and His seat. Meditating thus, one will be blessed with His *darshan* (transcendental vision)."

Chintamani loka should not considered an ordinary island like Hawaii. It is of pure consciousness. It is of effulgence. It is of mellow sweetness. It is inconceivable to the human mind, but could be seen in meditation in your heart, in the language of feeling, in your *bhava loka*, the *loka* of feelings and experience. That triangle is in you at the base of the spine where the *muladhara chakra* is. That island is where the entire nervous system, all the *nadis* in the astral body, are completely connected. It is the source of all energy and the energy of procreation as well. And that is where Ganesha is dwelling in the *trikuna* in our body.

Ganesha Gita

OM NAMO VISHNU SVAROOPAAYA
NAMASTAE RUDRA ROOPINAE
NAMASTAE BRAHMA ROOPAAYA
NAMO ANANTA SVAROOPINAE

    OM. Salutations to Thee, O Lord Ganesha, You are Vishnu; You are Rudra (Shiva), salutations! You are Brahma, the creator, salutations! Your names and forms are infinite, salutations!

In the Holy Ganesha Gita, Lord Ganesha taught to His devotee, Bhaktavarenya, about Himself thus:

1. SHIVAE VISHNAU CHA SHAKTAU CHA
   SURYAE MAYI NARAADHIPA
   YAABHEDA BUDDHIR YOGAHA
   SA SAMYAG YOGO MATO MAMA

   AHAMAEVA JADYASMAAT
   SRIJAAMI PAALAYAAMI CHA
   KRITVAA NAANAAVIDHAM VISHAM
   SAMHARAAMI SVALEELAYAA

    O King Varenya, there is no difference between Shiva, Vishnu, Shakti, Surya and Myself; to know that we are One is to realize the Truth. That is what I call *Samyag Yoga*. Assuming different forms I create, sustain and dissolve endless universes by My *leela* (the divine play).

LORD GANESHA

2. AHAMAEVA MAHAVISHNU
   AHAMAEVA SADAA SHIVAHA
   AHAMAEVA MAHAA SHAKTIR
   AHAMAEVA ARYAMAA PRIYA

   AHAMAEKO NRINAAM NAATHO
   HATAHA PANCHA VIDHAHA PURAA
   AJNAANAAN MAAM NA JAANANTI
   JAGATKAARANA KAARANAM

   O dear King! I am Mahavishnu, I am Sadaashiva, I am Mahashakti and I am Sun God. I am the supreme Master of all beings, and in ancient times, I myself manifested in the five main forms as Vishnu, Shiva, Shakti, Sun and Ganesha; that is Myself. I am the cause of the origin of the universe. Due to ignorance of My true form, they know Me not.

3. MATTOGNIRAAPO DHARANI MATTA AAKAASHA MAARUTAN
   BRAHMAA VISHNUSCHA RUDRASCHA LOKAPAALA DISHO DASHA
   VASAVO MANAVO GAAVO MANAVAHA PASHAVOPI CHA
   SARITAHA SAAGARAA YAKSHAA VRIKSHAHA PAKSHIGANAA API

   It is from Me that the fire, water, earth, sky, wind, Brahma, Vishnu, Rudra, celestials, ten quarters, Vasu and other guardian deities, Manu, the father of men, human beings, the bovine race or cattle, all animals, rivers, oceans, *yakshaas*, the demi-gods, trees, the entire plant kingdom and the entire bird kingdom have been created.

4. TATHAIKA VIMSHATCHI SVARGO NAAGAAHA SAPTA VANAANICHA
   MANUSHYAHA PARVATAAHA SAADHYAAHA SIDDHAA
   RAKSHOGANAAS TATHAHA
   AHAM SAAKSHEE JAGACHKSHUR ALIPTAHA SARVA KARMABHIHI
   AVIKAARO APAMAEYO AHAM AVYAKTO VISHWAGO AVYAHA

   Similarly, heavenly abodes, the reptile kingdom, the seven islands and forests, mountains, *saadhyas* (angels) and *siddhas* (perfected beings), and *rakshasas* (demons) are created by Me. I am the solar deity, the witness of this world. I am detached and beyond all karma. I am beyond duality, causeless, the unmanifested, all-pervading, indestructible principle.

5. AHAMAEVA PARAM BRAHMA
   AVYAYA ANANDAATMAKAM NRIPA
   MOHAYAT AKHILAAM MAYA
   SHRESTAAN MAMANARAANAMUN

   AJNO AVYEYO AHAM BHUTAATMAAN
   AADIRESHVARA EVA CHA
   AASTHAAY TRIGUNAAM MAAYAM
   BHAVAAMI BAHU YONISHU

   I am the Supreme Reality, formless and blissful. Highly evolved ones also get deluded by My *maya*, the illusory power. I have no birth, I am indestructible, I am the Self (*Atma*) of all beings and I am *Eshwara*, the Supreme Lord of the entire creation. Making My *maya* or energy as the executrix, I Myself manifest in the form of all beings.

6. ADHARMOPACHAYA DHARMAAPACHAYO MI YADAA BHAVAET
   SADHOON SAMRAKSHITUM DUSTAAM STHAADITUM
   SAMBHAVAAMYAHAM
   UCCHIDYAA ADHARMA NICHAYAM DHARMAM
   SAMSTHAAPAYAAMICHA

Mysticism

HANMI DUSTAAMSCHA DAIYAAMSCHA NAANAA LEELAAKARA MUDAA

Whenever unrighteousness predominates and virtue declines, then for the protection of the saints and the good, and for the destruction of the wicked demons, I take incarnation. I shall restore and uphold Dharma by uprooting unrighteousness. Such are my different *leelas* of bliss.

(From *Ganeshpuraanam, Ganesha Gita 1: 21-29; 3:9-11*)

Different Kinds of Ganesha Gayatri

1. EKADANTAAYA VIDHMAHAE
   VAKRATUNDAAYA DHEEMAHI
   TANNO DANTI PRACHODAYAAT (*Ganapati Upanishad*)

   I know the one-tusked Lord teaching me the oneness. I know the curve-faced one straightening my path. May that elephant-headed God bless me with enlightenment.

2. OM TATPURUSHAAYA VIDHMAHAE
   VAKRATUNDAAYA DHEEMAHI
   TANNO DANTI PRACHODAYAAT (*Narayana Upanishad*)

   I know that transcendental person. May that curve-faced one guide me. May lord Ganesha of elephant head inspire and illumine my mind.

3. OM TAT KARAATAAYA VIDHMAHAE
   HASTI MUKHAAYA DHEEMAHI
   TANNO DANTI PRACHODAYAT (*Maibraayani Samhita 2:6-9*)

   I know the mysterious Lord. May His elephant face guide me. May Lord Ganesha illumine my intellect.

Ganesha Mantras

Ganesha mantras are *siddhi* mantras. Each mantra contains certain specific powers of Lord Ganesha. When chanted with the proper *pranayama* (rhythmic breathing) and sincere devotion, they will yield good results. In general, Ganesha mantras will ward off all evil and bless the devotee with abundance, prudence and success. Evil spirits dare not enter the home or the mind of the devotee where Ganesha mantras are recited. Some such mantras are given below for the spiritual benefit of the readers.

One more point to remember is that one should bathe or wash the limbs before sitting for repetition of the mantra. Also, one should do three or more *pranayama* before beginning the mantra. The minimum repetition of the mantra should be one full rosary or 108 times. When this is done at a rigid hour and place regularly for 48 days, it becomes an "*upaasana*" which means intense meditation which will yield *siddhi* or spiritual powers. The warning given is that one should use those powers only for healing the sick and other such selfless actions for the benefit of mankind. These powers should not be misused. Misuse of power may bring the curse of the deity.

1. OM GAM GANAPATAYAE NAMAHA

This is a mantra from Ganapati Upanishad. One may always use it before beginning a journey, a new course in school, new career or job, or before entering into any new contract or business so that impediments are removed and your endeavor may be crowned with success.

LORD GANESHA

2. OM NAMO BHAGAVATAE GAJAANANAAYA NAMAHA

This is a devotional mantra personifying the all-pervading consciousness of Ganesha. This mantra is very efficacious to have the darshan of Ganesha or to feel his immediate presence as a person.

3. OM SRI GANESHAAYA NAMAHA

This mantra is usually taught to all children for their good education. It increases their memory power and they become successful in their examinations. Of course, people of any age may use this mantra when taking courses in a school or university and for success in attaining their degree.

4. OM VAKRATUNDAAYA HUM

This is a very powerful mantra as discussed in the Ganesha Puraana. When something is not working properly, individually or universally, nationally or internationally, or when the minds of the people get curved and negative, the attention of Ganesha may be drawn by this mantra to straighten their ways. The HUM symbolizes "Delay no more, my Lord, in straightening the paths of the curve-minded ones." This mantra is used many times in the Ganesha Puraana to curb the atrocities of cruel demons. In addition, this mantra could also be used for healing any spinal deficiency such as curvature of the spine or curved limbs. Dedicate 1008 repetitions of this holy word to straighten and heal such deficiencies.

5. OM KSHIPRA PRASADAYA NAMAHA

That *kshipra* means instantaneous. If some danger or something is coming your way and you don't know how to get rid of that trouble, with true devotion, practice this mantra for quick blessing.

**6. OM SHREEM HREEM KLEEM GLAUM GAM GANAPATAYAE
VARA VARADA SARVA JANAMAI VASHAMANAAYA SWAHA**

There are several *bija* (seed) mantras in this mantra. Among other things, it means "shower Your blessings, I offer my ego as an oblation."

7. OM SUMUKHAAYA NAMAHA

This mantra has a lot of meaning, but to make it simple, it means you will be always very beautiful in soul, in spirit, in face, everything. By meditating on that mantra, very pleasing manners and a beauty comes on you. Along with that comes peace which constantly dances in your eyes, and the words which you speak are all filled with that power of love.

8. OM AEKADANTAAYA NAMAHA

Aekadanta refers to one tusk in the elephant face, which means God broke the duality and made you to have a one-pointed mind. Whoever has that oneness of mind and single-minded devotion will achieve everything.

9. OM KAPILAAYA NAMAHA

Kapila means that you are able to give color therapy. You are able to create colors around yourself and around others, bathe them in that color and heal them. As per the mantra you create, so will you create the colors. Another meaning is "wish cow," the "cow of plenty." It means that whatever you wish, that comes true. There is a wish-cow inside you. Whatever you wish, especially for healing others, comes true immediately.

10. OM GAJAKARNAKAAYA NAMAHA

The ears of Ganesha, the elephant, are constantly fanning, which means people may talk a lot, but you are not receiving inside anything other than that which is important. It also means that you can sit anywhere and tune this cosmic television (the body) with seven channels

Mysticism

(*chakras*) and all 72,000 *nadis*, to any *loka* and be able to hear ancestors, angels, the voice of God, or the voice of prophets. That kind of inner ear you will develop through this mantra.

11. OM LAMBODHARAAYA NAMAHA
Which means you feel that you are this universe. It means that all the universes are within you. Like an entire tree is in the seed, the whole universe is in the sound of creation which is OM and that OM consciousness in you makes you feel that you are the universe. Therefore, if you say, realizing the oneness with the universe, "*shanti*" to the world everyday, then the grace of God will come and there will be world peace, universal peace. It is the universes within OM and OM within you.

12. OM VIKATAAYA NAMAHA
Means realizing this world as a dream or a drama. When you are in that high consciousness, this whole world looks like a dream. All of us have taken a role. We have to play our role in life as wife or husband or kids or citizens as per the role which we have taken. When an actor bitten by a sponge cobra which is brought on the stage falls, the entire audience cries, but that boy who has fallen knows that it was not a real cobra and that he is not dead. Life is a drama—definitely life in this material world, this physical world of ego is a drama. But inside, like the boy on the stage who is very happy knowing that he didn't die by the bite of the sponge cobra, like that, the truth never dies in us; it is immortal. So everything else you consider as drama. That consciousness comes to you by knowing this mantra.

13. OM VIGHNA NASHANAAYA NAMAHA
Invokes the Lord to remove every impediment in your life and in your works. By constantly knowing this mantra, all obstacles and blocked energy in you also is released.

14. OM VINAYAKAAYA NAMAHA
Vinayakaya is the name of Ganesha in the golden age. So by realizing this mantra, your life will have a golden age. In your office, in your work, you'll be the boss. Vinayaka means something under control. Vinayaka means the Lord of problems.

15. OM DHUMRAKETUVAE NAMAHA
Halley's Comet is called Dhumraketu in the *Vedas*. Whenever Halley's Comet appears, on the whole planet earth and in other places also, there will be fear and terror. The guiding Masters and those who have the wisdom to face it will all withdraw to the higher worlds. Important people die during that time, and bloodshed and various other problems come. To overcome that, it's important for us to remember this mantra for world peace.

16. OM GANADHYAKSHAAYA NAMAHA
This mantra is so important. Suppose you have a group, a country, neighbors, or any kind of group therapy, group healing or a whole country needing healing, then you have to bring that entire group to your mind's arena and say this mantra. A group healing takes place by this mantra.

17. OM BHALACHANDRAAYA NAMAHA
In Sanskrit, *bhala* means the forehead center. *Chandra* means the crescent moon. *Bhalachandra* means that *chakra* from where the nectar drips. That is the secret of all healing. It is to feel yourself as Shiva. Identifying yourself with the Truth and feeling constantly that you are carrying the crescent moon, the symbol of growth and nectar and peace.

18. OM GAJAANANAAYA NAMAHA
This means to have upon your trunk an elephant head. It means the ego is cut off and in its place, OM is kept. This means to have a head filled with infinite consciousness.

LORD GANESHA

Sri Ganapati-Atharva-Sheersham
or Ganesha Kavacham

OM SAHANAAVAVATU
SAHA NAU BHUNAKTU
SAHA VEERYAM KARAVAAVAHAI
TEJASVINAA VADHEETAAMASTU MAA VIDVISHAAVAHAI
OM SHANTIHI SHANTIHI SHANTIHI

ITI GANAPATI ATHARVA SHEERSHAM SAMAAPTAAM

OM BHADRAM KARNAEBHIHI SHRINUYAAMA DEVAA
BHADRAM PASHYAEMAAKSHIBHIRYAJATRAAHA
STHIRAIRANGAISTUSTUVAAM SASTANOOBHIR VYASHAEMA
DEVAHITAM YADAAYUHU

OM SHANTIHI SHANTIHI SHANTIHI
   OM. That which is auspicious, may we hear with our ears. That which is sacred, may we see with our eyes. May we sing Your glories and enjoy good health with strong limbs and body that is allotted to us by You, O God. OM, peace, peace, peace.

SVASTI NA INDRO VRIDDHA SHRAVAHA
SVASTINAHA POOSHAA VEDAAHA
SVASTI NASTAARKSHYO ARISTANEMIHI
SVASTI NO BRIHASPATIR DADHAATU

OM SHANTIHI SHANTIHI SHANTIHI
   May Indra, the lord of the *devas*, the all-knowing god Poosha (sun) and Taarkshya (Garuda, the eagle vehicle of Vishnu) who removes all calamities, and Brihaspati, the presiding deity over the intellect and guru of the celestials—all these being the high powers of almighty God—protect us and bestow prosperity. May we be free from the triple afflictions coming from the worlds above, within and without. OM, peace, peace, peace.

1. HARIHI OM
   NAMASTE GANAPATAYAE, TVAMAEVA PRATYAKSHAM TATTVAMASI
   TVAMAEVAM KEVALAM KARTAASI
   TVAMAEVAM KEVALAM DHARTAASI
   TVAMAEVA KEVALAM HARTAASI
   TVAMAEVA SARVAM KHALVIDAM BRAHMAASI
   TVAM SAAKSHAAD ATMAASI NITYAM
   Harihi OM.
   Salutations to Thee, O Lord Ganapati, Thou art the living Truth. Adorations to Thee, O living God, O embodiment of the great saying, "Thou art That." Thou art the creator; supporter Thou art; Thou art the dissolver of the universe. All this is pervaded by Thee, and Thou art eternal Atman.

2. RITAM VACHMI
   SATYAM VACHMI
   I speak that which is right. I speak that which is true.

Mysticism

3. AVA TVAM MAAM
   AVA VAKTAARAM
   AVA SHROTAARAM
   AVA DAATAARAM
   AVA DHAATAARAM
   AVAANOOCHAANAMAVA SHISHYAM
   AVA PASCHAATAAT
   AVA PURASTAAT
   AVOTTARAATTAAT
   AVA DAKSHINAATTAAT
   AVA CHORDHVAATTAAT
   AVAADHARAATTAAT
   SARVATO MAAM PAAHI PAAHI SAMANTAAT

   I see and glorify Thy transcendental form and listen to Thy great virtues. I adore Thee and worship Thee. I have dedicated my life for studying Thy great deeds. Protect me from the west and the east, from the north and the south, from above and below. Protect me from all calamities. Look at me, my Lord, protect me.

4. TVAM VAANGMAYASTVAM CHINMAYAHA
   TVAMAANANDA-MAYASTVAM BRAHMAMAYAHA
   TVAM SACCHIDAANANDAA ADVITEEYOSI
   TVAM PRATYAKSHAM BRAHMAASI
   TVAM JNAANAMAYO VIJNAANAMAYOSI

   Thou art the embodiment of all eloquence and wisdom. Thou art pure consciousness. Thou art the embodiment of bliss. Thou art Brahman. Thou art Truth, knowledge and bliss absolute and Thou art One without a second. Thou art the visible God. Thou art knowledge and Thou art wisdom.

5. SARVAM JAGADIDAM TVATTO JAAYATAE
   SARVAM JAGADIDAM TVATTASTISHTATHI
   SARVAM JAGADIDAM TVAYI LAYAMAESHYATI
   SARVAM JAGADIDAM TVAYI PRATYAETI
   TVAM BHUMIR AAPO ANALO ANILO NABHAHA
   TVAM CHATVAARI VAAKPADAANI

   This whole universe has emerged from Thee. This whole universe is sustained and maintained by Thee. This whole creation is dissolved by Thy power. This whole universe merges back into Thee. Thou art the earth, water, fire, air and the sky. Thou art the source of words and eloquence.

6. TVAM GUNATRAYAATEETAHA
   TVAM DEHATRAYAATEETAHA
   TVAM KAALABAYAATEETAHA
   TVAM MULAADHAARA STHITOSI NITYAM
   TVAM SHAKTI TRAYAATMAKAHA
   TVAM YOGINO DHYAAYANTI NITYAM
   TVAM BRAHMAA TVAM VISHNUSTVAM RUDRASTVAM INDRASTVAM
   AGNISTVAM VAAYUSTVAM SURYASTVAM CHANDRAMAASTVAM
   BRAHMA BHUR BHUVAHA SVAROM

   Thou art beyond the three *gunas* known as *sattva* (poise), *rajas* (passion), and *tamas* (ignorance). Thou art beyond the triple bodies known as physical, subtle and causal and the three states of consciousness (wakeful, dream and deep sleep). Thou art beyond past, present and future. *Mulaadhaara chakra*, the root-support mystical center at the base of the spine is Your

LORD GANESHA

eternal dwelling place. Thou art the embodiment of three powers known as *jnana shakti* (wisdom power), *icchhaa shakti* (will power) and *kriyaa shakti* (creative power). The great yogis always meditate on Thee. Thou art Brahma, Vishnu and Shiva. Thou art Agni (the fire god), Vaayu (the wind god) and Surya (the sun god). Thou art Chandra (the moon god) and Brahma that pervades the earth, space and heaven. Thou art OM.

7. GANAADIM PURVAMUCCHAARYA VARNAADIM TADANANTARAM
   ANUSHVAARAHA PARATARAHA
   ARADHAENDULASITAM
   TAARAENA RUDDHAM
   AETATTAVA MANU SVAROOPAM
   GAKAARAHA POORVAROOPAM
   AKAARO MADHYAMA ROOPAM
   ANUSVAARASCHAANTYA ROOPAM
   BINDUR UTTARA ROOPAM
   NAADAHA SANDHAANAM
   SAMHITAA SANDHIHI
   SA AESHA GANESHA-VIDYAA
   GANAKA RISHIHI
   NICHRAD GAAYATRI CCHANDAHA
   GANAPATIR DEVATAA
   OM GAM GANAPATAYAE NAMAHA

The first letter of the word "Gana" is "GA." That I utter first. Then is the nasal sound "M." When chanted together, they become "GAM," the seed syllable of Thee, O Lord Ganesha. This appears like the beautiful crescent moon. This is Thy transcendental form. "GA" forms the first letter; "A" the middle letter and the nasal sound "M" forms the last letter. This sound "GAM" is the essence of all sounds. I meditate on *naada*, the cosmic sound. I meditate on the holy scriptures. For this *Ganesha-vidya* (wisdom science on Ganesha), the sage is Ganaka, Gayatri is the meter. Ganapati is the presiding deity of this mantra, and the greatest mantra of Ganesha is OM GAM GANAPATAYAE NAMAHA.

8. AEKADANTAAYA VIDHMAHAE
   VAKRATUNDAAYA DHIMAHI
   TANNO DANTI PRACHODAYAT

I recognize the one-tusked elephant-headed Lord. I meditate on His twisted trunk symbolizing OM. May that one-tusked Lord enlighten and inspire me. (This is the Ganesha-Gayatri.)

9. AEKADANTAM CHATURHASTAM PAASHAM ANKUSHA DHAARINAM
   RADAMCHA VARADAM HASTAIR BIBHRAANAM MUSHAKADHVAJAM
   RAKTAM LAMBODARAM SHURPAKARNAKAM RAKTAVAASASAM
   RAKTAAGANDHAANULIPTAANGAM RAKTAPUSHPAIHI SUPOOJITAM
   BHAKTAANUKAMPINAM DEVAM JAGATKAARANAM ACHYUTAM
   AAVIRBHUTAM CHA SRISHTYAADAU PRIKRITAEHE
   PURUSHAATPARAM
   AEVAM DHYAAYATI YO NITYAM SA YOGI YOGINAAM VARAHA

I meditate on the one-tusked Lord Ganesha's face. He has four arms. He is holding a noose with His upper right hand and He holds the goad with His upper left hand. In His lower left hand, He is holding one tusk and He is showing the gesture of benediction with His lower right hand. He has a banner of the mouse. His color is red. He is of big belly carrying all the *lokas* in it. His ears resemble winnowing baskets. He is clad with red-colored clothes. His whole body is smeared with red sandalwood paste and He is worshipped with red flowers. He melts for His devotees and protects them. He is the primal cause of this universe. He is the

Mysticism

deathless principle. He manifested before the creation of this universe. He is beyond *prakriti*, the primordial energy and *purusha*, the individual soul.

Whoever meditates on Him thus everyday, that yogi is the greatest among yogis.

10. NAMO VRAATAPATAYAE
    NAMO GANAPATAYAE
    NAMAHA PRAMATHAPATAYAE
    NAMASTE ASTU LAMBODARAAYAIKADANTAAYA VIGHNA NAASHINAE
    SHIVA SUTAAYA
    SRI VARADA MURTAYAE NAMAHA

    Salutations to the Lord of the divine species. Salutations to the Lord of the *ganas*. Salutations to the Lord of the attendants of Shiva. Salutations to the cosmic-bellied One, the one-tusked elephant Lord, the remover of obstacles, the son of Lord Shiva. Salutations to One who showers His blessings!

11. AETADATHARVA SHEERSHAM YODHEETAE
    SA BRAHMABHUYAAYA KALPATAE
    SA SARVTAHA SUKHAMAEDHATAE
    SA SARVA VIGHNAIR NA BAADHYATAE
    SA PANCHA MAHAA PAAPAAT PRAMUCCHYATAE
    SAAYAMADHEEYAANO DIVASA KRITAM PAAPAM NAASHAYATI
    PRAATARADHEEYAANO RAATRI KRITAM PAAPAM NAASHAYATI
    SAAYAMPRAATAHA PRAYUNJAANO APAAPO BHAVATI
    SARVATRAADHEEYAANOPA VIGHNO BHAVATI
    DHARMA ARTHA KAAMA MOKSHAM CHA VINDATI
    IDAM ATHARVA SHEESHAM ASHISHYAAYA NA DAEYAM
    YO YADI MOHAADDAASYATI
    SA PAAPEEYAAN BHAVATI
    SAHASRAAVARTANAAT
    YAM YAM KAAMAMADHEETAE
    TAM TAMANAENA SAADHAYAET

    Whoever recites this prayer known as *Atharva-Sheersha* will attain the Brahmahood. He will never meet with any obstacles or calamities. He will be happy always. He will be free from the five great sins known as killing a child, killing a woman, killing a cow, killing a brahmin and attempting to commit suicide. By reciting this prayer in the evening, he becomes free from the sins incurred during the day. By reciting this prayer in the morning, he becomes free from the bad karmas done during the previous night. Those who recite this prayer both morning and evening become free from all karma and attain virtue, wealth, love and liberation.

    One should not teach this holy prayer to people who have no faith in God. If this *Atharva-Sheersha* prayer is taught only for the sake of money, one will lose its blessings. With devotion, if one recites this prayer one thousand times, all his wishes will be fulfilled.

12. ANAENA GANAPATIM ABHISHINCHATI
    SA VAAGMEE BHAVATI
    CHATURTHYAAMANASHNAN JAPATI
    SA VIDYAAVAAN BHAVATI
    ITI ATHARVANA VAAKYAM
    BRAHMAADYAACHARANAM VIDYAAT
    NA BIBHETI KADAACHANAETI

    Those who do the *abhisheka* or bathing of Lord Ganesha's image by reciting this prayer attain eloquence. One gets divine knowledge if one observes fasting and recites this *Atharva-Sheersha* prayer on Chaturthi day (the fourth day of each fortnight which is a special day of Lord Ganesha). Sage Atharvan revealed this text for the good of the mankind. When one

LORD GANESHA

recognizes the greatness of this prayer, the veil of *maya* will disappear and one will be able to see God and become free from fear.

13. YO DURVAAMKURAIRYAJATI
    SA VAISHRAVANOPAMO BHAVATI
    YO TAAJAIR YAJATI SA YASHOVAAN BHAVATI
    SA MEDHAAVAAN BHAVATI
    YO MODAKA SAHASRAENA YAJATI SA VAANCHITA
    PHALAMAVAAPNOTI
    YAHA SAAJYA SAMIDBHIR YAJATI SA SARVAM LABHATAE SA
    SARVAM LABHATAE
    ASTAU BRAHMANAAN SAMYAG GRAAHAYITVAA
    SURYA VARCHASVEE BHAVATI
    SURYA GRIHAE MAHAANADYAAM PRATIMAA SANNIDHAU VAA
    JAPTVAA
    SIDDHA MANTRO BHAVATI
    MAHAA VIGHNAAT PRAMUCCHYATAE
    MAHAA DOSHAAT PRAMUCCHYATAE
    MAHAA PAAPAAT PRAMUCCHYATAE
    SA SARVAVID BHAVATI SA SARVAVID BHAVATI
    YA AEVAM VEDA
    ITI UPANISHAT

Durvaa grass is dear to Ganesha. Whoever offers the durvaa grass to Ganesha with devotion becomes as wealthy as Kubera, the king of *yakshas*. Offering parched grain to Ganesha brings wisdom and fame. Offering one thousand sweet balls called "*modaka*" to Ganesha brings the fulfillment of all wishes. One gains supreme happiness and desired objects by pouring oblations of clarified butter into the fire while chanting Ganesha mantra.

One attains radiance like the sun god by teaching this *Atharva-Sheersha* to eight deserving disciples. Realization of a mantra deity comes to one who recites this prayer in a holy place during the solar eclipse. All obstacles will be removed from him. He becomes free from all sins and mistakes. He gains the highest wisdom. All his wishes come true. Yes, all his wishes come true. This is the declaration of the Vedas. This is the declaration of the Upanishads. So be it!

Thus ends the great prayer known as *Ganapati Atharva-Sheersham*.

OM SHANTIHI SHANTIHI SHANTIHI

Part III–Mythology

Philosophy, mysticism, and mythology. All are interrelated. The stories of God's divine pastimes look like ordinary stories, but they could be elaborated on for years, eons, life after life, because they are related to you and me. They are not somebody else's story. They have great symbolic meaning but require thought with full mind and concentration. Whoever listens to these stories of God will be blessed with happiness and peace. Whoever understands the inner and outer meanings of these stories becomes free from ignorance and achieves his goal.

STORIES OF LORD GANESHA

The Birth of Lord Ganesha (from Shiva Puraana)

In every cycle (*kaalpa*), the story of the birth of Ganesha is told in different ways. The story of the birth of Ganesha in this cycle, *Shveta-varaaha kalpa* (Divine Boar Cycle), is narrated thus:

Jayaa and Vijayaa, two friends of Shakti Parvati, once discussed with Her that She should create a son to head all of the *ganas* of Shiva. Parvati, pleased with the suggestion, resolved to carry it out. The great goddess thought, "There must be a son of my own who will be expert in his duties. He must not disobey my orders."

Thinking thus, goddess Parvati created a person by Her mere will from the dust or dirt of Her own cosmic body. She, being the primordial energy herself, created a boy from the three gunas or triple modes of nature known as *sattva* (poise), *rajas* (passion), and *tamas* (inertia). The boy was spotless and handsome in every limb of His body. He was huge in size and had the brilliance of a thousand suns. He was strong and full of valor.

Shakti Parvati blessed Him and said, "You are my beloved son. You shall carry out my orders obediently." Saying thus, Parvati presented Him with ornaments and clothes.

Ganesha made obeisance to Her and said, "My dear Mother, give me any duty. I shall accomplish whatever you command."

Parvati said, "Ganesha, guard my gates from today onwards. You are my own son. Do not allow anyone into my home without my permission." Accordingly, She gave Him a hard stick, kissed and placed Him, armed with that staff, as the gatekeeper at the entrance to Her palace.

Now Parvati began taking Her bath free from worry. At this very moment, Lord Shiva, Her husband, returned to His home and was about to enter the gate. Ganesha stopped Him and said, "without my Mother's permission, you cannot go in now. She is bathing. Wait until She finishes Her bath so I might obtain Her permission for you."

Shiva flew into a rage and said, "Who are you, O wicked knave? Don't you know that I am Shiva, the Lord of the universe? I am the husband of Parvati. This is my abode. Who are you to forbid me to enter?" Speaking thus, Shiva attempted to go inside. Ganesha got angry and struck Him with his hard stick several times. Lord Shiva, furious, stood outside the home and

LORD GANESHA

commanded His *ganas* (attendants) to inquire into the matter. (While following these worldly conversations, we should not forget that the Lord is playing a wonderful sport or *leela*.)

The *Shivaganas* came and spoke to Ganesha. "Listen," they said, "we are the servants of Shiva. We have come here to inquire about you and throw you out. This is Shiva's abode. You had better go away from here."

Ganesha ignored their speech and stood at the gate fearlessly. At the command of Shiva, His *ganas*, gnashing their teeth and armed with different kinds of weapons, rushed toward him. Nandi the bull caught hold of one leg and began pulling it. Bhringi caught hold of His other leg. But before they could topple Him, Ganesha struck a blow at their hands and got His legs free.

Standing at the gate, He held a big iron mace and smashed the attendants of Shiva. With crushed foreheads, broken hands, smashed backs, shattered teeth, fractured knees and blasted shoulders, the *ganas* of Shiva, thousands in number, fled in different directions to protect themselves!

Sage Narada, looking on, urged Lord Vishnu, Brahma and Indra to come there at once with all the *devatas*. Knowing this to be the *leela*, or the play of Shiva and Shakti, for a specific purpose, all the gods, headed by Brahma, came to attack Ganesha.

To assist Her son, Mother Parvati created two great *shaktis*. One *shakti*, assuming a fierce form, stood at the gate and opened her mouth as wide as the cavern of a mountain. The other *shakti* assumed a huge form as a terrible goddess ready to punish Ganesha's opponents.

The weapons hurled by the gods and *Shivaganas* were swallowed by the goddess with the wide-open mouth. Lord Ganesha won the battle single-handed. Gasping frequently for breath, being utterly shaken by His blows, the *devas* retreated and gathered around Lord Shiva.

Lord Shiva returned with a desire to fight Ganesha to the death. When Shiva lifted His trident, Lord Ganesha struck His hand with great power. The trident fell and with great anger, Lord Shiva took up His bow, Pinaka.

Ganesha felled Shiva's bow to the ground with His iron club, and struck His five hands also. Shiva took up the trident with the other five hands. The five-faced Shiva with His ten arms could not manage to fight with this boy of great *shakti*. Securing permission from Lord Shiva, Lord Vishnu created clouds of illusion and split the iron club of Ganesha by means of His discus. Then the son of Parvati took up His staff and struck Vishnu, who dramatizing great pain, fell to the ground. But He got up quickly and resumed the fight. Immediately, Lord Shiva saw His opportunity and cut off Ganesha's head with His trident.

Sage Narada broke the sad news to Parvati of the death of Her son. Parvati came running to Shiva and cried bitterly. "Oh, what shall I do? Where shall I go? Alas! How can this great misery be dispelled now?"

Lamenting, goddess Parvati became furious and angrily created hundreds of thousands of *shaktis* out of Her body instantaneously. Speaking with great fury, she cried, "O *shaktis*, devour forcibly all these *devatas*, *yakshas* and other *ganas* who have assisted Shiva in killing my son!"

Mythology

At once, the different kinds of *shaktis*, like *Karalis* (the terrific), *Kubjakas* (the hump-backed), *Khanjas* (the lame), *Lambashirshas* (the tall-headed) and the other multitudinous powers of goddess Parvati took up the gods with their hands and threw them into their mouths.

Seeing this, Shiva, Brahma, Vishnu, Indra, the *ganas* and sages headed by Sage Narada, appealed to goddess Parvati. They bowed to Her again and again and propitiated Her with many hymns. They said this prayer, "O Universal Mother, be pleased. Obeisance to You. You are the primordial *shakti*, and the source of creation. By Your anger, the three worlds are scorched. Shower Your grace and bless the world with peace."

The Divine Mother was pleased with their prayer and said, "If my son Ganesha regains life, is given first place among the *devas* and is first to be worshipped, then there will be no more destruction. There will be universal peace. Give him the power that before any action, any endeavor, anywhere, if they remember Ganesha, and offer the prayers to him, their works will be successful, and they will have no trouble or problems."

The gods agreed and intimated to Lord Shiva the wish of Parvati. Lord Shiva said, "It shall be done according to Her wish for the peace of all. Now you *devas* wash the headless body of Ganesha and I will go in the southern direction. Whatever person or creature I meet first, I shall cut off his head and fit it to this body."

Lord Shiva rushed with His trident towards the southern direction. The great god knew there was a demon of darkness called Gajasura sleeping in the southern direction who had destroyed many sages and fire sacrifices. He cut off the head of the sleeping elephant demon (*gajasura*) and carried it back.

The *devas* retrieved the body of Ganesha and after washing it well, took the head of the elephant that Lord Shiva brought and fitted it to the body. After joining it, the gods made obeisance to Shiva. Lord Brahma and Lord Vishnu, on the advice of Lord Shiva, sprinkled holy water upon the body of Ganesha. Immediately, the boy Ganesha woke up as if from a sleep.

Ganesha, with the face of an elephant, the trunk of a human and red complexion, gave joy to everyone. Goddess Parvati was delighted about Her son coming back to life and blessed the world with peace. Brahma, Vishnu and Shiva, the holy Trinity, and all the gods (*devatas*) crowned Ganesha as the supreme leader of the *ganas*, the angels, archangels, *siddhas*, *devas*, planets, divine and human species.

Goddess Parvati bestowed on Him all the *siddhis* (supernatural powers) and blessed Him lovingly. She said, "My dear son, Ganesha, you will receive worship first before all the gods and even before the Trinity. Vermilion will be your color and you will be worshipped with vermilion (*sindhwa*) by all devotees everywhere. All wishes of human beings shall be fulfilled by worshipping you with the sixteen modes of worship. All obstacles of theirs shall come to an end."

Thus, Mother Parvati blessed Her son. Then, to show the way of worship of Ganesha, She herself offered worship to Him. By this worship, all obstacles of the *devas* came to an end. Peace reigned in all the *lokas*.

Then Mother Parvati placed Ganesha on her lap. Brahma, Vishnu and Shiva blessed Ganesha and worshipped Him. They jointly declared to the *devas*, "Ganesha is the remover of

LORD GANESHA

all obstacles. He is the giver of all fruits from all rites—*vidya* (wisdom), *buddhi* (intelligence), and *siddhis* (the attainments or fulfillment). He shall be worshipped first and we shall be worshipped next or the fruit of all fire sacrifices and rites will be lost. This is the Truth."

Saying thus, Shiva, Vishnu and Brahma worshipped Ganesha respectfully with flowers, rice, sandalwood paste, fruits, food, etc. Thereafter, all the *devatas* and *ganas* also worshipped Him with devotion. So it was that the entire kingdom of heaven, the Trinity and their wives and all the denizens of heaven, proclaimed Ganesha as the presiding deity over all beings.

Lord Shiva himself conferred very special boons on Lord Ganesha. "O Ganesha, whoever worships you devoutly with songs and acts of service will achieve success in all their endeavors. Their obstacles will be shattered. Your worship vow (*vrita*) could be observed by people of all castes and especially by women for the welfare of their family and children. They will all be blessed with prosperity and good fortune."

Thus Lord Shiva blessed Ganesha. Celestial musicians sang. Celestial nymphs danced and there were flowers showered upon Ganesha. With the installation of Ganesha as the foremost deity to be worshipped, the whole universe attained peace. Brahma, Vishnu and all the gods, after paying homage to Shiva and Parvati, returned to their abodes.

Whoever listens to or reads this story of Ganesha shall have their wishes fulfilled. The sick will be healed, the poor will become rich, the childless will beget children. Those who want enlightenment and peace will obtain the same by the blessings of Lord Ganesha.

We are all like the image made by the Mother in this body. We are all given a job and a duty and as per the law, we do it. Then when the ego manifests, Shiva consciousness comes and cuts off our ego and darkness. A demon is sleeping in every one of us, the demon of darkness and ignorance, and when that head is chopped off, the Light alone is brought and thereby kept so our head is filled with the light.

Different Versions of the Story of the Birth of Ganesha Due to His Avataras in Different Kalpaas (Cycles)

In the holy *Padma-Puraana* the manifestation of Ganesha is explained thus:

Once upon a time, universal Mother Parvati applied fragrant oil to Her celestial body to take an oil bath. During that oil massage, she collected the dirt of Her cosmic body and made out of it an image with a human trunk with an elephant face. This means Shakti Parvati, being the primordial energy, used the clay to prepare an image with a man's body and an elephant head (the symbol of man's ascension to infinite consciousness).

As a part of Her divine play, She offered that image in the river Ganges. The touch of Mother Ganges made that image alive and Mother Ganga (presiding deity of the river Ganges) called Him her son and blessed Him. Then She saw that little son growing into a colossal form. Knowing the will of God, Mother Ganga handed over the son to Shakti Parvati who also called Him as her son.

Devas came and worshipped Him calling Him "Gaangaeya," the son of Ganga, and "Parvati-Nandana," the son of Parvati. Thus they worshipped Him with the mantra

Mythology

"*Dvai-Maaturaaya Namaha*" which means "we worship Him who has two mothers." The Trinity appointed Him as the head of the *ganas*. Hence, the name "Ganesha" or Ganapati came to Him.

The Story of Ganesha's Manifestation (from Linga Puraana)

Devas (celestials, the son of Aditi) and *asuraas* (demons, the sons of Diti) always fought (fight between good and evil). *Asuraas* used to please Lord Shiva through their austere penance and get special boons to defeat the *devas*. To solve this problem, Bhrihaspati, the teacher of the *devas* approached Lord Shiva and appealed to Him. "O God of gods, Mahadeva, You are known as 'Bholanath', the munificent giver. Taking advantage of this, the demons do penance and receive great boons and gifts from you and become invincible. Thus, the *devas* are suffering a lot. To overcome this problem, we request you to create a son of yours with a specific power of bringing obstacles to *asuraas* in their endeavor to destroy the good. May that son of yours be the sole authority in removing all obstacles. May He remove the obstacles of those who totally surrender themselves to Him."

Lord Shiva said, "*Tatastu* (so be it)" and disappeared.

After some time, the *devas* gathered at Kailasa Mountain for the blessings. Shiva and Parvati gave them the *darshan* and blessed them saying, "OM." At that hour, the cosmic sound of OM was heard from the supreme heavens and there appeared Ganesha—the *avatar* of OM—the Son of God Shiva. OM became Ganesha. He manifested with a transcendental body that resembled the human body with an elephant face, the symbol of OM, which means infinite consciousness.

In this manifestation, He was holding *trishula* or the trident instead of the goad. In the other hand He was holding *pasha* or the noose.

To give joy to the whole universe, Lord Ganesha danced before Shiva and Shakti. *Devas* poured the flower showers and rejoiced. Many celestials who were present offered their salutations to Lord Ganesha.

This dancing aspect of Ganesha is called "Nritya-Ganapati." Parvati presented Him with red clothes. Lord Shiva gave Him the Gayatri thread and the Gayatri mantra. Lord Shiva made His son to sit on His lap and blessed Him saying:

TAVA AVATAARAE DAITUAANAAM
VINAASHAAYA MAMAATMAJA
DAVAANAAM UPAKAARAARTHAM
DVIJAANAAM BRAHMA VAADINAAM

"O my son Ganesha, this incarnation of Yours is for the destruction of demons and for the protection of the *devas*. You create trouble in those who go against *dharma*, bringing them to their knees. And You remove all the troubles of Your devotees who walk in the path of *dharma*."

So saying, Shiva blessed His son. Ganesha saluted His parents and said, "*Tatastu*."

LORD GANESHA

The Origin of Ganesha According to Varaaha Puraana

When *devas* and sages saw that the unrighteous demons were attaining success and those who were doing righteous deeds were constantly curbed by the demons and barbarians, they sought refuge in Rudra (Shiva). The *devas* prayed to Rudra to create a great being for obstructing the actions of demons and for bringing impediments to the bad people.

Lord Shiva, pleased with the prayers of the *devas*, looked at His dazzling spouse, Uma Parvati, the primordial energy. Then four colossal shining bodies appeared without heads, one on earth, one in water, one in fire and one in air. But Rudra did not see one in the sky. Rudra was angry. Therefore, He roared, "Manifest, manifest, O great being, manifest with an elephant face (the symbol of OM), a pot belly (cosmos) and with the sacred thread of serpents (universal energy)."

When Rudra shook His body, there appeared innumerable *ganas* (attendants of Shiva).

The Creator Brahma appeared and declared, "O *devas*, rejoice. Now this great being created by Shiva and Uma will be known as Ganapati (Ganesha), the Lord of *ganas*. He will bring obstacles to the demons and all those who try to kill or defeat the good." Brahma prayed to Rudra, "O Shiva, Mahadeva, may this great being with the elephant head be the chief of all the *ganas*, *devas* and planets. May He occupy the earth, water, fire, air and the sky, making all the elements as His body and the sky as His head. May this Lord Ganesha receive the first worship from all on earth and in Heaven."

Lord Shiva said, "*Tatastu*, so be it."

Shiva and Uma blessed their son, "O Ganesha, may You bring success to your devotees, those who walk in the path of *dharma*, in all their undertakings. May You bring obstacles to those who forget to worship You and to the demons."

Ganesha said, "*Tatastu*, so be it."

Then the *devas* praised Lord Ganesha to remove all obstacles from them. Lord Ganesha blessed them.

Ganapati Khanda (from Brahma-Vaivarta Puraana)

In the *Brahma-Vaivarta Puraana*, another version of the incarnation of Ganesha is vividly discussed. When Shakti Parvati approached her husband, Shiva, for the blessing of a divine child, Shiva taught her a *vrita* (worship vow) called "Punyaka Vrita." Shiva said, "O Devi, this *vrita* will certainly fulfill your wishes. This *vrita* will bless you with a divine child who will be worshipped throughout the entire universe.

"Among pilgrimage centers, Pushkara (where the only temple of Brahma is located); among the flowers, the celestial *parijaata*; among the leaves, *tulasi* (basil); among the *yugas*, Krita Yuga (the Golden Age); and, among *vritas*, this 'Punyaka Vrita' is the greatest. Therefore, O Devi, you observe this discipline. This *vrita* pleases Sri Krishna, who is your own elder brother and the Lord of the Universe."

Saying thus, Lord Shiva took Parvati to the bank of the Ganges and imparted the great mantra of Mahavishnu (Krishna). Parvati conducted this *vrita* for one year with great devotion.

Lord Krishna was pleased with the *vrita*. He appeared before Her with His transcendental form and gave the blessing to Parvati to have an extraordinary baby son who would be worshipped even by the Trinity. Then Sri Krishna disappeared.

After a while, an old priest appeared to Her saying that he was very hungry. Parvati asked him who he was. The old brahmin began narrating the greatness of *bhakti* (devotion) to Sri Krishna and said, "O Shakti Parvati, in every cycle Lord Sri Krishna becomes your son Ganesha and displays His *leela* (the divine play)." Then the brahmin priest also disappeared.

Lord Shiva and Parvati searched for him everywhere but could not find him. From the heavens, a voice declared, "Do not search for him outside. He is Lord Krishna and even now, has taken the form of your child. He is in your inner chambers, lying there as your baby. Go see and feed milk to him."

When Parvati went to Her inner chambers, She saw an extraordinarily beautiful child, with a face like her older brother Krishna, lying there playing and calling out to Her, "Uma, Uma." This sight gave Her great joy. She realized that the old brahmin was none other than Krishna Himself—the same Lord Krishna who came now as baby Ganesha. He was filled with radiant light, with a full moon-like face and joyful countenance.

She called Lord Shiva and showed Him the supernatural baby which had appeared on Her bed by the power of the Punyaka Vrita. They both fondled the child, kissed Him and blessed Him saying, "O Divine Child, You are the fruit of all austerities. You are the embodiment of joy, love and peace."

Thereafter, Shiva and Parvati gave munificent charity to the *brahmanas*, *siddhas* and sages. At their invitation, all the *devas* came to Kailasa. Mahavishnu blessed the baby saying, "O dear Ganesha, may You live long and be equal to Your father Shiva in knowledge, and equal to Me in power. May You be the Lord of all the *siddhis*."

Brahma also said blessings. "Dear Ganesha, may Your name and fame fill the universe. May You occupy the first position and worship among gods."

God of Dharma said, "O Son of Shakti, may You be the embodiment of *dharma* and all great virtues. May You be the all-knowing, compassionate, protecting god of Your devotees."

Lord Shiva said blessings. "My dearest son, may You be benevolent, intelligent and wise. May You be the abode of peace like myself."

Goddess Lakshmi also blessed Him. "Ganesha, wherever people offer You worship and prayers, I will shower prosperity on them. May You get a noble wife."

Goddess Saraswati said, "Ganesha, I bless You with the power of knowledge, poetic ability, memory, and right discrimination."

Goddess Gayatri (Savitri) said, "Ganesha, I am the mother of the *Vedas*. I bless You to be supreme among those who know the *Vedas*."

Mountain god Hemavan blessed him, saying, "O my grandson, Ganesha, may You shine like Krishna (Vishnu) by constantly meditating on Him."

Goddess Menaka (Hemavan's wife) said, "O my grandson, Ganesha, I bless You to be like an ocean in sublimity, as beautiful as Cupid, wealthy like Lord Vishnu and righteous like Dharma Devataa."

Goddess Vasundara (Mother Earth) blessed him. "Ganesha, I bless You to be forgiving like me; may You be the shelter of Your devotees, remover of obstacles and the abode of peace."

Finally, His own Mother, Goddess Parvati blessed him. "O my dear son, Ganesha, may You be the Lord of the yogis, like Your father. May You be the bestower of supernatural powers, perfect, and the embodiment of all blessings. May You be deathless, wealthy and extremely intelligent and clever."

All the sages and saints blessed the baby as well.

Then, Lord Narayana took his seat on a celestial throne studded with precious gems. To His right sat Lord Shiva, and to His left, Brahma. The front seat was occupied by the god of *dharma*. Just next to him, the sun, moon, denizens of heaven, sages and saints, Hemavan, Menaka, and the others took their seats.

At the same hour, Shanaischara, the presiding deity over Saturn arrived to see Ganesha. That day his face was looking humble. His eyes were half-closed, and his tongue was engaged in chanting Sri Krishna mantra. He was shining like the blue flames of a fire ablaze and wearing a yellow robe.

He first bowed before Lords Vishnu, Shiva and Brahma. Then he made obeisance to his father, the sun god, to Dharma, the *devas*, and the sages. He asked their permission and entered inside the palace to bless the baby Ganesha.

There he bowed before Mother Parvati who was also sitting on a throne studded with gems. Her five female attendants were fanning Her gently. The divine Parvati asked Shanaischara to sit and asked him, "O presiding deity over Saturn, how have you been? Why are you constantly looking down at the earth and not looking at Me or my dear baby Ganesha? What is the reason? I would like to know!"

Shanaischara said, "O Divine Mother, in my opinion, karma is all-powerful. Souls enjoy or suffer as per their karma. As per good or bad karma, souls enjoy heaven or hell or are born as human beings or animals; born wealthy or poor; live with good health or sickness. As per only good karma, one enjoys a family life with a good wife and children or with one's bad karma one has a bad family life, with a quarrelsome spouse, no children or love.

"O Divine Mother, in this context I want to tell You about my own life. Since childhood, I was completely dedicated to Sri Krishna (Mahavishnu) and had no desire for a family. I always live a life of meditation and austerity.

"Then my father persuaded me to marry a beautiful woman. She was the daughter of Chitraratha. To obey my father, I married her. She was also a devotee of God who always talked and prayed to God Vishnu.

"One day, when I was in deep meditation, my young wife approached me with a desire for a son. But I had no bodily consciousness. It seems she got upset, frustrated and angry and she pronounced a curse on me. 'O Shani, from now onwards, you will be considered as inauspicious. On whosoever you look, may that person be destroyed.'

"I was shaken suddenly from my meditation and when I woke up, I fulfilled her desire. But she had no power to relieve me from that curse. Though she felt very bad about it, she could not help. Since that time, I am afraid to look at anyone lest they be destroyed. That is why I never look at anyone but keep my eyes downcast."

Hearing these words, Parvati smiled and the others who were in the room burst into laughter. They did not understand the seriousness of the words of Shani. Mother Parvati insisted that Shanaischara look at Her beautiful son and bless Him, but Shani definitely knew it would be disastrous to directly look at baby Ganesha.

Mother Parvati again said, "O Shani, look at Me; look at my dear son and bless us during this happy occasion." So Shani decided to look at Her son but not at Her. He made the God of *dharma* a witness and lifting his face, came near baby Ganesha. He looked directly at the divine child. As was expected, the head of the beautiful child was severed from the trunk and fell on the thighs of Parvati. Then instantaneously, it rose high up to Goloka, the transcendental abode of God, and there merged in the Blue Light.

Seeing the headless body, Parvati fell unconscious. When she gathered Her senses, She saw all the *devas*, *siddhas*, *ganas* and celestials standing around Her like statues, breathless and calm. Sensing the catastrophe, Lord Mahavishnu mounted on His eagle Garuda and went in the northern direction to the bank of the river Pushpabhadra.

He saw a great male elephant sleeping with its head facing northwards and its body facing south. He severed the head of that elephant quickly and brought it to the abode of Parvati on His eagle vehicle. Joining the elephant head to the trunk of the baby Ganesha, He uttered the mantra HUM and restored Ganesha to life. Then He consoled His sister Parvati and handed Ganesha back over to Her.

Looking angrily at Shanaischara, Parvati cursed him by saying, "May you live without your limbs." Immediately all the limbs of Shani disappeared and he faded into his loka.

When Lord Vishnu severed the head of the elephant and mounted on Garuda, it is said the female elephant with its young ones appealed to the Lord to restore the life of her husband. Then the compassionate Vishnu destroyed Gajaasura's (the demon disguised in the form of an elephant) head and fixed it back to the trunk of that elephant and blessed that elephant and its family to live with joy up to a cycle (*kaalpa*).

Lord Vishnu worshipped Ganesha with all sixteen modes of *puja* and said, "O Lord Ganesha, I conducted your *puja* first; hereafter let everyone worship You first. May You be worshipped by all in the entire universe and may You be the Lord of yogis." Saying thus, Sri Hari (Vishnu) offered His garland to Ganesha along with the wisdom and all *siddhis* or supernatural powers. Lord Vishnu also gave Him eight names: Vighnesha, Ganesha, Heramba, Gajaanana, Lambodara, Ekadanta, Shoorpakarna and Vinaayaka.

Thereafter, in the presence of all the gods, Ganesha's mother, Shakti Parvati, made Ganesha sit comfortably on a celestial throne and made the great sages bathe Him with 100 gold vessels (*kalashas*) full of Ganges water as they recited the Vedic mantras. After that, Ganesha

LORD GANESHA

wore the divine clothes given by His Mother. The sages also did His *puja* with all sixteen modes (*shodachopachara*) described in the *Vedas*. Brahma, Vishnu and Shiva, Hemavan, Mena, Indra and all the gods participated in the *puja*. They chanted this great mantra of Ganesha:

OM SHREEM HREEM KLEEM GANESHVARAAYA
BRAHMAROOPAAYA CHAARAVAE
SARVA SIDDHI PRADESHAAYA
VIGHNESHAAYA NAMO NAMAHA

In this mantra there are 32 Sanskrit letters. This mantra blesses one with fulfillment of all wishes and the four aims of life known as wealth (*artha*); love (*kaama*); virtue (*dharma*) and liberation (*moksha*). This mantra brings fulfillment, attainment and bestows supernatural powers. By repeating it 500,000 times with devotion, a man attains perfection and becomes a *mantra siddha* (adept in mantra). Whatever he says becomes a blessing. He becomes versatile, a great poet, guru to the gurus, attains all the *siddhis* or divine powers and the master of the universe. God channels through such a saint and blesses humanity. Just by remembering such a guru, people attain prosperity and happiness. This is the declaration of Sage Vyaasa in the book *Brahma-vaivarta Puraana*.

To relieve him from the curse of Divine Mother and as an armor of protection to him, all the *devas* and human beings, Shanaischara, the presiding deity over the planet Saturn, requested Mahavishnu to impart to him the prayer and meditation on Ganesha.

Lord Vishnu taught Shani the *Ganesha Kavacha* (Armor of Ganesha hymn) which blesses one with total protection, and said, "If a man with great reverence does the *japa* (repetition) of this *kavacha* one million times, he conquers death and becomes physically immortal, living forever." This is the declaration of Lord Vishnu in the great epic. "All sins come to an end by recitation of this *kavacha* of Ganesha and all evil spirits run away wherever this hymn is recited. Even as serpents dare not approach Garuda, the great eagle, similarly no sickness—mental or physical—or any kind of grief could ever approach a man or woman who receives this armor hymn. This hymn is to be imparted by the guru to a deserving, humble disciple.

"O Shanaischara, the title of this hymn is *Samsaara Mohana* or the most beautiful hymn in the world. Prajaapati (Progenitor, the mind-born son of Brahma) is the sage who heard this mantra in his meditations. The meter of this hymn is called Brihati and Lord Ganesha is its presiding deity. Wealth, love, virtue and liberation are oblations to this sacred hymn."

Saying thus, Lord Vishnu imparted this exalted *kavacha* to Shanaischara and to the whole world.

Samsaara-mohana Ganesha Kavacha

1. SAMSAARA MOHANASYAASYA KAVACHASYA PRAJAAPATHIHI
   RISHISHCHHANDASYA BRIHATI DEVO LAMBODARAHA SVAYAM
   DHARMAARTHA KAAMA MOKSHESHU VINIYOGAHA PRAKEERTITAHA
   SARVESHAAM KAVACHAANAAMCHA, SAARABHUTAMIDAM MUNAE
   May the above mantra protect my head. May this 32-lettered hymn protect my forehead.

2. OM HREEM KLEEM SHREEM GAM
   ETI CHA SANTATAM PAATU LOCHANAM
   TAALUKAM PAATU VIGHNAESHAHA SATATAM DHARANI TALAE

Mythology

May the above mantra protect my eyes always. Throughout my life on earth, may Lord Ganesha protect my eyesight.

3. OM HREEM SHREEM KLEEM
   ETI CHA SANTATAM PAATU NAASHIKAAM
   OM GAUM GAM SHOORPANKARNAAYA SWAHA
   PAATWADHARAM MAMA DANTAANI TAALUKAAM
   JIVHAAM PAATU MAE SHODASHAAKSHARAHA

   May the above mantra protect my nose and lips always. May these 16 letters protect my teeth, mouth and tongue always.

4. OM LAM SHREEM LAMBODARAAYA
   ETI SWAHA GANDAM SADAAVATU
   OM KLEEM HREEM VIGHNANAASHAAYA SWAHA
   KARNAM SADDAVATU

   May the above mantra protect my temples and jaws. May it protect and heal both of my ears always.

5. OM SHREEM GAM GAJAANANAAYA
   ETI SWAHA SKANDHAM SADAAVATU
   OM HREEM VINAAYAKAAYA
   ETI SWAHA PRASTAM SADAAVATU

   May the above mantra protect my shoulders always. May it protect my back always.

6. OM KLEEM HREEM
   ETI KANKARAM PAATU VAKSHAHSTHALAM CHA GAM
   KARAU PAADAU SADAA PATU
   SARVAANGAM VIGHNA NIGHNA KRIT

   May the above mantra protect my neck. May it protect my chest (heart), arms, legs and all of my limbs.

7. PRAACHYAAM LAMBODARAHA PAATU
   AAGNAEYYAAM VIGHNA NAAYAKAHA
   DAKSHINAE PAATU VIGHNAESHO
   NAIVATYAAM TU GAJAANANAHA

   May Lambodara protect me in the eastern direction and may Vighnanaayaka protect me from the southeast. May Vighnaesha protect me in the southern direction, and in the southwest may Gajaanana protect me.

8. PASCHIMAE PAARVATI PUTRO
   VAAYAVYAAM SHARAKARAATMAJAHA
   KRISHNASYAAMSHESHCHOTTARAE CHA
   PARIPURNATAMASYA CHA

   May the son of Parvati protect me from the west and in the northwest may the son of Shankara protect me. In the northern direction may Krishna's part-manifestation protect me.

9. AESHAANYAAM AEKADANTASCHA HERAMBAHA PAATU
   CHORDHVATAHA
   ADHO GANAADHIPAHA PAATU SARVA POOJYASCHA SARVADAHA
   SVAPNAE JAAGARANAE CHAIVA PAATU MAAM YOGINAAM GURUHU

   May Aekadanta protect me in the northeast. May Lord Heramba protect me from above. May the all-worshipful Ganesha protect me from all directions and below. May that Guru of the yogis protect me while I am sleeping and in my wakeful states. May He protect me always in all directions and in all states of consciousness—both here and hereafter.

10. ETI TAE KATHITAM BATSA
    SARVA MANTRANGHA VIGRAHAM
    SAMSAARA MOHANAM NAAMA KAVACHAM PARAMAADBHUTAM
    SRI KRISHNAENA PURAA DATTAM GOLOKAE RAASAMANDALAE
    VRINDAAVANAE VINEETAYA MAHYAM DINAKARAATMAJA
    MAYAA DATTAM CHA TUBHYAM CHA YASMAI KASMAI NA DAASYASI
    PARAM VARAM SARVA POOJYAM SARVA SANKATAA TAARANAM
    GUROOMABHYARCHYA VIDHIVAT KAVACHAM DHAARASAETTU SAHA
    KANTAE VAA DAKSHINAE BAAHAU SOOPI VISHNUR NA SAMSHAYAHA
    ASHVAMAEDHA SAHASRAANI, VAAJAPAEYA SHATAANICHA
    GRIHAENDRA KAVACHASYAASYA KALAAM NAARHANTI SHODASHEEM
    IDAM KAVAACHAMAJNAATVAA YO BHAVAET SHANKARAATMAJAM
    SHATA LAKSHA PRAJAPTOPI NA MANTRAHA SIDDHI DAAYAKAHA
Ganapati Khanda 13: 71-96

Lord Vishnu said, "O Shani, thus is taught to you the entire body of mantra which is Ganesha Himself in the form of this Hymn Armor. This was originally taught by Krishna Himself in Goloka just before He began His "Rasa Dance," the dance of love, the energy of which sustains the universe. This is a supremely worshipful mantra, to be received by a deserving and humble disciple through a mantra guru in a great initiation.

"This brings the realization of Lord Ganesha. Without complete devotion to Ganesha, if you do the *japa* any number of times, it will not be useful. If you do the *japa* with devotion, you will attain the highest blessings."

So saying, Lord Vishnu blessed Shani and departed to His divine abode. Practicing this hymn, Shanaischara obtained the blessings of Ganesha and His Mother, Shakti.

Chaturthi

Ganesha Chaturthi is the birthday of Lord Ganesha. It falls on the fourth day of the bright fortnight of the month of Bhadrapada which falls in the months of August-September.

During one of His birthdays, His mother, Shakti Parvati, cooked for Him twenty-one types of delicious food and a lot of sweet porridge. Ganesha ate so much that even His big belly could not contain it. Mounting His little mouse, He embarked on His nightly rounds. His mouse suddenly stumbled upon seeing a huge snake. To adjust His belly, Ganesha put the snake on as a belt 'round His stomach.

All of a sudden, He heard from the sky someone laughing at Him. He looked up and saw the moon mocking Him. Ganesha, infuriated, broke off one of His two tusks and hurled it at the moon. The moon hid himself behind the clouds. Immediately Ganesha pronounced a curse on him saying, "Let no one look at your face on my birthday. If anyone, knowingly or unknowingly, looks at you, they will be completely misunderstood in the family circle and neighborhood for no reason whatsoever."

The symbology behind the mouse and snake and Ganesha's big belly and its relationship to the moon on His birthday is highly philosophic. The whole cosmos is like the belly of God. Shakti Parvati is the primordial energy who cooks twenty-one types of dishes, meaning twenty-one expansions: seven *lokas* above, seven *lokas* below and seven oceans, all of which

Mythology

are inside the cosmic belly of Ganesha, held together by the cosmic energy *kundalini* symbolized as a huge snake which Ganesha ties around Him.

The mouse is nothing but our ego. Ganesha, using the ego as vehicle, represents the fact in every one of us that our great Self or consciousness controls the ego and uses it as a vehicle or instrument in daily efforts. In other words, one who has controlled the ego has Ganesha consciousness or God-consciousness.

Now the moon on that day, that is, Ganesha's birthday, is malefic and will not allow the mind of man to concentrate on God. That is why Ganesha punished him with His tusk and made it well known to all people by warning them of the danger of looking at the moon on such an auspicious day as His birth. In other words, it is an astrological fact that on that day, the moon creates bad moods in human beings. In case someone accidentally looks at the moon, he could atone for it by listening to the part of the Bhagavatam story where Krishna saw the moon on Ganesha's birthday and was misunderstood—even the great God was misunderstood!—by all 16,108 gopis, all three divisions of army, the entire Yadavas, and his own brother Balarama.

The story that is described in the Bhagavatam, Book Ten, Discourse 56 is as follows:

During the time of Sri Krishna there was a king called Satrajita. He worshipped the sun god for a long time and attained his grace. The sun appeared before him and gave him a precious gem called Syamantaka. King Satrajita returned to Dwaraka city with pomp and glory, wearing that gem around his neck. People who saw him, shining brilliantly like the sun, mistook him to be the sun god himself. They ran to Sri Krishna saying that the solar deity was coming to visit Him. The all-knowing Lord Krishna burst into laughter and said that it is not the sun god, only Satrajita who is wearing the gem given as a blessing to him.

King Satrajita invited gurus and priests and installed the Syamantaka gem in a beautiful shrine inside his palace. This extraordinary gem yielded a large amount of gold every day and the wealth of Satrajita was abundant.

Now Satrajita had a younger brother called Prasena. With the permission of his elder brother, Prasena decked that gem around his neck and went for hunting into a formidable forest. A ferocious lion killed Prasena and acquired the precious gem. At the same time, Lord Jambavan, one of the physically immortal beings born in *Krita yuga* continued to live in *Dwapara Yuga* as a great hero in the form of a bear. He killed the lion, took away the precious gem, and handed it over to his beautiful daughter called Jambavati.

In Dwaraka city, Satrajita came to know of the death of his younger brother in the forest and accused Sri Krishna of killing his brother and taking away the Syamantaka gem. Krishna's own brother, Balarama, and all His family members misunderstood Him for the first time. Krishna knew that all that was happening was due to His looking at the moon on Ganesha's birthday. Even though the Supreme Lord has no blame or blemish, unless He Himself shows a way to get out of the trouble, people will have no example. After He solves a problem, then that becomes the story for people to read or hear to help in conquering their own problems.

That is why Sri Krishna forthwith started His journey to the forest. He saw the lion and Prasena dead and marched towards the cave of the great bear, Jambavan, by following its footprints. Sri Krishna found the precious gem in the hands of children who were playing there and decided to take it away. After a very heavy fight with the hero Jambavan, Sri Krishna vanquished him in a severe battle.

Jambavan prayed to Sri Rama saying that he had never been defeated by a man and that God, Rama, should come to his rescue. Lo, what he saw next was Sri Rama there instead of Sri Krishna! Sri Rama said, "Hey, Jambavan, you couldn't recognize my *avatara*? I am incarnate in this *Dwapara yuga* as Sri Krishna. Due to your great services in my past incarnation in *Treta yuga*, I came to your cave to visit you and say the blessings." Jambavan saluted the Lord again and again and begged for forgiveness. He requested Lord Sri Krishna to accept his beautiful daughter, Jambavati, as one of His queens. And with great devotion, Jambavan handed over the Syamantaka gem to Sri Krishna.

Krishna returned to Dwaraka with two gems, the Syamantaka gem and the gem of a girl, Jambavati. People rejoiced at His conquest and Krishna dispelled the doubts of His family members and the citizens by showing the gem to them. Then He invited King Satrajita to His palace. In the presence of everyone, he returned the precious gem and narrated all the stories behind the gem and how He had brought it back.

King Satrajita felt very unhappy for misunderstanding the Lord of the universe. To expiate his sin, he decided to hand over to Sri Krishna his beautiful daughter, Satyabhama, and the precious gem. Seeing his genuine devotion, Lord Krishna accepted Satyabhama as one of His eight main queens.

Shukabrahma, narrating this story to King Parikshita said that whosoever simply reads or listens to this blessed story filled with the *leelas* of the Lord, will get rid of all evil reputation and misunderstandings and attain joy and peace.

The Marriage of Lord Ganesha

Shiva and Parvati were very happy at the services rendered by their son Ganesha. For the destruction of the demon Taraka Asura, a second son was born to them. His name was Skanda. Because He had six faces, He was known as "Shanmukha." And as He was born when the "*kritloka*" stars were auspicious, He was also known as "Kartekeya." The whole universe adored Him with the name "Subrahmanya," as He blessed His devotees with the knowledge of Brahman.

The universal parents, Shiva and Parvati, thought of marriage for their two sons, Ganesha and Subrahmanya, as they had attained youth—the right time for marriage. When their parents revealed the decision for them to marry, the two boys began quarreling.

One said, "marry me first!"

"No," the other rejoined, "marry me first!"

To pacify them, Shiva and Parvati devised a plan, called them near, and spoke to them thus, "O good sons, we love both of you equally. To settle your quarrel, we have made a decision. Between the two of you, whoever returns here first after going around the entire Mother Earth shall be married first."

Mythology

On hearing these words, Lord Subrahmanya immediately set off on His peacock with great speed to go around the earth quickly and return earlier than Ganesha. To their wonderment, Lord Ganesha just stood near Lord Shiva and Shakti Parvati without making any preparations to leave. Instead, He requested that His divine parents occupy the two seats He provided and prayed to them to accept His worship service. Shiva and Shakti readily agreed to this and sat on those seats.

Lord Ganesha worshipped both of them with great devotion, circumambulated seven times and made obeisance to them seven times. As He completed His seventh salutation, Lord Subrahmanya arrived, completing His journey around the entire earth. Now Subrahmanya demanded that His marriage be celebrated first because He had gone around the earth and returned to them first, as per their command. Lord Ganesha never went around the earth at all.

At this point, Lord Ganesha said, "O Divine Mother, O Universal Father, the *Vedas* declare that whoever goes around or circumnavigates his parents obtains the fruit of *bhu-pradakshina* or circling around the entire earth. When this blessing is applicable even by going around earthly parents, how much more it should be when the circumnavigation is done to you, O Divine Parents. By going around you seven times, I have gone around not only the earth, but the whole universe! Therefore, celebrate my marriage without any delay."

On hearing Ganesha's intelligent words, Shiva and Parvati were pleased and at once decided to celebrate His marriage first. Prajapati Vishwaroopa's two beautiful daughters, one called Buddhi and the other called Siddhi, were selected to marry Lord Ganesha. The divine sculptor Vishwakarma made all the arrangements for the marriage by constructing a beautiful marriage hall. Lord Shiva and Parvati celebrated the marriage of Ganesha to Buddhi and Siddhi, who bore Him two beautiful sons named Labha and Kshema respectively.

Ganesha is an eternal *brahmachari* (celibate). All the gods are, but they "marry" sometimes so that we people on mundane earth will understand. Thus, Ganesha married two beautiful daughters of Brahma the Creator, and they are called "Buddhi" and "Siddhi." The illumined mind, and attainment. The energies or powers of God are His wives. And out of these two wives, Ganesha had two children. One is called Kshema. Another is called Labha. Labha means profit, gain of the highest wealth. And Kshema means complete protection of that highest wealth.

Lord Subrahmanya, who silently observed all this, bade farewell to His parents and brother and went to the Krauncha Mountain near Lake Manasa in Kailasa Mountain. (In *Skanda Puraana*, the story of Subrahmanya is narrated, where it is explained that after the marriage of Ganesha, Subrahmanya also was married to two beautiful wives named Valli and Devasena.)

A Story of Three Demons

Once upon a time, there were three demons of darkness. They wanted more and more power for themselves. They propitiated Brahma the Creator with tamasic concentration and completely selfish motives to usurp the throne of God and the angels. Because of their tamasic concentration, Brahma appeared to them. They said, "we should be invincible and invulnerable, incapable of being defeated by any one at any time anywhere in all the universes!"

LORD GANESHA

Brahma the Creator thought, "I should put some tricky boon here. If I give them all these powers, then they will usurp the throne!" The Creator granted their request, saying, "I give you those boons with one exception. You will build three cities in the air, one of gold, one of silver and one of iron. Those three cities will be like huge planets. They will revolve and have their own nine planets and their own satellites, their own sun, moon, etc. But once in ten thousand years, these three cities will come together and during that time, with only one arrow, Shiva will be capable of bringing the destruction to you. Shiva's arrow has to hit exactly at the moment the three cities come together. Then alone will you all be gone forever, reduced to ashes. Otherwise, it will take another ten thousand years for them to come together; other than Shiva's arrow hitting at that moment when the three cities come together, you shall not be destroyed by anyone at any time, anywhere, for sure. Saying thus, the Creator disappeared.

The demons, puffed up with pride, controlled all the angels and archangels. They created their own suns and moons to revolve around them, became invincible, invulnerable, inexhaustible, and enjoyed all the heavenly treats, the celestial nymphs and dances and everything. All the *devas* were concerned. They never knew what to do. In agony, they remembered that if we propitiate Ganesha, our troubles will come to an end and so they propitiated this Son of God.

Thus the *devas* offered a prayer. Ganesha, pleased with the prayer, immediately requested His father Shiva to take up the sharp *pashupata astra*, the mantra arrow, to destroy all this terrorism in the upper and lower regions.

Shiva saw that the time was right, because the three cities had come together after ten thousand years. That moment is of great importance, so he made the Meru Mountain his bow and the serpentine energy, Vasuki, the string of the bow, and Mahavishnu Himself as the *pashupata*, the whole earth and the universe as his chariot, and the four *Vedas*—the four revelations—as his horses. He drew back the bow, ready for that very moment when the arrow had to hit the target and destroy the three cities to bring the freedom.

Then he tried to release the arrow, but something was wrong. Though the moment was right, and He was the great God Shiva, still, however he tried, the arrow was not moving from the bow. In the form of the arrow, Mahavishnu Himself was there. Shiva asked, "what is wrong? Why are we not moving?"

Lord Vishnu said, "Look! Look at the tip of the sharp arrow. See there, like a small little chickpea, your son Ganesha is sitting and he's not allowing me to move to destroy the demons!"

Shiva, surprised, addressed Ganesha. "Why are you bringing trouble to me, my son?"

"Well," replied Ganesha, "you have given me the power that before any action, especially big projects like this, you have to remember me. I will not allow even my Dad to go ahead with the project unless I am worshipped first!"

Then the Trinity declared to the whole of the world, "OH! He is not only the trouble-remover, but the trouble-maker as well!" Therefore, the Trinity offered the great prayer to Lord Ganesha.

Only after telling 'Jai!' to Him did He give the way. And in the millionth fraction of a moment in which this took place, He made the arrow hit the target with his blessings and thus came the end to the three cities and the demons who were ruling over angels and human beings.

The three cities means your three bodies—the gross, the astral and the causal. And the ego is trying to rule in these cities, the cities which are meant for the realization of truth. The ego wants to rule in three capacities in these three cities, the wakeful in the gross (the physical), the dream in the astral, and the dreamless deep sleep in the causal. It takes ten thousand lives or more, or ten thousand hours, or months, or years, until you come across the the Guru, the initiation, the mantra and the faith. When all these are combined together, then you can destroy the three cities, which means to be detached from the body consciousness and go beyond body consciousness.

When Shiva conquered the three cities, trumpets were blown, flowers were showered, and sages like Tumbura and Narada danced above the clouds singing the glory of Shiva and Ganesha!

Sri Ganesha Comes to the Aid of Sage Vyaasa

Sitting on the banks of the river Ganges in his *ashrama* called Badarika Ashrama, the immortal Sage Vyaasa contemplated writing the entire wisdom of the *Vedas* and the entire culture and history of ancient India in a book form called the *Mahabharata*. Because of the velocity of his thoughts, he needed a powerful scribe to write down his dictations. Vyaasa meditated on Brahma, the Creator. When Brahma appeared, Vyaasa asked him about the scribe. Brahma suggested the name of Lord Ganesha whose help is needed in all great writings and works.

Accordingly, Sage Vyaasa prayed to Lord Ganesha and the living Lord appeared before him. Vyaasa questioned, "O Lord, would you kindly write down my dictation on *Mahabharata*?"

Ganesha smiled and said, "I will. I will, provided there is no pause or interruption."

Vyaasa said, "My Lord, I pray that you write down my dictation only after knowing its esoteric and exoteric meaning."

Ganesha readily agreed. When Sage Vyaasa saw Ganesha writing down the dictation with the same velocity as his thoughts, he found no time to compose his new thoughts. Therefore, he dictated some verses containing 108 meanings. When Ganesha would take a minute or two to go through the 108 meanings, Vyaasa would compose another thousand stanzas in his mighty mind. Thus was written the magnum opus called *Mahabharata*, which became the national epic of India.

"All knowledge that is found in all holy books is found in *Mahabharata*. that which is not found in this book cannot be found in any other book." Such is the declaration of Sage Vyaasa.

This shows that for every great work, we need Lord Ganesha's grace. It also enlightens us to the the truth that Ganesha is a living God who appears and personally attends to the needs of His devotees!

Sri Ganesha Puraanam

We meditate on Lord Ganesha who is the word OM. OM is His true form. All saints meditate on Him as OM. May Ganesha, the embodiment of OM, bless us all!

Chapter I

In ancient times, the kingdom of Saurashtra was ruled by a king called Somakaantha. He was well-versed in the *Vedas* and other holy texts. He was practicing the *Sanatana Dharma*, the love of God. In intelligence, he was equal to Brihaspati, the teacher of celestials. In wealth, he was equal to Kubera, the treasurer of God. In patience, he was like Mother Earth; and he was sublime like the ocean. He was radiant like the sun, cool like the moon, beautiful like Cupid, and powerful like the fire.

He had five ministers called Roopavantaa, Vidyaadheesha, Kshanankara, Jnaanagameya and Subala. They counselled the king wisely and with their assistance, the king ruled over the country with *dharma*.

The emperor Somakaantha had a virtuous and beautiful queen called Sudharma. Even celestial nymphs envied her beauty. She was chaste and pure and followed her husband in practicing *dharma*, like a shadow following a man.

The had a powerful and beautiful son called Hemakanta. Thus, with a happy family, the benevolent king ruled over his country bringing peace and prosperity to his people.

(Here ends the first chapter.)

Chapter II

Sage Suta narrated this story to Sage Shaunaka and other sages:

"O sages, as the years rolled by, unfortunately King Somakaantha was attacked with leprosy. His body was filled with wounds and puss formations and bleeding. He was filled with grief and so was his family.

"He called a meeting with his cabinet ministers and decided to coronate his son Hemakanta on the throne and go to the forest to do the *tapas* (austere penance) to put an end to his karma. He spoke to them thus: 'O ministers, when I do not have health, what is the use of wealth or palace? All my beauty, fortitude, benevolence and powers have come to an end. I know this is the result of the bad karma of my past lives and I have no blame for anyone. I alone have to suffer this and therefore I am coronating my son as king. I will go the the forest and seek refuge in God.'

"Hearing these words, the cabinet members and all of his subjects cried bitterly saying that they would follow their king to the formidable forest and be with him.

"Seeing this agony, Queen Sudharma Devi said, 'O ministers, you all should assist our son Hemakanta who will be installed as the king. You should all serve the country with *dharma* following the example of my husband, the king. As per my *dharma*, I will be following my husband and serve him in the forest.'

"Hemakanta, their son said, 'O my divine parents, I will not live here without you. Like the lamp without oil, body without lifebreath, this kingdom will die without your presence.'

"The king consoled all of them saying they should follow God's *dharma* and discharge their duties for the welfare of all beings.

"He blessed his son to carry on the duties of a king and counselled him on how to discharge his duties."

(Here ends the second chapter.)

Chapter III

"King Somakaantha imparted these instructions to his son Hemakanta. 'My dear son, every day get up very early in the morning at the auspicious time known as *Brahmi muhurta* (approximately 3:45 a.m. to 4:45 a.m., which is the best time for meditation). After the elimination, cleaning and bathing, use the meditation clothes and enter the shrine. Sit in lotus posture or a comfortable posture with upright position; meditate on Guru and Ganesha first. Then offer a prayer to our family deity and Mother Earth. Recite this prayer with devotion, understanding the meaning thereof. This will bring you the blessings of prosperity and peace.'

Morning Prayer:

1. **PRAATAR NAMAAMI GANANAATHAM ASHESHA HAETAM BRAHMAADI DEVA VARADAM SAKALA AAGAMAADYAM;
DHARMA ARTHA KAAMA PHALADAM BHAVA-MOKSHA HAETAM;
VAACHAAMA AGOCHARAN ANAADIM ANANTA-ROOPAM**
    At morning, I meditate on Lord Ganesha with this prayer: O my Lord Ganesha! You are the source of this entire universe of sentient beings and insentient matter. You have blessed Brahma, archangels and angels by fulfilling their wishes. You are propitiated by all the *Vedas* and holy scriptures. You are the bestower of *dharma* (virtue), *artha* (wealth) *kaama* (love) and *moksha* (liberation) to Your votaries. You are beyond words and mind. You are eternal and the infinite Truth. Salutations!

2. **PRAATAR NAMAAMI KAMALAAPATIM UGRA VEERYAM;
NAANAAVATAARA NIRATAM NIJARAKSHANAAYA;
KSHEERAABDIVAASAM AMARAADHIPA BANDHAM AESHAM;
PAAPAAPAHAM RIPUHARAM BHAVA-MUKTI HAETAM**
    I meditate on Lord Mahavishnu, the spouse of Mahalakshmi—the goddess of wealth, the almighty Lord who incarnates again and again for the protection of the good and the destruction of the wicked. I meditate on Vishnu whose abode is the ocean of milk (the human heart), One who releases us from the bondage of karma and rebirth. I offer my morning salutations to Lord Vishnu with all my heart.

3. **PRAATAR NAMAAMI GIRIJAAPATIM INDUMAULIM;
VYAAGHRAAJINAAVRITAMUDAS TADAYAM NANDJAE;
NARAYANAENDRA VARADAM SURASIDDHA JUSTAM;
SARPAAM TRISHULA DAMAROON DADHATAM PURAARIM**
    I meditate on Lord Shiva in my morning prayers, the spouse of Girija (Shakti), One who has the crescent moon decked upon His forehead; One who is clad with the tiger skin; One whose mind's eye-fire reduced Cupid to ashes; One who is propitiated by Vishnu, Indra and other celestials on whom He bestows the great boons. To the Lord who has serpents as His

ornaments, trident and drum as His weapons; to One who has destroyed the demon Tripuraas; to that Parashiva, I salute again and again. May He bless me.

4. PRAATAR NAMAAMI DEENA NAATHAM AGHAAPAHAARAM;
   GAADAANDHAKAARA HARAM UTTAMA LOKA VANDYAM;
   VEDATRAYAATMAKA MUDASTASURAARI NAAYAM;
   JNANAIKA HAETAM URUSHAKTIM UDAARABHAAARAM

Every morning I offer my salutations to the sun god who dispels the darkness from this world by his light; he destroys our sins and blesses us. He is propitiated by the denizens of heaven and other great *lokas* above. He is the embodiment of the *Vedas*. He is dispeller of the magic of the demons. He is the bestower of pure knowledge and is of extraordinary prowess and strength. To him, I salute again and again. May he bless me.

5. PRAATAR NAMAAMI GIRIJAAM BHAVABHUTI HAETAM;
   SAMSAARA SINDHU PARAPAARATARIM TRINAETRAAM;
   TAATVAADI KARANA MUDSTAASURAARI NAAYAAM;
   MAAYENAYEEM SURAMUNEENDRA NUTAAM SURAESHEEM

I meditate on Goddess Girija (Shakti), the daughter of Mount Himalayas. She is the source of the highest wealth of Lord Shiva. It is this Divine Mother who takes us across the ocean of rebirth. She is Mahaamaaya (delusion and remover of delusion). She is the embodiment of the pure knowledge of Brahman. She is the supreme Goddess (Devi) who is propitiated by *devas* and sages. I make my obeisance to that Divine Mother. May She bless me.

"Thus King Somakaantha taught his son the power of prayer and worship of God and gave him advice for the secret of ruling the country successfully by following the way of Truth."

(Here ends the third chapter.)

Chapter IV

"Following the advice of the king, the priests and the cabinet members made all the arrangements for the coronation of Hemakanta and King Somakaantha coronated him as the king at an auspicious hour.

"King Somakaantha called all the cabinet ministers and advised them to take care of his kingdom and his son, the newly coronated king. 'Watch for the wellbeing of our people.' Saying thus, he bid farewell to everyone and went to the forest with his two ministers called Sobala and Jnaanagameya, and with his noble queen called Sudharma.

"Walking a great distance in the forest, they reached a beautiful *ashrama*. Bathing in the holy lake, the king and the queen rested underneath a tree while the ministers went to bring edible roots and fruits for their meal. While the queen was serving her husband, she saw a radiant boy and she inquired who he was. The boy said, 'I am from the *ashrama* nearby. My father is the great sage Bhrigu and my mother is Puloma. My name is Chyavana. O Mother, tell me who are you and who is this man and why is he suffering with great agony?'

"Queen Sudharma explained all that had happened and the sudden leprosy, pain and bad odor to the king's body and the afflictions they were undergoing. She appealed to the young hermit to find a way to relieve their pain and the hermit promised her that he would find a way out of the calamity.

Mythology

"Son Chyavana went running to the *ashrama* where he met his father, Sage Bhrigu, and narrated the pathetic story of the great king and queen. Sage Bhrigu sent his son to bring the royal couple to the *ashrama*. By this time the cabinet ministers had returned to the king with the fruits and edible roots, so all of them followed Chyavana to the hermitage of Sage Bhrigu. They saluted the great guru and offered him fruits and flowers. The king bathed the lotus feet of Bhrigu with his tears and appealed to him to relieve his pain and agony. Sage Bhrigu consoled him by saying, 'God is with us. Everything will be all right. All of you partake the divine food and rest tonight peacefully in our ashrama. Tomorrow, after the morning disciplines of bathing and meditation, you all come to this shrine where the entire problem will be tackled and solved by the grace of Lord Ganesha.'

(Here ends the fourth chapter.)

Chapter V–VIII

"Sage Bhrigu conducted his morning spiritual disciplines and received King Somakaantha and Queen Sudharma and the ministers in his *ashrama*. As per the request of the king, the sage began telling him about his past life:

'There was a wealthy merchant named Chidrupa in a city called Kolhaara, near Mount Vindhya. He had a chaste wife called Sulochana who was obedient to *dharma*. O King Somakaantha, you were their son in that past life. Your name was Kaamanda at that time. Late in their life, you were born and being the only son, they had deep attachment for you. When you grew up they married you to a beautiful woman called Kutumbini. You had seven sons and five daughters born of her.

'In due course of time, your parents died and you spent all their wealth carelessly Your so-called friends deceived you. You never heard the noble advice of your chaste wife. You even sold the house and spent all that money as well.

'Having nowhere to live, your wife had to take all of your children to her parents' house to protect and educate them. Thus she had to live in her parents' home.

'You became very cruel and like a mad man, you wandered about aimlessly, looting the wealth of the people and mercilessly killing many. Spending your time and money in gambling and drinking, you went on committing many heinous sins. All people became afraid of you. Building a hut in the forest, you lived like a man-hunter killing all those who used to journey through that forest. Again, you amassed a large amount of money. You old father-in-law brought your family and children and left them with you in that forest.

'One day, a good Brahmin priest called Guna Vardhana was passing through that forest. As soon as you saw him, you decided to kill him and held his hand. That priest appealed to you again and again not to kill him. He also told you the consequence would be horrible for you in the next life. But you listened not to him. Thus, in your past life you killed women, children, old people and many animals. Finally, you killed a Brahmin also.

'After a few years, you became old and crippled. Then you sent for some Brahmin priests and requested them to take *dhaan* (charity) from you. They declined and said that all your money was sinfully earned and they might have to share your bad karma if they received money from you. When the Brahmins returned to their hermitages, you confessed and prayed to Lord Ganesha. You decided to renovate an old Ganesha temple and spent most of your money in rebuilding that temple. The rest of your wealth was shared by your family and children.

After a while, you died a miserable death. Immediately, the messengers of death took you to hell and punished you mercilessly for all the wrongs you did. When still more karma was there to suffer, Yama, the god of death, asked you whether you would like to go through the punishment for all your bad karma or if you would like to enjoy the blessings of your good karma. You said you would like to enjoy the results of your good karma.

'Accordingly, you were sent to this world in this life to enjoy as the King of Saurashtra, or King Somakaantha. The blessings of renovating the old Ganesha temple made you to be born as a king and to have such a noble woman as your queen. Out of mercy for you, I have narrated all the details of your past life.'

"King Somakaantha could not believe that he did so many bad deeds in his past life. He doubted Sage Bhrigu's readings and sat there like a stone. Within moments after the king began doubting the words of the sage, several birds emerged from the body of the king and began eating his body. As the pain became unbearable, the king surrendered to Sage Bhrigu and prayed for forgiveness and protection. Immediately, the great sage roared the HUM mantra, all the birds disappeared and the king became peaceful."

(Here ends Chapters five through eight.)

Chapter IX

"Sage Bhrigu said, 'O King, all your pain will disappear and you will be freed from this leprosy and grief if you listen with devotion to the great epic called *Ganesha Puraana*. I will show you the power of Ganesha mantra. Hear now . . . .' Saying thus, Sage Bhrigu chanted the 108 holy Names of Ganesha and sprinkled the charged water upon the body of the king. Immediately, a dark dwarf manifested from the exhaled breath of the king and began growing into colossal form. With his mouth agape and his tongue stretching out of his mouth, that bloodshot-eyed demon created terror in the hearts of all.

"Sage Bhrigu asked him who he was and he replied that he was the personification of the sins which the king had committed in his past life. 'O Sage, Lord Ganesha's mantra and the sprinkling of that charged water on the body of the king made me to quit his body. Now I am very hungry. Give me food or else I shall devour King Somakaantha and all those who are with him. Also, O Sage, as you made me to quit his body, show me now a place where I can dwell.'

"So the sage commanded that evil spirit to enter into a dry tree outside his *ashrama* and eat the dry leaves which had fallen around the tree. 'If you move from the tree,' the sage said, 'I shall reduce you to ashes!'

"The evil spirit occupied the tree but was arrogant. Seeing this, the king fell flat at the feet of the sage and begged him to bestow the knowledge of *Ganesha Puraana*.

"Sage Bhrigu made the king and his queen bathe in the holy lake called Bhrigu-Sheetha and utter the mantra of his commitment to listen to the *Ganesha Puraana*.

Mythology

"The king uttered the *sankalpa kriya* (decision) to listen to the *Ganesha Puraana* through the guru Sage Bhrigu. At that very moment, his leprosy completely disappeared and he became hale and healthy. Now Sage Bhrigu took him and the queen, along with his ministers, to the shrine and conducted the worship of Lord Ganesha. After that, all of them sat comfortably as Sage Bhrigu began the great discourse.

"Sage Bhrigu said, 'Listen with devotion, O King. This wisdom of the *Puraana* was originally imparted by the creator Brahma to Sage Vyaasa. The great Vyaasa taught this to me. The same knowledge I shall impart to you as you have complete faith now in Lord Ganesha. As you grow in merits by listening to this *Puraana*, so shall grow that mango tree which was reduced to ashes by me. If that tree grows fully green, you will attain God-realization and you will be free from all sins.'

OM AVYAYASYA APRAMAEYASYA NIRGUNASYA MIRAAKRITAEHA
MANOVAGANIRUPAYASYA KEVALAANANDA ROOPINAHA

Lord Ganesha is eternal Truth. He is the great Self in the heart of all beings. He is beyond *maya* or the great illusion and beyond the triple modes of nature. He is incomprehensible to the mind and speech. He is One without a second and of blissful nature.

'Only by the grace of Lord Ganesha is one able to narrate His stories, glories and philosophy. Sage Mudgala narrated this *Puraana* to the progenitor Daksha who attained peace by listening to it.

'This wisdom should not be imparted to doubtful people. Those who have sincere devotion alone are entitled to listen to this *Puraana*.'"

Here ends the ninth chapter.

Chapter X

"Sage Bhrigu continued.

'Once upon a time, Sage Vyaasa approached the creator Brahma and said, "O Lord Brahma, my intelligence and memory power have disappeared. I cannot write or dictate the *Puraanas* anymore. Please guide me in what I should do."

'Brahma replied, "O Sage Vyaasa, don't you know that all troubles come by forgetting Lord Ganesha?"

AARAMBHAE SARVA KAARYAANAAM, PRAVAESHAE VAAPI
NIRGAMAE
SHRAUTAE SMAARTHAE LAUKOKAE
YO ASMRITO VIGHNAM KAROTI CHA

Definitely, there will be obstacles in everything unless one remembers and pays homage to Lord Ganesha. In all undertakings, journeys, beginnings of works or projects, entering a new home or any new building; in traditional, Vedic, scriptural or social activities, there will be impediments unless one remembers and worships Lord Ganesha.

'O Sage Vyaasa, take refuge in Ganesha. Please Him through hymns and worship. If He is pleased, you are able to accomplish all your works. Otherwise, you may strive for a thousand years, but there will be no fulfillment.'

LORD GANESHA

"Hearing these words of Brahma, Vyaasa requested him to narrate *Ganesha Leela*, the glories of Ganesha and His incarnations (*avataras*)."

(Here ends the tenth chapter.)

Chapter XI

"As per Sage Vyaasa's request, Brahmadeva narrated the stories of Ganesha.

"Brahma said, 'Listen, O sage, among seven billion Ganesha mantras, His one-lettered mantra OM is the greatest. After the purificatory rites you should meditate on this mantra along with rhythmic breathing (*pranayama*). Mentally seeing His form, you should repeat OM. As you go on meditating on Lord Ganesha with the help of OM, Ganesha will definitely appear to you. You ask the Lord to stay in your heart forever. Ganesha will bless you with that boon. Once He stays in your heart, you will have perfect wisdom. You are able to see the past, present and future and you will be able to write all the *Puraanas* and the scriptural texts.'

"Listening to the words of Brahma, Sage Vyaasa took a pledge of propitiating Sri Ganesha. Saluting Brahma again and again, he requested Brahma to tell him more about Lord Ganesha and His mantras."

Here ends the eleventh chapter.

Chapter XII

"The creator Brahma narrated the story of Lord Ganesha to Sage Vyaasa thus:

'Hear, O Sage Vyaasa! I have told you earlier that Lord Ganesha is the embodiment of the cosmic sound 'OM.' Without OM, no mantra yields the desired result. All this is OM and OM is Ganesha. Even the Trinity had a revelation of OM Ganesha during the universal dissolution.

'The entire creation follows a cyclic beginning and cyclic rest once in 4,320,000,000 human years. When the cyclic rest appeared, the cosmos became chaos. Fierce winds began blowing from all sides and all the mountains crumbled to pieces. Twelve *adityas* (aspects of the sun) joined together and burned everything in creation, drying all the waters of the oceans and rivers. Cataclysmic fire reduced everything to ashes. Thereafter, the great clouds called Samvartaka poured very heavy rains. The waters reached the very summit of Mount Meru, deluging everything. Thus the universal destruction took place during that cosmic dissolution.

'To show to the angels and to humanity the greatness of the Word—the OM which is Ganesha—the holy Trinity themselves dramatized fear and began chanting the Pranava Japa, OM-OM-OM. As they prayed with deep devotion, there appeared an effulgent light with the brilliance of billions of suns. In the midst of that light, Lord Ganesha appeared shining like a gold mountain. He had four arms which were holding celestial weapons. His elephant face was shining with one white tusk. The Holy Trinity saluted Lord Ganesha again and again and offered an extraordinary prayer eulogizing the Lord.'"

Here ends the 12th chapter.

Mythology

Chapter XIII

"The Holy Trinity—Brahma, Vishnu and Shiva—glorified Lord OM Ganesha thus:

1. AJAM NIRVIKALPAM NIRAAKAARAMAEKAM
   NIRAANANDAM ADVAITAM AANANDAPOORNANAM
   PARAM NIRGUNAM NIRVISHAESHAM NIREEHAM
   PARABRAHMA ROOPAM GANESHAM BHAJEMA

   Salutations to Lord Ganesha who is birthless and deathless, devoid of deformity, One without a second, the embodiment of bliss, higher than the highest, beyond maya and the three qualities of nature, eternal, and always contented. To the transcendental God Ganesha, we salute; we propitiate.

2. GUNAATEETAM AADYAM CHIDAANANDA ROOPAM
   CHIDAABHAASAKAM SARVAGAM JNAANAGAMYAM
   MUNIDHYEYAM AAKAASHROOPAM RAESHAM
   PARABRAHMA ROOPAM GANESHAM BHAJEMA

   We propitiate Lord Ganesha who is beyond the three gunas, the Primal Being, whose form is pure consciousness, who shines in the serene mind, who is all-pervading and realized through divine knowledge. Sages meditate on Him as the all-pervading sky. To that Parabrahma Ganesha, the transcendental Lord, we salute.

3. JAGAT KAARANAM KAARANAJNAANA ROOPAM
   SURAADIM SUKHAADIM YUGAADIM GANESHAM
   JAGADVYAAPANAM VISHWA VANDYAM SURESHAM
   PARABRAHMA ROOPAM GANESHAM BHAJEMA

   We salute Lord Ganesha, who is the creator, sustainer and dissolver of the universe. He is the cause of all the causes. He is the source of happiness and the creator of all angels and ages, the *yugas*. He is the Lord of all *ganas*, the species; He is the all-pervading principle, adored and worshipped by all, Lord of celestials. To that transcendental Lord, we make our obeisance.

4. RAJO YOGATO BRAHMA ROOPAM SHRUTIJNAM
   SADAA KAARYASAKTAM HRIDAACHINTYA ROOPAM
   JAGATKAARAKAM SARVA VIDYA NIDHAANAM
   PARABRAHMA ROOPAM GANESHAM NATAASMAHA

   Assuming the *rajo guna*—the creative passion—He assumes the name Brahma; He is the knower of the *Vedas*. Assuming the form of Vishnu, He protects the world. He is unthinkable and the abode of all wisdom; He is Shiva. To that transcendental Lord Ganesha, we salute.

5. SADAA SATTVAYOGAM MUDAA KREEDAMAANAM
   SURAAREEN HARANTAM JAGATPAALAYANTAM
   ANAEKAAVATAARAM NIJAAJNAANAHAARAM
   SADAA VISHNU ROOPAM GANESHAM NAMAAMAHA

   Salutations to Lord Ganesha who assumes the quality of poise known as *sattva guna* and takes the form of Vishnu. Destroying the demons, Lord Vishnu upholds *dharma* for the protection of the universe. For this cause He takes different *avataras* or incarnations and removes the veil of ignorance from His devotees. To that Ganesha who is Vishnu, we make our obeisance.

6. TAMO YOGINAM RUDRA ROOPAM TRINETRAM
   JAGADDHAARAKAM TAARAKAM JNAANA HAETUM
   ANAEKAAGAMAISVAM JANAM BODHAYANTAM
   SADAA SHIVA ROOPAM GANESHAM NAMAAMAHA

LORD GANESHA

We adore Lord Ganesha who assumes the *tamo guna* and the name Rudra (Shiva) to dissolve the ignorance of souls. Thus, the three-eyed Lord who is the witness consciousness reveals the divine knowledge which takes the souls across the ocean of rebirth. To that Ganesha, who is Shiva Himself, we make our obeisance.

7. TAMASTHOMAHAARAM JANAAJNAANAHAARAM
   TRAYEE VEDASAARAM PARABRAHMAM PAARAM
   MUNIJNAANAKAARAM VIDURAE VIKAARAM
   SADDAA BRAHMA ROOPAM GANESHAM NAMAAMAHA

Salutations to Lord Ganesha who is Brahman and the dispeller of the ignorance of His votaries. He is the meaning of all the Vedic wisdom. He reveals the Truth to the saints and sages who adore Him. To that Ganesha, the pure Brahman, we make our obeisance.

8. NIJAIROSHADHEE TARPAYANTAM KARAUGHAIHI
   SOUROUGHAAN KALAABHIHI SUDHAASRAAVINEEBHIHI
   DINAESHAAMSHEE SANTAAPAHAARAM DVIJAESHAM
   SHASHAANKA SVAROOPAM GANESHAM NAMAAMAHA

Salutations to Lord Ganesha, who assumes the form of the moon and nourishes the entire plant kingdom. Through His nectarian soothing rays, He brings joy to the denizens of heaven by removing the scorching heat of the sun. To that full moon-like Ganesha, the king of the stellar kingdom, we make our obeisance.

9. PRAKAASHA SVAROOPAM NABHO-VAAYA ROOPAM
   VIKAARAADI HAETUM KALAAKAALA BHOOTAM
   ANAEKA KRIYAANAEKA SHAKTI-SVAROOPAM
   SADAA SHAKTI ROOPAM GANESHAM NAMAAMAHA

Salutations to Lord Ganesha who is the illuminating principle. He is the sky, the wind and the source of creation. For the different functions of the universe, He assumes different forms and conducts the whole universe perfectly. Him we adore again and again.

10. PRADHAANA SVAROOPAM MAHATATTVA ROOPAM
    DHARAAVAARI ROOPAM DIGEESHAADI ROOPAM
    ASAT SATSVAROOPAM JAGAD HAETUBHOOTAM
    SADAA VISHWA-ROOPAM GANESHAM NATAHASMAHA

Salutations to Lord Ganesha who assumes the form of primordial energy, cosmic intelligence, earth, water, the directions and the guardian deities. He appears as matter and energy, sentient and insentient, remaining always as the substratum of the whole universe. To that Ganesha of cosmic form, we make our obeisance.

11. TVADEEYAE MANAHA STHAAPAYAED ANGHRIYUGMAE
    JANO VIGHNA SANGHAANNA PEEDAAM LABHAET
    LASAT SURYABIMBAE VISHAALAE STHITOYAM
    JANO DHVAANTA BAADHAAM KATHAM VA LABHAET

O Lord Ganesha, people should keep their minds on Your lotus feet firmly. If they do, they will never be troubled by unbearable obstacles. How could there be the agony of darkness when the sun is shining? How could troubles haunt them who propitiate You!

12. VAYAM BHRAAMITAAS SARVATHAA JNAANA-YOGAT
    ALABDHAASTAVAANGHRIM BAHOON VARSHA POOGAAN
    EDAANEEMAVAAPTAHA TAVAIVA PRASAADAAT
    PRAPANNAAN SADAA PAAHI VISHWAMBHARAADYA

Deluded by ignorance, without seeing Thy lotus feet for a long time, we have been i grief. It is by Thy grace we had Your *darshan* and feel blessed! O Lord Ganesha, the support of the universe, bless us, bless all and protect everybody. Salutations!

'Lord Ganesha was very much pleased at this great prayer and called the prayer '*Sthava-Raja*' which means 'King of all the prayers.' He also blessed this hymn and said, "Whoever recites everyday this hymn in praise of Me in the morning, at midday and in the evening with devotion, I will bless him with abundance, good family, good children and happiness here and hereafter. His soul will attain My immortal Kingdom of Heaven.

"After this blessing, Lord Ganesha revealed limitless universes to Brahma within His cosmic belly, inhaling him inside His belly. Seeing endless universes and celestials there, Brahma glorified Lord Ganesha again. Lord Ganesha brought Brahma out along with His exhalation. After this, as the Holy Trinity was watching, Lord Ganesha disappeared then and there. Brahma, Vishnu and Shiva returned to their celestial abodes."

Here ends the 13th chapter.

Chapter XIV

"Brahma became egotistical feeling that he could create the whole world but he was confronted with various obstacles and troubles. Then he realized that without the help of Lord Ganesha, one could never attain success in any endeavor. Therefore, he recited the Ganesha mantra with true devotion. As he meditated on Ganesha's transcendental form, he heard the voice of Lord Ganesha telling him, 'Look at the banyan tree. Look at it.'"

Here ends the 14th chapter.

Chapter XV

"Sage Bhrigu narrated the story to King Somakaantha as it was explained by Brahma to Sage Vyaasa.

"Brahma told Vyaasa his experience. 'O Sage Vyaasa, I was carried away by the celestial current in the vastness of space. And, as per the voice of Ganesha, I saw the great banyan tree. When the whole universe was destroyed through the cataclysmic flood, how could this one banyan tree remain without being destroyed?

As I was thinking this, a sweet voice emerged from the banyan tree. I saw a beautiful little boy upon the tree. He wore a beautiful crest-jewel on his head and shining earrings. He was clad in red robes and wore a cobra belt. He had a celestial human body with a one-tusked elephant head. Gently, he touched my head with His trunk and initiated me with His monosyllabic mantra "OM" and asked me to do the *tapas* or penance.'

"Brahma did the austere penance for a long time and was again blessed with the *darshan* of Lord Ganesha. Ganesha gave him the knowledge to create the universe and removed all his troubles and obstacles. Thereafter Brahma worshipped Lord Ganesha and offered two beautiful divine *shaktis* to Ganesha. It is said the two celestial ladies appeared there while he was doing the *puja* to Lord Ganesha. They are known as *buddhi* (prudence) and *siddhi* (prosperity) who are the two powers or 'wives' of Ganesha. Lord Ganesha blessed Brahma and disappeared with His powers. Brahma was now able to create the universe without any obstacle."

Whoever recites, reads or listens to this story will be blessed with prudence and prosperity.

Here ends the 15th chapter.

Chapter XVI

"Sage Bhrigu continued the story. 'O King Somakaantha, listen. By the blessings of Lord Ganesha, Brahma created seven sons from his cosmic mind. He asked his mind-born sons to create and and expand the creation. But his sons took to the path of meditation and austerity, attaining Self-realization.

'Again Brahma created seven sons from his mind. Even these sons took to the spiritual path and attained the Truth.

'So Brahma expanded the creation himself. From his mouth, *brahmanas* were born. From his shoulder, the *kshatriyas* or warrior class; from his thighs, *vaishyas* or the merchant class; and from his feet, the *shudras* or the working class was born.

'Again, from his mouth he created the fire god; from his mind, the moon; from his eyes, the sun; from his ears *prana* or the breath was born. The atmospheric region emerged from his navel; paradise from his head; earth from his feet; the directions through his ears and the entire universe from different parts of his limbs he created.

'Once, when Lord Vishnu was reclining over the ocean of milk and entered into yogic trance (*yoga-nidra*), Brahma, who was born of Vishnu's navel lotus, was threatened by the demons of duality called Madhu and Kaitabha. Brahma appealed to the divine Mother Shakti to awaken Mahavishnu for the destruction of those demons. Goddess Shakti agreed to do so."

Here ends the 16th chapter.

Chapter XVII

"Shakti awakened Lord Vishnu who fought the demons without success. Lord Vishnu assumed the form of a celestial musician and sang before Lord Shiva. Lord Shiva knew that it was Vishnu and told him to propitiate Lord Ganesha to get out of troubles and win the victory over the demons Madhu and Kaitabha."

Here ends the 17th chapter.

Chapter XVIII

"Lord Vishnu, to show the way of meditation, went to a holy place and meditated for a long time with devotion on the six-lettered mantra '*Vakratundaaya Hum*.' Ganesha appeared and Lord Vishnu glorified Him. Ganesha said to Vishnu that there will be no more obstacles, and He could go ahead and fight with the demons. That place where Lord Ganesha appeared to Lord Vishnu has become the great pilgrimage center called '*Siddhi-kshetra*.'

"Lord Vishnu resumed the battle with the demons. Egotistically, the demons said to Lord Vishnu that they would be happy to confer boons on Him. Lord Vishnu said,'then let my *sudarshana* disc chop off your heads.' As Lord Vishnu was saying these words, His weapon flew from His hand and hovered near the two demons. Then they had the knowledge of God and prayed for *moksha* (liberation). The celestial disc cut off their heads and their souls attained liberation.

"Lord Vishnu glorified Lord Ganesha for His success.

"God is one; Names are many. These are all stories of the divine play or the *leelas* of God."

Here ends the 18th and final chapter.

Ganesha Puraana, Volume 4

In Vidarbhe country, there was a village called Madisha. There, a butcher called Bheema used to kill animals mercilessly and protect his family. He also used to kill *brahmanas* and others who travelled through that forest.

On a festival day, with the desire to make more money by selling the meat, he went to the forest very early in the morning for the purpose of slaying many animals. After great success in his endeavor and while he was returning, he saw a colossal demon called Pingaaksha approaching. Out of fear, the butcher threw all the dead animals down, along with his weapons, and climbed a holy tree called *shamee*. As the demon was chasing him, the butcher hit him with a branch of that holy tree.

One leaf from that branch was carried away by the wind and fell on the head of Lord Ganesha's living image. Ganesha is always pleased when someone worships Him with *shamee* leaves. Due to some meritorious deeds of both the butcher and the demon, the leaf which fell on Ganesha brought them the highest blessings.

Lord Ganesha's messengers came to them in their chariot of light. Both the demon and the butcher, free of sin, left their mortal bodies and assuming divine bodies, ascended to Ganesha *loka*, the abode of Ganesha. Lord Ganesha blessed them with immortality. The message is, Lord Ganesha is easily pleased with some gesture of loving devotion.

How did the *shamee* leaves become dear to Ganesha? There is a beautiful story behind it. There was a king called Priya-vrita. He had two queens. The first queen was called Keerti and the second queen's name was Prabha.

Somehow, the king had deep attachment to the younger queen Prabha and he almost neglected the elder queen Keerti. Queen Prabha had a son whom they named Padmanaatha. When he grew into a young man, the king married him to the daughter of the king of Paanchaala.

The king appointed his elder queen Keerti to serve the newly-wedded couple. Finding fault with her, the younger queen kicked her mercilessly. Queen Keerti decided to drink poison and put an end to her life.

Before she could quaff the poison, her family guru Sridevu came. He initiated her with Ganesha mantra and asked her to worship Ganesha who would remove all her troubles. Accordingly, she worshipped the Lord with sixteen modes of worship and offered her prayers thus:

"O Lord Ganesha, You are the support of this whole universe. You are Brahma, Vishnu and Shiva. You are the fire god (Agni), the moon god (Chandra), the god of death (Yama), the treasurer of God, (Kubera), the god of waters (Varuna) and the wind god (Vaayu).

"You are the oceans, rivers, trees, creepers and flowers. You are happiness and misery and the cause of both. You are the trouble-maker and the one who frees us from troubles. You are the cosmos and the cosmic truth. You are the bestower of progeny, and the fulfiller of all our wishes. You are the womb of creation and You are the redeemer of *maya*. You are the primordial energy (*prakriti*) and You are consciousness (*Purusha*). You are attributeless

Brahman. You are the past, present and future. You are the protector; You are the destroyer of the enemies of *dharma*. You are the sacrifice and the Lord of sacrifice. You are knowledge and the knower. You are the omnipotent, omniscient, omnipresent Lord. O all-pervading truth, Lord of creation, You are the mantra, the Word. I surrender myself totally to Your lotus feet. Protect me!"

As queen Keerti could not obtain the holy grass (*durvaa*) to worship the Lord on that day, she worshipped with *shamee* leaves not knowing that they are dear to Lord Ganesha. (According to scripture, *tulasi* leaves are dear to Lord Vishnu, *bilva* leaves are dear to Lord Shiva and *shamee* leaves are dear to Lord Ganesha.)

Pleased with her devotional prayer and the offering of *shamee* leaves, the blessed Lord Ganesha appeared to her in a divine dream and said, "O Keerti Rani, I am pleased with your prayer and worship, especially the *puja* in which you offered me the holy *shamee* leaves. By my blessings, your husband King Priya-vrita will now love you and all prosperity shall smile on you. You will be blessed with a noble son. You should name him 'Kshipra Prasadana' which is one of my names. At the age of four, he will die due to poisoning, but at that very moment, I will send my devotee Gritsamada who will restore him by the power of my mantra. All your troubles have come to an end. Peace and prosperity will prevail in your family hereafter. Whoever reads, recites or listens to the prayer you composed will receive my complete blessings. Progeny, wealth, knowledge and devotion come to them by the virtue of this prayer and finally, they attain my abode of bliss."

Saying thus, Lord Ganesha disappeared. The queen awoke from the dream and made several salutations to Lord Ganesha's *murti*. As per the blessings of Lord Ganesha, King Priya-vrita got attracted towards her and all her misery came to an end. A beautiful son was born to them whom they named Kshipra Prasadana as per the instruction of Lord Ganesha.

When the boy was four years old, the younger queen Prabha gave him food mixed with poison. Everyone, including the king, were prostrate with grief. Sage Gritsamada was sent by Lord Ganesha. He asked Queen Keerti to offer the merit of the *puja* done to Ganesha with *shamee* leaves and to sprinkle the holy water with the leaves upon the dead body of her son. The sage uttered the mantras while this was performed and the son was restored to life. The king came to understand that it was his younger queen Prabha who poisoned his son. Immediately, he exiled her to the forest, never again to return to the kingdom.

Thus, by the power of Ganesha *puja* with the offering of *shamee* leaves, the dead son was restored and thereafter, they all lived happily.

Ganesha Puraana, Volume 6
(Incarnation as Mayuraeshvara)

Once upon a time, there was a king called Chakrapaani. He ruled over the country of Videha. The city Gandaki was the capital of that country. The king ruled the country very efficiently. He had many divine virtues and was loved and honored by his subjects. His kingdom was filled with wealth and prosperity.

He had two important cabinet ministers as his supporters. Their names were Samba and Subodhana. His queen was named Ugre. She was very beautiful and possessed divine virtues. In spite of all these blessings, they had one great worry in life. Although many children had

LORD GANESHA

been born to them, all had died at a very young age. They did several kinds of benevolent deeds and still their pain was not relieved. So they decided to go to the forest to perform austere penance for God-realization. They promised the cabinet ministers and the noble citizens of Videha that they would return if God blessed them with progeny.

Saying thus, they handed over the responsibility of ruling the country to the ministers and prepared to depart to the forest. There came at that time a great sage called Shaunaka. He blessed the royal couple and initiated them in a worship vow of the sun god called '*Surya-Naaraayana-vrita*.' The sage taught them the mystic mantras of the sun as follows:

1. OM MITRAAYA NAMAHA
2. OM RAVAYAE NAMAHA
3. OM SURYAAYA NAMAHA
4. OM BHAANAVAE NAMAHA
5. OM KHAGAAYA NAMAHA
6. OM PUSHNAE NAMAHA
7. OM HIRANYA-GARBHAAYA NAMAHA
8. OM MAREECHAYAE NAMAHA
9. OM AADITYAAYA NAMAHA
10. OM SAVITRAE NAMAHA
11. OM ARKAAYA NAMAHA
12. OM BHAASKARAAYA NAMAHA

Then the sage said, "For each mantra, O King, you should salute the sun god. The sun is pleased with salutations. You should feed 100,000 *brahmins* per day for one month with great devotion. You should maintain celibacy during this spiritual discipline. At the conclusion of this *vrita* (vow), you should munificently distribute cows, gold and clothes to the *brahmins* and sages. Then, with the blessings of the sun god, you will have a son who will be long-lived with fame and name, and having great devotion to the solar deity." Saying thus, the great sage Shaunaka disappeared then and there.

The royal couple observed the spiritual discipline with great devotion. Both of them maintained strict celibacy. One or two days before the conclusion of the discipline, the queen dreamed that a beautiful *brahmin* was enjoying her and she suddenly woke up overwhelmed with a desire for enjoyment. In a half-awake, half-sleep state, she requested the king to fulfill her desire but the king maintained his discipline of celibacy.

Then the sun god came disguised as King Chakrapaani, fulfilled the queen's desire and disappeared. After a while, the queen got up and began teasing the king about breaking his vow of celibacy before the month-long vow was finished. The king said, "In the name of the sun god, I have not broken my vow. This may be a dream you had."

The queen was frightened at these words. After a few days, she spoke to the king. "I saw you in my dream fulfilling my desire. Now I am pregnant and I don't understand who might have looked like you!"

The noble king consoled her by saying, "The solar deity was pleased with our discipline and therefore, he himself might have assumed my form in your dream and blessed you. Now, as per the word of Sage Shaunaka, a son will be born to us. I am delighted. You should feel very glad also."

Mythology

Hearing these words, the queen felt delighted. As she was carrying the energy of the sun in her womb, scorching heat manifested in her. She smeared sandalwood paste all over her body in order to feel cool, but no matter what she did, the scorching of the fire continued. Unable to bear it any longer, she went to the bank of the Sindhu River and released the energy of the sun there. She returned, sobbing, and explained everything to her husband, King Chakrapaani.

There on the bank of the river Sindhu, this energy of the sun assumed the form of a colossal baby. He had three eyes like Lord Shiva and held a disc in one hand and a trident in the other. When he cried, all three worlds were shaken. Possessing a terrible form which began growing quickly into great stature, he wanted to empty the ocean and suffocate the celestials. The ocean king got alarmed and took that colossal baby back to the king and queen, explaining that it was their child.

Queen Ugre lifted the child and began feeding him with the milk of her breast. After a few days, the king organized the naming ceremony. The child was called Sindhu after the name of the river on whose bank he was born. The king and queen distributed a lot of their wealth to the *brahmins* and others during that joyous occasion.

As a boy, he was tall and strong and began uprooting huge trees playfully. When he went to the forest, cruel animals ran away out of fear as the colossal child used to hurl huge rocks at them. Once he even leapt to the moon and stopped the moon's movement for a while before he returned to earth. He killed a powerful elephant with a strong blow of his fist to the elephant's head and kicked a mountain around like a ball. His parents concluded that their son was a demon.

The boy Sindhu grew up, attained colossal size and became very powerful. He developed a desire to usurp the throne of the *devas* and rule over all three worlds. So he asked the blessings of his parents to allow him to go to the mountains to propitiate God and get the powers. The king and queen blessed him and wished him success. As a mark of respect, he circumambulated his parents and departed for the forests and mountains to conduct severe penance.

He selected a beautiful place by a lake with pure waters flowing and began his austerities. Standing on one toe with uplifted arms, he said prayers to his guru Shukraacharaya and meditated on the mantra of the sun god given by him. He stood like a mountain, still, formidable and silent, concentrating on the effulgence of the solar deity. Rain or shine, cold or heat, hunger or thirst could not stop him from his severe penance. Withholding his breath, sustaining his body only by air or *prana*, he continued his meditation uninterruptedly even when ants built an anthill on his colossal body mistaking it to be a mountain. But he had no body consciousness at all.

A fire of *tapasya* emerged from the crown of his head and began burning all the upper *lokas*. The sun, who is the source of heat, himself felt scorched by the fire of Sindhu's austerity. Without any delay, the sun god appeared to him and sprinkled nectar on him to make him come out of his meditation. Seeing the solar deity, Sindhu fell prostrate on the ground. The sun said, "My son, ask the boon of your choice."

Sindhu praised the sun god. "O Lord Surya, salutations unto you. You are the witness of the entire universe. You are the life of the entire world. I and my entire family are blessed by your holy presence. Bless me with these boons: I should not die in the hands of anyone; I should conquer my opponents in every battle; I should be always invincible and conquer the *devas*, never meeting death through those celestials."

The sun god granted those boons and said, "You'll never meet death by the denizens of heaven nor human beings. Nor will you die through the agency of any animal or reptile. Here I give you a small container of nectar. As long as you have this nectarian container around your neck, no one will be able to kill you. If someone is able to take this away from your neck, then you will die in his hands. It looks to me that God Himself may have to take incarnation to kill you. It is impossible for anyone else to destroy you. You shall rule the three worlds and be invulnerable. Enjoy to your heart's content." Saying thus, the solar deity returned to his place.

Rejoicing, Sindhu returned to his parents who received him with great delight. He elaborately explained to them all that had happened and told of the great gifts he had received from the sun god.

Seeing the time as opportune, King Chakrapaani coronated his strong and able son and joyfully left for the forest with his queen to contemplate upon God for the rest of his life. Sindhu became the king and appointed able people to take care of the country's affairs. With a great desire to expand his power and bring all countries under his dominion, he set out with his powerful military to conquer. Demons followed his chariot on elephants and horses, armed with all their celestial weapons. The whole world trembled as they marched and thousands of kings paid their tribute, surrendering themselves to demon Sindhu.

Very powerful demons like Shumbha, Nishumbha, Vritra, Prachanda, Kaala, Kadambaasura, Shambara, Kamalaasura, Kolaasura and others became his main advisers. Among them, Kolaasura appealed to him to conquer the *devas* and subjugate all fourteen *lokas*. The other demons joined their voices with Kolaasura and praised Sindhu as the one Lord of the universe. Sindhu honored all of them by distributing very costly presents among them.

Then he gave the orders to the demon advisers and his mighty military to fight with the *devas* and to conquer them. By their magical powers, they ascended to Devaloka (Paradise) and began looting and fighting. Indra, the head of the *devas*, was alarmed. His ministers said, "O Lord Indra, it seems that this demon Sindhu is all-powerful. We have to think properly before we fight with him."

As they were talking, a thousand arrows of demon Sindhu attacked them. Indra flew into a rage and killed thousand of demons with his *Vajraayudha* (the thunderbolt). He hit Sindhu on his head and made Sindhu fall on the ground, unconscious, for some time.

After a while, the demon-king awoke, roared like a lion and struck the vehicle of Indra, the mighty elephant Iraavata, with his fist. The stroke broke the head of the elephant and blood flowed like a river. Suddenly, the demon rushed towards Indra to dash him to the ground. Lo! Indra used his *anima siddhi* to assume a minute form and escaped. Leaving everything behind, along with the celestials, he went to Vaikunta, the *loka* of Lord Vishnu, to appeal to Him to relieve them from this trouble. In the meantime, Sindhu usurped the throne of Indra and appointed all the demon heroes to different high positions to rule over Paradise.

Indra and the denizens of heaven went to Vaikunta Loka and fell at the lotus feet of Lord Mahavishnu, saying, "God, you know all of our difficulties. All the *devas* were bested in battle

Mythology

with the demons and their chief, Sindhu, has taken over our kingdom. We have taken refuge in You. Kindly protect us."

Lord Vishnu gave them the promise that He would vanquish the demons and restore their kingdom. He mounted on His eagle vehicle called Garuda, the supreme among the celestial birds, and arrived to fight with the demons. All the denizens of heaven and Indra followed Him.

Demon-king Sindhu burst into laughter hearing of the return of the *devas* in the company of Lord Vishnu. He dispatched his large army to attack the *devas* and himself came to fight with Lord Vishnu. Indra, the head of the angels, Agni (the fire god), Varuna (the god of waters), the presiding deities over the nine planets, the celestial twin physicians known as the Ashvini *devataas*, and the other *devas* began fighting with the demons.

Demon Prachanda began fighting with Varuna; demon Kamala fought with the lord of wealth, Kubera; Indra fought with the demon Vritraasura; Vaayu the wind god attacked demon Nishumbha. Another colossal demon known as Shumbha began fighting with Lord Vishnu Himself! Agni, the fire god, fought with the demon Chanda; the moon god, Chandra, fought with the demon Munda; the god of Mars, Mangala, fought with the demon Kadambha; the demon Shambara fought with Madana (or Cupid, the god of love). The demon Kaala attacked the Ashvini *devataas*, the twin physicians. Thus, the battle became fierce as each one among them was expert in warfare and each one had the mystical chant-arrows!

Demon Vritra and Indra fought for a long time. Finally Indra struck Vritra with his thunderbolt weapon called Vajraayudha and the demon fell to the ground vomiting blood. After a little while, he struck Indra with his fist and Indra ran away from the battlefield. When the *asuras* (demons) surrounded Indra on all sides, Indra used a mantra and disappeared from their sight. When Indra disappeared, the other *devas* were overcome with fear and ran away in different directions.

Seeing this, Lord Vishnu sent powerful Garuda into battle and wielding His own celestial weapon, the *sudarshana* disc, He Himself destroyed innumerable demons. Those whom Vishnu destroyed, by His blessings, attained liberation (*moksha*).

When the ferocious demons called Chanda, Munda, Shumbha and Nishumbha came to attack Lord Vishnu, He made short their lives by striking powerful blows upon their chests with His fist and threw their bodies into a river. In spite of such punishment, those four *asuras* returned and rejoined the demons' army.

In the meantime, Lord Vishnu punished the demons Vritra and Prachanda, Kaala and Kamala, by dashing them to the planet earth. The Lord severed the heads of demons Bhaumaasura and Kadambaasura with His celestial disc. Using His mace called Kaumodaki, Lord Vishnu destroyed demon Kolaasura.

Seeing the destruction of his friends, the head of the demons, Sindhu, came on his golden chariot and stood in front of Vishnu to fight with Him. All eight guardian deities, including Indra, appeared to assist Lord Vishnu. Demon Sindhu made each one of them unconscious by hitting them with his powerful fist. Thus Indra, Agni, Yama, Nirati, Varuna, Vaayu, Kubera, Ishaana and the presiding deities over the planets—the moon, Mars, Mercury, Jupiter, Venus, Saturn, Rahu and Ketu—were defeated by the colossal demon. He didn't attack the sun because earlier you have read how he was born by the blessings of the sun god.

LORD GANESHA

Finally, he tried to attack Mahavishnu but all of his weapons were reduced to ashes the moment they approached Lord Vishnu. Lord Vishnu knew that the demon was invincible by virtue of the blessings of the sun god and the '*amrita-kalasha*' (nectarian vessel) kept 'round his neck. That is why Mahavishnu stopped the war and said, "O Sindhu, I am very much pleased with your heroic deeds. Ask of me any boon of your choice."

Hearing these words of praise from the almighty Lord, Sindhu said, "O Supreme God Vishnu, if You are really pleased with me, then I pray that You, along with Lord Shiva, Brahma and the *devas* come and dwell in my city called Gandaki which is on the banks of the holy river Gandaki." Seeing his devotion, Mahavishnu could not say 'no.' He went with Sindhu and his entourage to stay at Gandaki!

As time passed, the *devas* jointly approached Mahavishnu and said, "Our Lord, demons are ruling Paradise and the heavens. You came to destroy them and restore our kingdom to us. Instead, now You made us the demon's slaves by coming to his city and staying here as his guest. We are very much confused. Kingly enlighten us."

Lord Vishnu said, "O *devas*, you are all aware of the highest boons which the demon obtained from the sun god and Brahma. It is only for some time that he will rule over Paradise and the other *lokas*. His own unrighteousness and sinful deeds will weaken him and bring his destruction. Patience is the key. Pray and meditate and wait for the right time. Your time will come and you will win."

Demon Sindhu got puffed up with pride and thought, "All the Trinity are under my control. I am the invincible Lord of the universe. None is equal to me." Thinking thus, he issued an order that no one should worship God and that everyone should worship him for he was God. All the temples and images of God should be destroyed and new temples were to be built where his image would be installed so that everyone could worship him. If anyone transgressed this order, he would be punished with death instantaneously. All the demons began carrying out his order creating terror on planet earth and in the other *lokas*. They destroyed all the temples and hermitages and threw all the holy images and symbols of God into the river. In their place, they built new temples, installed the image of demon Sindhu and began worshipping him.

All the sages took resort in Mount Meru. The cosmos became chaotic without *dharma* and the religious observances. Timely rains stopped and drought appeared everywhere. The whole earth was filled with demons who destroyed the innocent people who tried to practice *dharma*.

After a period of penance and patience, all the *devas* gathered in a place and asked their guru, Brihaspati, to guide them. The sage said, "There is only one way for our success. We should pray together to Lord Vinaayaka Ganesha with devotion and worship Him. The time is very auspicious to invoke Ganesha. It is the Maagha month (September) and Tuesday during the dark fortnight. This is the birthday of Lord Ganesha. You should prepare a beautiful ten-armed Ganesha from clay. His hands should hold all His celestial weapons. On either side of Him, you should make clay images of His two powers called *siddhi* and *buddhi*. By offering sixteen modes of worship, you should please and glorify Him with hymns and prayers. The lion is His vehicle in His aspect called Gajaanana. Lord Ganesha will be pleased with our devotion and He will destroy demon Sindhu and his followers and will bring peace in the whole universe."

Mythology

All the *devas* heeded the words of wisdom spoken by guru Brihaspati and worshipped Lord Ganesha with all sixteen modes of worship. Thereafter, they jointly offered this prayer:

1. DEENAANAATHA DAYA SINDHO
   YOGI-HRITPADMA SAMSTHITHAHA;
   AADI-MADHYAANTYA RAHITA
   SVAROOPAAYA NAMO NAMAHA

   O Lord of the forlorn, Ocean of Mercy, dweller in the heart of the yogis, You have no beginning, middle nor end. We offer our salutations unto You!

2. JAGADBHAASA, CHIDABHAASA
   JNAANA GAMYA NAMO NAMAHA
   MUNIMAANASA VISHTAAYA
   NAMO DAITYA VIGHAATINAE

   You are the Light of this world; You are the pure consciousness in the heart of all beings; You are revealed through divine knowledge. You always dwell in the shrine of the hearts of sages. You are the destroyer of demons. Salutations unto You!

3. TRILOKASHA, GUNAATEETA
   GUNA-KSHOBHA NAMO NAMAHA
   TRAILOKYA PAALANA VIBHO
   VISHWA-VYAAPI NAMO NAMAHA

   You are the Lord of three worlds. You are beyond the *trigunas* (triple modes of nature. Imbalancing the *sattva* (poise), *rajas* (passion) and *tamas* (inactivity), you create the whole universe. You are the sustainer of the three *lokas*. O all-pervading God, salutations unto You!

4. MAAYAATEETAAYA BHAKTAANAAM
   KAARMA POORAAYA TAE NAMAHA;
   SOMA SURYAAGNI-NETRAAYA
   NAMO VISHWAMBHARAAYA TAE

   You are beyond maya. You always fulfill the wishes of Your ardent devotees. Having the sun, moon and the fire as Your three eyes, You support the entire universe. O all-pervading Lord, salutations!

5. AMAEYA SHAKTAYAE TUBHYAM
   NAMASTAE CHANDRA MAULAYAE;
   CHANDRA GAURAAYA SHUDDHAAYA
   SHUDDHA JNAANA KRITAE NAMAHA

   Infinite are Your powers which none can ever fathom. You have adorned the moon on Your forehead. Bright and as soothing as the moon, You are pure truth. You are the bestower of highest knowledge to the devoted souls. Salutations!

As they were praying, a supra-terrestrial effulgent light manifested. In the midst of that dazzling light, they saw Lord Vinaayaka sitting on a lion. He had ten arms and in each hand he held a celestial weapon. Decked with costly gems that illumined all ten quarters, His body was smeared with sandalwood paste. He was wearing a snake-belt 'round His belly and His ankles had golden ankle bells which jingled. His musk-pigmented forehead was shining brightly.

All the *devas* fell at His lotus feet and glorified Him with many hymns and prayers. Lord Ganesha blessed them saying, "O *devas*, I am pleased with your devotional prayers. I know that the whole universe is suffocating under the thumb of demon Sindhu and all of you are afflicted. Therefore, I have decided to take another *avatara* called 'Mayureshvara' at Kailasa as

LORD GANESHA

the son of Shiva and Shakti Parvati. I will destroy all the demons and protect all of you who are pious. Your kingdom will be restored to you. Regaining your Paradise and your respective positions, you will all live peacefully.

"In *Kritayuga* (golden age), my *avatara* was known as 'Vinaayaka Mahotkata.' Having a lion as my vehicle, using my ten arms with ten weapons, I destroyed the demons and protected the pious. Now in the *Tretayuga* (silver age), I will appear with white color as 'Mayureshvara' with six arms and having the peacock as my vehicle. Similarly, in *Dwaaparayuga* (copper age), I will manifest with red color having four arms. I will use the mouse as my vehicle and will be known as 'Gajaanana.' Again in *Kaliyuga* (iron age), I will appear with black color and with two arms. My vehicle will be a horse and I will be known then as 'Dhumraketu.'

"All these *avataras* I take are for the establishment of *dharma* by destroying the dark powers and for sustaining good souls. Your difficulties will be over soon. You have my blessings!" Saying thus, Lord Ganesha disappeared.

Whoever listens to, reads or recites this story of Ganesha will enjoy health and wealth in this life and reach the heavens after death.

Seeing the dangers of the demon Sindhu's rule, Lord Shiva and Shakti left Kailasa mountain and went to a quiet pilgrimage place called Trisandhya along with their seven crore (70 million) *ganas* (attendants) and settled there. Seeing this, all the sages followed them and fell at the feet of Shiva, asking Him to protect them and their austerities.

Lord Shiva gave them the promise of protection and said, "I would like to stay here with all of you and meditate on my own Self. You should all pray and meditate and conduct your austerities so that the spiritual power that is generated by this penance will end the demoniac rule." Saying thus, Shiva taught Ganesha mantra to Shakti Parvati and sent her to a mountain called Lekhanaadri to meditate. This is for the incarnation of Lord Ganesha as Mayureshvara.

Shakti Parvati went to the holy mountain and began her severe penance, meditating on Ganesha. She continuously recited 'OM' which is the monosyllabic mystical sound of Ganesha. Giving up food and drink, sleep and rest, night and day she meditated on Lord Ganesha's mantra. At the end of a twelve year *tapasya* (penance), Lord Ganesha, also known as Gunesha (God of virtue), appeared in her presence. This time Ganesha appeared as Trinity—Brahma, Vishnu and Shiva—with three heads and one body in their original form.

Ganesha said, "O Mother Shakti, I am pleased with your austerity. Whatever boon you choose, the same will be granted to you."

Parvati said, "Ganesha, today my entire being was blessed with Your presence. All gods are in You and You are the supreme Lord. I pray that You be born in my womb as my son, please. This wish of mine is for the joy of all beings. Kindly fulfill my only wish!"

Ganesha said, "*Tatastu* (so be it)," and disappeared.

Shakti Parvati prepared a clay image of Ganesha as she saw him and built a temple around that living image. She called it '*Siddhi-kshetra*' which means those who meditate there will attain their wishes. She blessed that place and returned to Lord Shiva.

Mythology

Lord Shiva was in deep meditation. She fell at his feet and praised him. Lord Shiva slowly opened his eyes and blessed her. Shakti narrated all that had happened and the promise of Lord Ganesha to be born as her son.

Shiva said, "Parvati, the agony of the universe will come to an end by the incarnation of Ganesha in you. He alone is capable of destroying demon Sindhu and restoring the righteousness." Saying thus, he embraced his dazzling spouse Parvati.

Shakti Parvati meditated on Ganesha as Gunesha whose *darshan* she had earlier. Now she prepared another living image of that Gunesha and worshipped that *murti* with supreme devotion. Again the Lord appeared to her as a beautiful boy of transcendental effulgence and said, "As per my promise, I have appeared now as your son. I shall serve both you and Shiva as my divine parents and crush demon Sindhu and restore Paradise to the *devas*. After these main duties, I shall return to Svaananda Dhaama, my abode of bliss." Saying thus, he assumed the form of a little baby and began crying.

Hearing the cry of the baby, all the sages gathered around him. Parvati and her maidservants bathed the baby and fed him with milk. Lord Shiva came with his *ganas* to see and bless the baby. The child was transparent like a crystal hill. Lord Shiva addressed the sages. "O Sages, this child is the incarnation of the supreme Word, OM. He shall certainly fulfill the wishes of all the devotees and bring peace in the universe."

The sages said, "O Lord Shiva, this day, when he took his *avatara*, is the most auspicious day. This is the fourth day of the bright fortnight in the month of Bhaadrapada (September). It is a Monday; His zodiac is Leo. He will be of extreme valor and strength and will destroy the demons and restore *dharma*. This is the astrological reading of the child."

There was a festival of ten days. On the eleventh day, Lord Shiva and the sages named him as Gunesha, meaning 'one who orders the primordial energy of *trigunas* to create the universe' and also the 'abode of all divine virtues.' And it is this Gunesha who would assume the name Mayureshvara later for the destruction of demon Sindhu. Thus blessing the child Gunesha, the sages returned to their hermitages.

The secret spies of demon Sindhu carried the news to him of the incarnation of Ganesha at the hermitage of Lord Shiva as Gunesha. The spies said, "Our Lord Sindhu, there is a forest called Dandakaaranya. In the midst of the forest, there is a holy place called Trisandhya. Shiva is dwelling there with Shakti. They have an unusual baby born to them. It has six arms. Its splendor eclipses thousands of suns and moons. All the sages and Shiva named the child as Gunesha. They also predicted that he will kill all of us and restore Paradise to the *devas*. We are terror-stricken. Therefore, we have come to you to convey this news. Lord Shiva's seventy million attendants are keeping a guard on the child. Somehow, we escaped from them and came here to tell you of these events. Kindly protect us now by destroying that invincible child."

After this, all of them heard a heavenly voice say, "O demon Sindhu, your end is nearing. One who is destined to destroy you is born in a forest. Beware!"

Demon Sindhu and all his followers were terrified at the voice. It was like a bolt from the blue to them. Some of them fell unconscious with fear. For the first time in his life, Sindhu was very much disturbed. After a while, he gathered his strength and addressed the fear-stricken *asuras*. "O powerful warriors, there is no one equal to me in the three worlds. How can a lamb attack a lion? How can a mosquito kill an elephant? How can this silly child kill me? Now, some of you, using your magical powers, go and destroy that child wherever he is, and bring me the good news. Those who kill him will be highly rewarded."

Hearing this, several demons started to go to Trisandhya, the holy place where Ganesha took incarnation as Gunesha. The demons reached there after some time and waited for an opportunity to kill the boy.

Gunesha grew up like the crescent moon growing into full moon. Once Himavanta, the presiding deity over the Himalaya mountain and the father of Shakti Parvati, came to Trisandhya to see his grandson Gunesha. He brought with him some rich presents.

Parvati was beside herself with joy ineffable when she saw her father. She fell at his feet. Himavanta lifted her up, showering blessings on her. As he was very eager to see her son, she brought him and made him sit on his thigh. Himavanta was extremely happy to see his grandson. He adorned the child with the precious ornaments which he had brought. After decking him with jewels, a necklace, rings, etc., he gazed at his beauty again and again and was filled with a great joy. Then he said to his daughter, "O Parvati, this son of yours is not an ordinary baby. He is almighty God. He has come to relieve the burden of this earth by destroying evil forces.

"The moment I saw this child, my mind merged in him. I cannot think of anything else. I have found a great peace. I want to name him as Heramba which means 'remover of great obstacles' and 'bestower of happiness to his devotees.' Parvati, you must take care of your child with all alertness. May good betide you all."

After meeting Lord Shiva and partaking food, the king of the mountains left for his abode.

A few days elapsed. One day, Gunesha was playing by himself. Taking this opportunity, demon Gridhraasura, one of Sindhu's henchmen, assumed the form of a huge vulture of extraordinary strength, and rushed toward the boy, covered him with his wings and carried him away to the sky. The dust that was raised by the vulture made everyone's eyes blinded for some time, but when they could see again, they could not see the child. "Where is Gunesha?" they cried. "Where is the light of our house. Where is my child?" sobbed Shakti. When she lifted her eyes to the sky, she saw her son hanging from the beak of the huge vulture and she fainted, crying, "Please! Someone protect my child!"

As everyone was crying with agony, Gunesha, the supreme Lord, suffocated the vulture who fell, along with the boy, to earth. The vulture form disappeared and the dead demon was seen in his true color.

Shakti came running with the others and lifted her son and hugged him, caressed him and kissed him. All were wonderstruck at the strength of the child in killing the demon and returning to earth unharmed! It was clear to everyone that he was God. The attendants of Shiva came and threw the colossal body of the demon away in the mountains.

Whoever listens to this leela of Gunesha will never be hurt by demons!

Mythology

Baby Gunesha became one month old and the second month began. One day Parvati bathed her baby, made him sleep in his cradle and began singing a lullaby. Suddenly, she saw two big rats fighting with one another as they approached the cradle. Though she tried to drive them away with the aid of a stick, unfortunately they entered the cradle and began hurting her baby Gunesha. These were the two demons again sent by demon Sindhu to kill the child. Their names were Kshema and Kushala.

Suddenly, Gunesha opened his eyes and roared. Shakti fainted and everyone in that *ashrama* was alarmed. In the meantime, almighty Lord Gunesha squeezed both rats with his two hands and threw them on the ground. Assuming their true forms, both demons died vomiting blood. The attendants of Shiva once again threw their huge bodies away in the mountains. *Brahmins* sang peace hymns to the child. Parvati kissed her mysterious child and prayed for his protection.

Sages came and recited the *rakshoghna* mantras for the protection of the child from the demons and put a protective talisman around his neck. Until the end of the second month, there were no more untoward incidents. People thought the mantra medal was going to protect their Gunesha.

Now Gunesha entered his third month of growth. One day, Shakti was sleeping with her baby and a demon called Krura, assuming the form of a cat, entered the house. He managed to climb upon the bed, catch hold of the head of the little baby with his teeth and jump down.

Gunesha gave a big cry which awakened Shakti and others. They saw the cat holding the baby's head in its mouth. Parvati called the attendants to protect her child, but in the meantime, the demon attempted to bite the neck of Gunesha. Lo! Gunesha held the ears of the cat tightly and pulled those ears forcibly. Within seconds, the demon fell dead with a loud cry that shook the *ashrama*.

Parvati lifted her baby and went to a safer place where she bathed him gently. She kept a strict guard on the child herself and sang songs for him to rest.

Baby Gunesha entered his fourth month. That was the day when the northern solstice began. All married women came with their little children to Parvati's home to offer their respects to Parvati. All of their children began playing and the little babies, including Gunesha, crawled on the ground as the women got immersed in their festivities.

During that time, another demon called Baalaasura, assuming the form of a little child, began playing with the other children. Then he slowly moved towards Gunesha and began playing with him. Playfully, he began hitting him and pushing him. Then he held the neck of Gunesha and tried to choke him. Suddenly, Shakti saw this and asked the other women whose naughty child was fighting with Gunesha. They didn't know!

At that moment, the demon pressed the throat of Gunesha very forcibly. Gunesha then decided to destroy him and choked him to death. The demon fell dead in his true form, creating terror in the hearts of the people. All the women ran away to their homes with their children and Shakti invited the sages to remove all obstacles from her child through the hymns and prayers. Again the sages recited the powerful mantras for his protection and returned to their respective abodes.

LORD GANESHA

When Gunesha completed the fourth month and entered into the fifth, there came the great sage Marichi to see and bless the baby. Parvati and others made him sit comfortably and washed his feet. They offered him milk and fruits. The sage blessed all of them and said he had come to see Gunesha and bless him. In this connection, he said, "Shakti, one day when I was meditating, I saw your son Gunesha clearly. I had a mystic vision of him. To ascertain the truth of this experience, I have come here to see him and have the *darshan* of both Gunesha and Lord Shiva."

Hearing these words, Parvati was overwhelmed with joy, brought her son and handed him over to the sage. Sage Marichi made the child sit on his lap comfortably and began gazing at his transcendental beauty. It was He who appeared to the sage in his meditation.

The sage said, "O Shakti, I am convinced that your son is verily God. He is the one object of meditation of all the yogis. *Vedas* constantly praise Him. Sages renounce everything to realize Him. He is one without a second. He is Trinity. From time to time He assumes different forms to protect *dharma*. In the past, in *Kritayuga*, He assumed the form of Mahotkata Vinaayaka. In this *avatara*, He will be known as Mayureshvara, having the peacock as His vehicle. In *Dvapara* age, He will be known as Gajaanana and in *Kaliyuga*, His name will be Dhumraketu. He will be invincible. No one can ever destroy Him. Still, it is your duty to keep an eye of protection on Him always."

Shakti said, "O great sage, bless him with a special prayer of protection. Let that prayer protect my baby."

Sage Marichi entered into meditation and composed this prayer of protection to Gunesha and for the protection of all future children.

The Prayer of Protection

1. DHYAAYAET SIMHA GATAM VINAAYAKAMAMUM DIGBAAHUM AADYAE YUGAE
   TRETAAYAAM TU MAYURA-VAAHANAMAMUM SHADBAAHUKAM SIDDHIDAM
   DVAAPAARAETU GAJAANANAM YUGA BHUJAM RAKTAANGA-RAAGAM VIBHUM
   TISHYAETU DVIBHYJAM SITAANGA RUCHIRAM SARVAARTHAADAM SARVADAA

   We meditate on Mahotkata Vinaayaka of *Krita* age mounted upon a lion and having ten arms. We meditate on *Mayura-vaahana* who shines with six arms mounted upon a peacock in *Treta* age. We meditate on Gajaanana of red color with four arms in *Dvapara* age; and we meditate on Dhumraketu with two arms shining in the *Kali* age.

2. VINAAYAKAHA SHIKHAAM PAATU
   PARAMAATMAA PARAATPARAHA
   ATI SUNDARA KAAYASTU
   MASTAKAM SU-MAHOTKATAHA

   May Lord Vinaayaka protect the top of the head of this child. May the radiant Mahotkata protect his head.

Mythology

3. LALAATAM KAASHYAPAHA PAATU
   BHRUYUGAM TU MAHODARAHA
   NAYANAE BHAALACHANDRASTU
   GAJAASYASHOSOTA PALLAVOU

   May the son of Sage Kashyapa protect the forehead of this child. May Mahodara who has fourteen lokas in his belly protect the brow of this baby. May Lord Bhaalachandra protect the eyes. May the elephant-headed Gajaasya protect his lips.

4. JIVHAAM PAATU GANAKREEDAHA
   CHUBUKAM GIRIJAASUTAHA
   VAECHAM VINAAYAKAHA PAATU
   DANTAAN RAKSHATU DURMUKHAHA

   May Ganapati protect his tongue. May Girijaa's son protect his temples. May Vinaayaka protect his speech. May Sumukha protect his teeth.

5. SHRAVANAU PAASHAPAANISTU
   NAASIKAAM CHINTHITAARTHADAHA
   GANESHASTU MUKHAM KANTAM
   PAATU DEVO GANANJAYAHA

   One who is holding the noose, may He protect the ears of the child. May the fulfiller of the wishes of His devotees protect his nose. May Ganesha protect his face. May the victorious Lord protect his neck.

Ganesha Leela

Once upon a time, there lived in a town in Bengal a *brahmin* named Rudraketu well-versed in the *Vedas*. His chaste and beautiful wife, Sharada, was obedient to *dharma* and always worshipped God and gurus. They prayed for children and she conceived. After nine months she gave birth to twin children who were named Devaantaka and Naraantaaka. Rudraketu rejoiced and distributed wealth and food to the priests and astrologers who predicted that the children would be famous and powerful when they grew up.

As the children grew, they gave great happiness to their parents and relatives. Sage Narada blessed them and said, "They will be strong and mighty. I advise them both to go to the holy mountain and propitiate Lord Shiva." Then Narada initiated the twins with the five-lettered holy mantra OM NAMAH SHIVAAYA. After this, Sage Narada left for Brahmaloka chanting the Holy Name.

The young men, Devaantaka and Naraantaaka, went to the holy mountains and began their austere penance. They stood with one leg and after a few days stood on their toes with uplifted arms meditating on OM NAMAH SHIVAAYA. Lord Shiva was pleased with their austerity and devotion and appeared in their presence. They saw Lord Shiva mounted on the bull Nandi, wrapped in tiger skin, with five heads and ten arms, His head decked with the crescent moon and the river Ganges flowing from His matted locks. Serpents coiled 'round His body which was smeared with holy ashes.

Leaping with joy, Devaantaka and Naraantaaka fell prostrate at His lotus feet and prayed to the Lord. "O great God Shiva, we are extremely blessed with Your *darshan*. We feel this is a great blessing to our entire family. Our ancestors will attain heaven with the grace of Thine. We know that nothing is impossible to Thee. Kindly shower Your grace upon us."

LORD GANESHA

Lord Shiva, pleased, gave them permission to ask any boon of their choice.

With joined palms, the twins prayed, "O Lord Shiva, we want to be invincible and invulnerable in all three worlds. We should never meet death from celestials, demons, human beings, evil spirits or any creature created by the creator in this whole universe. Finally, we pray for devotion to Your lotus feet."

Lord Shiva granted the boons and disappeared. Devaantaka and Naraantaaka returned to their abode and narrated all that had happened to their parents who embraced their sons and rejoiced at the news of their great success.

Receiving the blessings of their parents and other priests, they set on their journey to conquer the three worlds. Devaantaka said to his brother that he would go to conquer the celestials in *Svargaloka* (Paradise). He requested Naraantaaka to conquer everyone on the planet earth and in *Patala*, the nether regions.

Seeing an auspicious moment, Devaantaka invaded Amaravate, the capital of Indra. He destroyed Nandanavana, the beautiful garden of the *devas*. He conquered the *devas* by the might of the boon of Shiva. He even cut off the most powerful weapon of Indra, the thunderbolt (*Vajraayudha*, the diamond weapon). All the *devas*, including Indra fled and sought shelter on Mt. Meru. Now Devaantaka ascended the throne of the celestial kingdom.

Here on earth, Naraantaaka and his *asura* army routed the kings in battle and Naraantaaka became the unquestioned emperor of the whole planet earth. He sent his demon army to conquer the nether regions of *naagas* (serpents) and the army took over that kingdom defeating everyone there. Thus he subjugated all the lower *lokas* and let them live peacefully without transgressing his laws.

Now both Naraantaaka and Devaantaka met one another and were very happy at the success of each other. Thus they began governing the whole world. All the sages and saints, *devas* and angels were suffocated by the rule of the demons and were praying to God to come for their protection.

Mahotkata Avatar of Lord Ganesha

Sage Kashyapa was the son of Marichi, the mind-born son of Brahma. His chaste wife Aditi, the mother of gods once approached him with a question. "O my Lord, I had these *devataas* and Indra as my children with you. I want to know how can I have the supreme God as my son?"

Sage Kashyapa saw her sincerity and blessed her with Vinaayaka mantra and initiated her by teaching her the disciplines of propitiating God to be pleased with her austerity. Worshipping the feet of her husband, Aditi took permission from him and went to a formidable forest to do severe penance to propitiate Vinaayaka. Bathing thrice a day, she meditated on the Lord without partaking any food or even a drop of water. She lived just by breathing air and with all her mind and heart, she propitiated Lord Vinaayaka. The power of this austere penance made all cruel animals to give up their animosity and live in love with one another.

As all the *lokas* above began burning by the power of her austerity, Lord Ganesha appeared before her as Vinaayaka, the splendor of whom could eclipse thousands of suns and moons. He

Mythology

had ten arms. His earrings were shining resplendent. Siddhi and Buddhi, His two queens were with Him. His auspicious neck was decked with a large garland of pearls. He was holding a hatchet in one hand and a lotus in the other. He had a gold waistcord and His forehead had a mark of musk. He had a serpent as a belt for His belly and He had divine robes on His celestial body.

Seeing the brilliant form of the Lord, Aditi entered into silence for some time and then the Lord spoke to her. "Aditi, O mother of gods, I am Vinaayaka whom you propitiated. Ask of me any boon of your choice."

Aditi saluted the Lord and said, "O God, You are the creator, preserver and destroyer of the whole universe. You are the ancient and eternal Truth. Kindly bless me to have You as my son. Let destruction of demons and protection of the pious take place through You and may You restore *dharma*."

Lord Vinaayaka granted the boon saying, "*Tatastu* (so be it). I will be born as your son. I shall destroy the demons and protect the good. I shall restore *dharma*." Saying thus, Lord Vinaayaka disappeared.

Aditi returned to her husband gladly and saluting him, she narrated all that had happened.

In the meantime, the rule of the demons Devaantaka and Naraantaaka had brought great affliction to the *devas*, sages and saints. All of them went to the creator Brahma with Mother Earth and explained their sad predicament. Brahma asked them to offer special prayers to Lord Vinaayaka. Now all of them, lead by Brahma, offered this prayer:

1. NAMO NAMASTE AKILA LOKANAATHA
   NAMO NAMASTE AKHILA LOKA DHAAMAN
   NAMO NAMASTE AKHILA LOKA KAARIN
   NAMO NAMASTE AKHILA LOKA HAARIN

2. NAMO NAMASTE SURASHATRU NAASHA
   NAMO NAMASTE HRITA BHAKTA PAASHA
   NAMO NAMASTE NIJABHAKTA POSHA
   NAMO NAMASTE LAUGHU BHAKTI TOSHA

3. NIRAAKRITAE NITYA NIRASTAMAAYA
   PARAATPARA BRAHMAMAYA SVAROOPA
   KSHARAAKSHARAATEETA GUNAIR VIHEENA
   DEENAANUKAMPIN BHAGAVAN NAMASTE

4. NIRAAMAYAAYAAKHILA KAAMAPOORA
   NIRANJANAAYAA AKHILA DAITYADAARIN
   NITYAAYA SATYAAYA PAROPAKAARIN
   SAMAAYA SARVATRA NAMO NAMASTE

   O Lord of all the *lokas*, salutations unto Thee! O Support of the universe, salutations again and again. O Creator of endless worlds and Dissolver of the whole creation, we make our obeisance to Thee. O Destroyer of the enemies of *devas*, and the redeemer of Thy devotees from bondage, salutations! Thou art the protector of Thy votaries and Thou art pleased with their simple devotion. Salutations! Having a transcendental form, Thou art formless, too; Thou art Brahman and Thou art beyond nature and souls.

LORD GANESHA

Thou art beyond all the modes of nature and merciful towards Thy devotees. Again and again, we salute unto Thee. Thou art pure spotless Brahman, destroyer of all demons. Thou art eternal Truth who extends help to the needy and all-pervasive. Salutations again and again.

O God Vinaayaka, the whole world is in trouble and devoid of fire sacrifices, oblations and prayers. We, the denizens of heaven are driven away by the demons and we live like animals in the caves of Mt. Meru. Protect us, O God, showing Thy mercy upon us.

Pleased with their prayers, Lord Ganesha sent His messenger who spoke to the *devas* from the high heavens. "O *devas*, do not be afraid any more. Lord Vinaayaka will take *avatar* in Aditi's womb at Sage Kashyapa's *ashrama to* protect all of you and earth. He will restore your heavenly abode. Do not worry."

All were pleased to hear the heavenly voice and saluting Brahma, they went back to their respective places. Brahma returned to His abode Satyaloka.

After some time, Sage Kashyapa's wife Aditi became pregnant. She was filled with the divine aura. After nine months, at an auspicious moment, there appeared a supernatural being from her. *Ganesha Puraana* discusses the beauty of this Supreme Person thus:

DASHA BHUJO BAHU BALAHA KARNA-KUNDALA MANDITAHA KASTURI VILASADBHAALO MUKUTA BHRAAJI-MASTAKAHA
SIDDHI BUDDHIYUTAHA KANTAE RATNA MAALAA VIBHOOSHITAHA
CHINTAAMANI LASAD VAKSHA JAPAAPUSHPAARUNAA DHARAHA
UNNASO BHRIKUTEE CHAARU LALAATO DANTA DEEPTIMAAN
DAEHA KAANTHYAA HATATAMAA DIVYAAMBARA YUTAHA SHUBHAHA

He looked extremely strong. He had ten arms. He had shining earrings and on His forehead, the musk pigment was seen. The splendor of His crown illumined the four directions. The goddess of prudence (Buddhi) and the goddess of fulfillment (Siddhi) were on either side of Him. A garland of gems added beauty to His neck. His bosom was brilliant with the wish-jewel and His lips were red like the japaa flowers. A prominent nose and beautiful brows added beauty to His face. His teeth were shining. The light emanating from His body dispelled darkness. Donning divine garments, the boy looked extremely beautiful.

Mother Aditi was besides herself with ineffable joy. The Supreme Being spoke to her. "O Mother Aditi, as per my promise during your austerities, I have come as your son. Destroying the demons and protecting the pious, I shall fulfill your wishes."

Mother Aditi prayed to Him. "O Eternal Truth, Transcendental Reality, I am a thousand times blessed to have You as my son. Now I pray that You play as my child, giving up this divine form to give me the joy as Your mother." As per her request, Lord Gajaanana appeared as a beautiful child and began crying. His cry reached all three worlds. The earth began trembling at the noise of the loud cry. Demons were terrified and celestials rejoiced at the *avatara* of Ganesha.

Sage Kashyapa was overjoyed at the *avatara* of Ganesha as his son and through the head priests, he conducted the proper rites of worship and gave food and wealth as charity to the *brahmanas* to bless the child.

Even as a child, Ganesha had a large stature and huge body. Therefore, Sage Kashyapa named him as Mahotkata, which means 'supernatural being of an unusual size.'

Mythology

There came at that time the great sages Vashista and Vaamadeva. Aditi and Kashyapa brought their son Mahotkata to them for blessings. Sage Vashista said, "Oh, this boy has 32 marks on his body which proves that he is an *avatar* of God. There will be many dangerous events happening during his childhood days. Several demons may try to kill him. But, being the *avatar* of Vinaayaka Ganesha, he will destroy the demons and bring peace to this universe." Sage Vashista and Vaamadeva worshipped the feet of Ganesha and prayed to Him thus:

PRAARTHAYAAMAASA SARVASTHAM, BHUBHAARA HARANAM KURU
SAADHUNAAM PAALANAM DEVA, DUSTA DAANAVA GHAATANAM

O God, the three worlds are scorched by the afflictions caused by the demons. Kindly save the world by destroying the demons and protecting Your votaries.

Saying thus, the sages saluted Ganesha again and again and left for their *ashramas*.

By the presence of Ganesha as Mahotkata, the sages became fearless and in all the hermitages, the hermits began the study of the *Vedas* and conducted fire sacrifices as before.

Leelas and Pranks of the Child Mahotkata

The demons felt threatened at the *avatara* of Ganesha as Mahotkata. They reasoned, "we should not allow him to grow and then destroy us and our kingdom. If we root out the sapling, then it will not grow into a tree. If we destroy him as a child, then he cannot destroy us."

The king of the demons dispatched a demoness called Virajaa to kill the boy Mahotkata. She came to the hermitage of Sage Kashyapa, but while trying to kill the boy, she herself was killed by him. Whoever dies by the hand of God will attain the divine abode; thus, Virajaa attained the supreme abode of Ganesha.

Threatened and alarmed by the death of Virajaa, the king of the demons sent two powerful demons called Udvata and Dhundhura to kill the boy. Those demons disguised themselves as two parrots and came to the boy to bite him with their poisonous beaks. They came at a time when Mother Aditi was breastfeeding the baby.

The moment the boy saw the parrots, he demanded that the birds be caught and given to him. Aditi wondered how she could catch the flying birds. Seeing this, the boy Mahotkata leapt up and caught both the parrots instantaneously. The two demons in the form of those parrots bit him all over his body and tried to escape from him by beating their wings. Ganesha Mahotkata squeezed both the birds until their life-breath departed. They fell dead on earth with their colossal demoniac forms.

Mother Aditi said prayers for the boy's protection as Sage Kashyapa chanted peace hymns. Knowing that other demons may again come and attack the boy, they kept a strict watch on Mahotkata.

Mahotkata grew up into a four year old lad. All the sages and saints around knew that He was the *avatar* of God and therefore they felt protected. Beautiful trees surrounded a lake there that contained pure water, but the sages were afraid to bathe due to the presence of a crocodile.

On an auspicious new moon day known as '*somaavati amaavaasya*,' Mother Aditi went to bathe in that lake, leaving her son on its shores. While she was bathing, Ganesha Mahotkata wanted to bathe also. So he jumped into the lake and was caught by the crocodile. Aditi cried loudly for the protection of her son. Aditi and many hermits tried to protect the boy, but in vain. After a while, as they were praying, they saw the power of Ganesha.

Lord Mahotkata fought with the crocodile and threw it on the ground with full force. The crocodile rolled on the ground and died. In the place of the crocodile, there arose a *gandharva* (celestial musician) called Chitraratha, the king of celestial musicians.

He saluted Lord Mahotkata Ganesha and said, "O Lord, I am Chitraratha. During my marriage, I welcomed every guest, but somehow, I neglected to welcome and worship the venerable Sage Bhrigu. He pronounced a curse upon me to be born as a crocodile. When I fell at his feet and offered prayers, the merciful sage softened the curse by saying that the moment You come into contact with Ganesha, you will gain your original celestial form." After this, the *gandharva* circumambulated Lord Ganesha and bid farewell to him. After receiving His blessings, he went back to his celestial abode.

All the sages glorified Ganesha. Mother Aditi embraced her son with great love and Sage Kashyapa and others rejoiced, hearing the news of Ganesha's victory.

Once upon a time, three celestial musicians called Haahaa, Huhu and Tumburu arrived at Sage Kashyapa's *ashram* singing the songs on God. Sage Kashyapa requested them to stay there for a day in his *ashram*. They agreed and went to bathe. After returning, they decided to worship and therefore, they kept the holy images of Lord Shiva, Vishnu, Vinaayaka, Surya and Shakti Parvati. When they closed their eyes and began meditating, the boy Mahotkata came and threw all the images into his mouth. When the *gandharvas* opened their eyes, they could not see any of the images. They conveyed the news to Sage Kashyapa. The sage and his wife scolded the boy to find out the truth of the images' disappearance.

"Where can I hide them?" he asked. "Look into my mouth!" Saying thus, Ganesha opened his mouth and lo! All of them saw in his mouth Mt. Kailasa and Lord Shiva, Vaikunta and Lord Vishnu, Satyaloka and Brahma, paradise and Indra, the forests, mountains, oceans, lakes, semi-gods, demi-gods, denizens of heaven and all the *lokas* above and below.

All the *gandharvas*, Aditi and Sage Kashyapa saw this cosmic form of Ganesha. All of them prayed for forgiveness of their ignorance. Now again, Mahotkata began playing like an innocent boy. Aditi blessed her son and wondered at the mystery of the Lord. The musicians Haahaa, Huhu and Tumburu fell at His feet again and again. Receiving blessings from Sage Kashyapa and Aditi, they left for their abodes.

Sacred Thread Ceremony (Upanayana Samskara) of Mahotkata

Mahotkata Ganesha became five years old. His father chose an auspicious day and time to perform his son's sacred thread ceremony. He invited all the *devas*, higher hierarchy and all the sages and saints.

To bring obstacles, five *asuras* (demons) also came disguising themselves as *brahmanas* by smearing their forehead with holy ashes and adorning their necks with the rosary of *rudraksha* beads. Their names were Vighaata, Pingaaksha, Vishaala, Pingala, and Chapala. They sat with the *brahmins* so that they could attack and harm Mahotkata Ganesha easily.

Mythology

After the elaborate *pujas* and chanting of the peace hymns, Ganesha was given the sacred thread and Gayatri mantra by his father. Mother Aditi blessed him by showering red rice on him. She was followed by all the *brahmins* who came to Ganesha to bless him with the *akshata* (red rice). Taking this opportunity, the five demons who had disguised themselves also came to Ganesha with the intention of killing him. When they were about to strike him with their weapons, Mahotkata Ganesha took a few grains of red rice, uttered some powerful mantras and threw the rice upon their heads. Instantaneously, all five of them fell on the ground, dead.

Devas and sages felt that this was not an ordinary boy. They said, "Who can destroy five powerful demons in a trice by throwing red rice on them? Who can put the power of destruction in a mantra other than God? This must be an incarnation of the Supreme!"

After this, they showered Him with flowers. Brahmarishi Vashista took the boy Mahotkata to the creator Brahma. Brahma blessed him with water from his sacred jar (*kamandalu*) and presented him a blossomed lotus that never fades. He gave Ganesha a special name known as Brahmanas-pati or 'Lord of all the divine beings.' Kubera worshipped Ganesha and named Him as Suraananda and presented Him with a necklace of gems. Varuna presented his *paasha*, the noose, and called him Sarva-priya, which means 'dear to all.' Lord Shiva presented Him with the trident and his drum and blessed Him with the names Viroopaaksha and Bhaalachandra which means 'mysterious-eyed one' and the 'effulgence of the moon.' Renuka, the mother of Parashurama, blessed Ganesha with the *parashu* (hatchet) and named him Parashu-hasta, which means the 'holder of the hatchet.' She gave him a lion as his vehicle and called him Simha-vaahana which means 'Lord whose vehicle is the lion.' Then she told him, "Vinaayaka, destroy the demons as soon as possible!"

The king of the oceans presented him a celestial garland called *muktaamaala* and named him Maalaadhara. The serpent god offered himself as his seat and called him Dhanirajaasana which means the 'Lord who has the serpent king as his seat.' Offering his burning power, Agni, the fire god, named him Dhanamjaya which means 'victory of wealth.' Vaayu, the wind god, gave him his power and the name Prabhanjana which means the 'great destroyer.' Thus, all the *devas* except Indra honored and worshipped him.

Indra thought, "When I am the lord of all the *devas*, everyone should honor me! Why should I honor and worship this boy?"

Sage Kashyapa told him, "Indra, this boy is not ordinary as you think. At a young age, he destroyed the demoness Virajaa. He killed two demons called Udvata and Prachanda who came disguised as parrots to destroy him. He released the celestial musician Chitra, who was a crocodile, just by his touch. He showed all the gods in Himself to the two *gandharvas* called Haahaa and Huhu. Right in our presence, he destroyed the five colossal demons who came here disguised as five priests. Don't you see that He is an incarnation of God?"

"But I have not seen myself any of his powers!" responded Indra. No sooner had he said this than there burst forth a hurricane smashing everything and everyone. Indra fell on his knees and looked at Mahotkata. Fire was emerging from His third eye. Indra saw infinite faces and forms of Ganesha. The sun, the moon and the fire were His three eyes. He saw endless universes emerging and merging in the pores of His body. Seeing such a universal form of Ganesha, Indra's ego was humbled and he fell at the feet of the Lord, glorified Him and begged for forgiveness.

LORD GANESHA

The hurricane stopped. Indra praised Him and worshipped His lotus feet. He presented Him with the goad (*ankusha*) and wish-tree (*kalpa-vriksha*) and called Him Vinaayaka which means the 'special leader of all the *devas*.' Following this, Indra, the *devas*, sages and saints went back to their abodes.

Mahotkata mastered all the holy wisdom and became an adept in all the sciences including archery. At the age of seven, He began riding on His lion, holding a *pasha* (noose), *ankusha* (goad), *parashu* (hatchet) and *padma* (lotus). He put a snake 'round His belly as His belt and decked Himself with the yellow silken robe and musk pigment on His forehead. He roamed about near His *ashram*. When He roared, it created terror in the hearts of the demons and sages felt completely protected by Him.

Sri Ganesha's Eight Important Avataras

Mudgala Puraana was written by Sage Mudgala. He writes that Ganesha's *avataras* are endless. Of them, the most important incarnations are eight in number. They are 1) Vakratunda, 2) Aekadanta, 3) Mahodara, 4) Gajaanana, 5) Lambodhara, 6) Vikataa, 7) Vighnaraaja and 8) Dhumravarna.

Vakratunda *avatara* took place for the destruction of Matsaraasura or the demon of jealousy. In this incarnation, Ganesha's vehicle was a lion. He was body-Brahman.

Aekadanta *avatara* manifested for the destruction of Madaasura, the demon of arrogance. Ganesha's vehicle in this *avatara* was the mouse. He was soul-Brahman.

Mahodara *avatara* was for the destruction of Mohaasura, the demon of infatuation. Mouse was the vehicle of the Lord and He was knowledge-Brahman.

Gajaanana *avatara* was for the destruction of Lobhaasura, the demon of greediness. Mouse was His vehicle and He was primordial energy or *saankhya*-Brahman.

Lambodhara *avatara* was for the destruction of Krodhaasura, the demon of anger. His vehicle was the mouse. He was *shakti*-Brahman.

Vikataa *avatara* was for the destruction of Kaamaasura, the demon of lust. His vehicle was the peacock and He was sun-Brahman.

Vighnaraaja *avatara* was for the destruction of Mamataasura, the demon of attachment. Serpent god Mahashesha was his vehicle. He was Vishnu-Brahman.

Dhumravarna or Dhumraketu *avatara* was for the destruction of Abhimaanaasura or the demon of ego. His vehicle again was the mouse. He was Shiva-Brahman.

Now we explain the main avatara among the eight, which is Vakratunda.

Matsaraasura or the demon of jealousy was born of Indra when he committed a mistake due to tamasic lethargy. This demon took the initiation of "OM NAMAH SHIVAAYA" mantra from Shukraacharya, the teacher of demons. He conducted austerities, repeating this five-syllabled mantra and obtained the *darshan* of Shiva and Shakti. Pleased with his devotion, Shiva blessed him to be invincible and fearless and then disappeared along with Shakti.

Mythology

The demon returned to his guru Shukraacharya, and with his blessings, became the ruler of the whole earth by conquering all the kings. then he went to the nether regions known as Patala and they, too, offered their throne to him. He went to paradise with his military and conquered all the guardian deities and Indra, the head of the angels. Now he began ruling all three worlds. His power was such that he even conquered the Trinity and appointed his sons to take over the whole universe. All this was due to the blessings of Shiva!

All the *devas* gathered to find out the solution. Lord Dattatreya came and he blessed the *devas* by imparting the monosyllabic Ganesha mantra "GAM" and asked them to propitiate Ganesha to ward off all evil. All the *devas* and Brahma, Vishnu and Shiva meditated on "GAM" mantra for a long time with total devotion. God Ganesha appeared before them with the "curved tusk" *avatara* known as Vakratunda. He promised the Trinity and the *devas* that He would destroy the demon Matsara and all dark powers.

Vakratunda willed that millions of powerful *ganas* manifest with celestial weapons and they appeared instantaneously. He marched with them to the palace of the demon Matsara and roared. The hearts of the demons were fear-stricken. Numberless demons fought with limitless *ganas*. The attendants of Ganesha bested the demons in the fierce battle. The *ganas* also destroyed the two powerful sons of the demon, Sundarapriya and Vishayapriya.

Hearing of the death of his two sons, demon Matsara began blazing with anger. He decided to destroy Vakratunda and all the *devas*. He came to the battlefield. But when he saw the brilliance of Vakratunda, he realized his folly and knew that his end had come. Therefore, he surrendered to Vakratunda Ganesha and glorified Him. Pleased with his devotion, Vakratunda blessed him with love and peace. Matsara the demon of hatred or jealousy now became a devotee of love. *Devas* were restored of their kingdom. Peace dwelt on earth and in the whole universe.

Whoever listens to this story, their heart will be filled with love and all hatred and jealousy will be transformed into devotion and peace.

Vakratunda's main mantra is "VAKRATUNDAAYA HUM." The creator Brahma meditated on this mantra and by the blessings of Ganesha, he was able to continue the work of creation successfully.

It is from a tremor of the body of Brahma that the *asura* or demon Dambha, the demon of arrogance was born. Like the demon Matsara, he also did austere penance and obtained the boon from Brahma to become invincible. He also conquered all the *lokas* and created chaos and confusion through unrighteousness. The *devas* once again went in total surrender to Vakratunda Ganesha. Ganesha appeared and promised all protection to them. He sent Indra himself as His emissary to the demon Dambha.

Indra came disguised to demon Dambha and told him the message of Vakratunda to return paradise to the *devas* and to come in total surrender to Him. At first, Dambha was very angry and decided to fight with Ganesha. But his guru Shukraacharya taught him the nature of Ganesha and His powers as the Lord of the universe. Then demon Dambha came in total surrender to Lord Vakratunda and the Lord blessed him with love and peace. He restored the kingdom of the *devas* and reestablished *dharma*.

LORD GANESHA

The message of these stories are that the demons of hatred and jealousy, arrogance and hypocrisy are in every human being. Lord Ganesha is OM or pure consciousness, the Paramatman or God in our heart. He is the supreme power of love! Jealousy and arrogance may gain momentary victory over dominions and things, but eventually, they will be subdued and transformed by the power of love. Philosophy is clothed in mythology and mysticism which helps people to understand their own minds and the eventual victory of light over darkness, love over jealousy and truth over arrogance.

Sri Ganesha Puja
Worship of Five Aspects of God—
The Position of Ganesha

GANESHA PUJANAE VIGHNAM
NIRMALAM JAGATAAM BHAVAET
NIRVYAADHIHI SURYA PUJAAYAAM
SHUCHIHI SRI VISHNUM PUJANAE

(Brahma Vaivartha Puraana, Ganapati Khanda 6:100)
Ganesha Puja roots out all obstacles if He is worshipped with devotion before you underake any endeavor. All illness of the body disappears by worshipping the Sun god. Purity, holiness and peace of mind result from worshipping Mahavishnu.

In all rituals and worship, the *puja* of five deities or five aspects of one God is emphasized. A great Sanskrit text called *Shabdakalpadruma Kosha* writes thus:

AADITYAM GANANAATHAMCHA
DEVEEM RUDRAM CHA KESHAVAM
PANCHA DAIVATAM ITYUKTAM
SARVA KARMASU PUJAYAET

Sun, Ganesha, Shakti, Shiva and Vishnu are the five aspects of Truth or God that are to be worshipped in every *puja* on all auspicious occasions.

These are the presiding deities over the five cosmic elements known as ether, air, fire, water and earth.

Presiding Deities

1. Lord Vishnu - Ether, sky (*akasha*)
2. Sun god - Air, life-principle (Vaayu)
3. Goddess Shakti - Fire, energy (Agni)
4. Lord Ganesha - Water (fulfilling energy)
5. Lord Shiva - Earth (one who blesses with longevity)

The authority of the scripture declares this in Sanskrit:

AAKAASHASYAADHIP VISHNUR
AGNAESHAHAIVA MAHESHVAREE
VAAYOHO SURYAHA KSHITAER ESHO
JEEVANASYA GANAADHIPAHA

The presiding deities over ether, air, fire, water and earth are Lord Vishnu, Sun, Shakti, Lord Ganesha and Lord Shiva, respectively.

The philosophy and symbology behind this is very interesting. Ethereal space or sky has the property or quality of sound (*shabda*). This is why Lord Vishnu, being the presiding deity over *akasha* (sky) is worshipped through sounds. This means He is propitiated through Vedic mantras and *kirtans* (song services).

The Sun god is the presiding deity of the principle of *vaayu* (air). That is why the sun is considered to be the life of the universe, and why the sun god is worshipped through salutations

LORD GANESHA

and *pranayama* (rhythmic breathing). Sun and the moon are the presiding deities of inhalaton and exhalation. *Pingala naadi shakti*, solar energy, flows through the right side of the spinal column (*sushumna*) and the lunar energy, *ida naada shakti,* flows through the left side. Thus, the *prana* (life breath) is connected with solar energy, the solar plexus, and the Sun. It is why the very first posture in yoga is the Sun Salutation (*Surya Namaskara*).

The presiding deity over Agni, fire, is Shakti or Goddess Durga. That is why one pours oblations into the fire whenever one propitiates Shakti as Gayatri, or the energy of any aspect of God. Doing Gana Homa, the fire ceremony of Lord Ganesha, one pours oblations to the power or energy of Ganesha. Thus, through oblations, Shakti is satisfied.

The presiding deity over the water principle is Lord Ganesha. *Manusmriti*, the Code of Manu, says that in the beginning of creation, there was nothing but the water principle with its presiding deity, Lord Ganesha. **AAPA EVA SASARJAADOU TAASU BEEJA-MAVAASRIJAM** (*Manusmriti, 1-8*).

In rituals during Ganesha's birthday, after keeping His clay image for five days, devotees then immerse His *murti* in water as He is the presiding deity even over Varuna, the god of waters.

Finally, Lord Shiva is considered to be the presiding deity over Mother Earth. Thus He is worshipped in the form of *lingam*, a round emblem of stone or clay (*Paarthiva-lingam*). For all the '*pashus*' (desire-bound souls), He is *pati* (Lord). Hence the name Pashupati came to Lord Shiva. He also blesses those who worship Him with long life and immortality.

Now, even among these five deities Ganesha is worshipped first. The holy Trinity—Brahma, Vishnu and Shiva—declared this to the whole universe when the elephant head was affixed to His human trunk.

The Power of Ganesha

Narada Purana discusses **GANESHAADI PANAHA DUATAABHYO NAMAHA** (*Narada Purana 3:65*) which means Ganesha is to be worshipped first among the five deities.

Four important blessings among the many which come to the devotee by worshipping Ganesha are:

1. **MAHAAVIGHNAAN PRAMUCHYATAE** which means the greatest obstacles are removed.

2. **MAHAAPAAPAAN PRAMUCHYATAE** which means the greatest sins are destroyed.

3. **SARVA DOSHAAN PRAMUCHYATAE** which means all mistkaes are forgiven and errors corrected.

4. **SA SARVAVID BHAVATI**, that is, Lord Ganesha blesses His devotees with right knowledge.

SRI GANESHA PUJA

After bathing, dressing and collecting all puja articles, one sits for worship.

SANKALPA — The Decision to do the Puja

SARVEBHYO DEVEBHYO NAMAHA
To all the deities, I offer my salutations.

SARVEBHYO BRAAHMANEBHYO NAMAHA
To all the brahmanas (the knowers of Brahman), I offer my salutations.

ACHMANA — Sip the Holy Water for Purification
Fill the copper cup with pure water. Holding the spoon in the left hand, pour a spoonful of water onto the right palm while holding the hand like a conch. Then sip the water, letting it run off the end of your palm into your mouth. After sipping from the right hand, run your hand over your forehead and the crown of your head. Repeat the sipping process three times, intoning the following mantras after each sipping of water:

OM SRI KESHAVAAYA SWAAHA
Salutations to Keshava. The fruit of this is eternal wisdom.

OM SRI NARAAYANAAYA SWAAHA
Salutations to Narayana. The fruit of this is final beatitude.

OM SRI MAADHAVAAYA SWAAHA
Salutations to Madhava. The fruit of this is prosperity.

Now continue chanting the rest of the twenty-four holy Names of Lord Vishnu:

OM GOVINDAAYA NAMAHA
Salutations to Govinda. The fruit of this is obstacles removed.

OM VISHNAVE NAMAHA
Salutations to Vishnu. The fruit of this is cosmic consciousness.

OM MADHUSUDANAAYA NAMAHA
Salutations to Madhusudana. The fruit of this is the eradication of the ego.

OM TRIVIKRAMAAYA NAMAHA
Salutations to Trivikrama. The fruit of this is knowledge of all worlds.

OM VAMANAAYA NAMAHA
Salutations to Vamana. The fruit of this is humility and virtues.

OM SRIDHARAAYA NAMAHA
Salutations to Sridhara. The fruit of this is wealth, both material and spiritual.

OM HRISHIKESHAAYA NAMAHA
Salutations to Hrishikesha. The fruit of this is control of the senses.

OM PADMANAABHAAYA NAMAHA
Salutations to Padmanabha. The fruit of this is realization in the navel lotus.

OM DAMODARAAYA NAMAHA
Salutations to Damodara. The fruit of this is realization of the form of God.

LORD GANESHA

OM SHANKARSHANAAYA NAMAHA
   Salutations to Shankarshana. The fruit of this is the highest attraction.

OM VAASUDEVAAYA NAMAHA
   Salutations to Vaasudeva. The fruit of this is the all-pervasiveness of God.

OM PRADYUMNAAYA NAMAHA
   Salutations to Pradyumna. The fruit of this is becoming the son of God.

OM ANIRUDDHAAYA NAMAHA
   Salutations to Aniruddha. The fruit of this is the light of God.

OM PURUSHOTHAMAAYA NAMAHA
   Salutations to Purushothama. The fruit of this is the realization of the supreme Person.

OM ADHOKSHAJAAYA NAMAHA
   Salutations to Adhokshaja. The fruit of this is the opening of the third eye between the eyebrows.

OM NARASIMHAAYA NAMAHA
   Salutations to Narasimha. The fruit of this is the destruction of evil propensities.

OM ACHYUTAAYA NAMAHA
   Salutations to Achyuta. The fruit of this is becoming invincible.

OM JANARDANAAYA NAMAHA
   Salutations to Janardana. The fruit of this is seeing God in all.

OM UPENDRAAYA NAMAHA
   Salutations to Upendra. The fruit of this is lordship.

OM HARIYAE NAMAHA
   Salutations to Hari. The fruit of this is transcendental bliss.

OM SRI KRISHNAAYA NAMAHA
   Salutations to Krishna. The fruit of this is the realization of Lord Krishna.

PRAANAYAMA — Rhythmic Breathing

Inhaling is known in Sanskrit as *puraka*. Holding the breath is known as *kumbhaka*. Exhaling is known as *rechaka*. These three processes together are known as *pranayama*.

Do three pranayamas: Plug the right nostril with the right thumb. Inhale deeply through the left nostril. Plug both the nostrils and hold the breath; while holding the breath, meditate on the inner light in the brow center. Now exhale through the right nostril. Inhale now through the right nostril. Plug both the nostrils and retain the breath. Meditate on the light in the brow center. Slowly exhale through the left nostril. Repeat this process three times.
Then chant:

OM PRANAVASYA PARABRAHMA RISHIHI
PARAMAATMAA DEVATAA
DAIVI GAAYATRI CHANDHAHA
PRANAAYAMAE VINIYOGAHA
   Parabrahma or the Transcendental Godhead Himself is the supreme Guru for the Pranava (OM), the Word. Paramatma, the all-pervading spirit of God Himself, is the presiding deity of the mantra. Gayatri is the meter. Meditating thus, we have offered our *pranayama*.

Sri Ganesha Puja

GAYATRI MANTRA

OM	The Word that is God
OM BHUH	God who is eternal
OM BHUVAHA	God who is the creator
OM SWAHA	God who is independent
OM MAHA	God who is worshipful
OM JANAHA	God who has no beginning
OM TAPAHA	God who is the light of wisdom
OM SATYAM	God who is the Truth;
OM TAT	That eternal God
SAVITUR	That creative principle of light manifesting through the sun
VARENYAM	That supreme God propitiated by the highest gods
BHARGO	The light that bestows wisdom, bliss and everlasting life
DEVASYA	The light of that effulgent God
DHEEMAHI	On That we meditate;
DHIYO	May our intellect
YONAHA	Be directed by that Lord
PRACHODAYAAT	Toward illumination.
OM APO	One who protects us from the waters karma
JYOTI	One who is the Light of all the lights
RASO	One who is the quintessence in everything
AMRITAM	One who blesses us with immortality
BRAHMA	That almighty God
BHUR BHUVAHA	Who is pervading in earth, atmosphere
SWAR	and heaven,
OM	May He bless us with enlightenment.

OM BHUR BHUVAHA SVAHA; OM TAT SAVITUR VARENYAM; BHARGO DEVASYA DHEEMAHI; DHIYO YONAHA PRACHODAYAAT
   O effulgent light that has given birth to all the *lokas* or spheres of consciousness, O God who appears through the shining sun, illumine our intellect.

Continue with the following mantra:

**PURVOKTA AEVAM GUNAVISHESHA VISHISTAAYAM PUNYATITHOU
ANANTHA KALYAANA GUNA PARIPURNA
KSHIRABDHISHAAYI SRI VISHNUPRERANAYA
SRI VISHNUPRIRTHYARTHAM VARTAMAANAE VYAVAHAARIKAE**
(mention the year)
**NAAMA SUMVATSARE DAKSHINAAYANAE VARSHA RITHOU
BHAADRAPADAMASAE SHUKLAPAKSHE CHATURTHYAM** *(mention the day)*
VAASARAE *(mention the name of the person conducting the puja)*
**ASMAAKAM SAHAKUTUMBAANAAM
STRI, PUTRA, POUTRA, DHANA, VIDYA, JAYA,
YASHAAYURAAROGYA ABHISHTA**

LORD GANESHA

SAKALAISHWARYAABHI VRIDHYARTHAM
SAKALAKARYESHU NIRVIGHNATA SIDDHYARTHAM
YATHAAMILITOPACHAARAIHI
SRI VARA SIDDHIVINAAYAKA DEVATAAMUDHISHYA GANESHA
PUJAAM KARISHYAE

As per the auspicious and specific time that is scheduled by the Lord at this highly meritorious hour, we are conducting the worship of Lord Ganesha who is none other than Vishnu, the abode of limitless virtues and perfection whose abode is the Ocean of Milk.

As per His will and to please Him, we conduct this *puja* of Lord Ganesha in this year (mention the year), on (mention the day) as conducted by (mention the name of the person conducting the *puja*), along with the family, children, grandchildren; and for wealth, wisdom, victory, fame, longevity, health, fulfillment of all wishes and growth of prosperity and for accomplishing all works without obstacles.

With the *puja* articles available, I am dedicating this worship specifically to Lord Ganesha, known as Sri Vara Siddhi Vinaayaka, the Lord who bestows the boons of supernatural powers and blessings of knowledge.

After saying these mantras, offer the water to the ground from your palm.

SHANKHYA PUJA — Worship of the Conch
Pour water into the conch from the kalasha and offer sandalwood powder, flowers and tulasi to the conch. Place your palms over the conch and chant the following mantras:

OM TWAM PURAA SAGAROTPANNO VISHNUNA VIDHRITAHA KARAE
MANITAHA SARVADEVAISHCHA PAANCHAJANYAM NAMOSTUTE

O Divine Conch, Panchajanya, thou art born of the ocean and became Lord Vishnu's weapon. Thou art revered by all the *devas*. Salutations to thee.

GARBHAA DEVAARINARINAAM VISHIRYANAE SAHASRADHA
TAVA NAADENA PAATAALAE PANCHAJANYAM NAMOSTUTE

O Divine Conch, when you were blown by Lord Vishnu it created terror in the nether regions in the hearts of demons and their families. Salutations.

TAVA NADAENA JIMUTA VIDRAVANTI SURAASURAHA
SHASHAANKAAYUTADIPTAABHA PAANCHAJANYAM NAMOSTUTE

O Divine Conch, when you sound, the *devas* rejoice and *asuras* (demons) tremble. You make the moon shine brightly. Salutations.

SHANKHAM CHANDRAARKADAIVATYAM MADHYE
VARUNADAIVATAM
PRASHTAE PRAJAAPATIM VINDYAADAGRAE GANGAASARASWATI

O Divine Conch, we invoke the sun and moon in you. In the middle of the conch we invoke Varuna, the god of waters. At the back of the conch we invoke Prajapati, the progenitor. At the top of the conch we invoke the holy rivers Ganges and Saraswati.

SHANKHADEVATAABHYO NAMAHA
GANDHAAKSHATAPUSHPAANI SAMARPAYAAMI

Salutations to the presiding deity over the conch. I offer sandalwood paste, red rice and flowers.

Sri Ganesha Puja

Upon completing the above mantras, offer salutations to the conch and again offer it sandalwood powder, flowers and red rice.

>APAVITRAHA PAVITROVAA SARVAAVATHAAM GATOPIVAA
>YAHA SMARAET PUNDARIKAAKSHAM SABAHYAABHYANTARAHA
>SHUCHIHI
>
>I sprinkle this holy water over my head, meditating on the lotus-eyed Lord, for inner and outer purity. In all conditions and environments, the holy water touched by the Lord purifies the impure one.

Then sprinkle the conch water over your head and on all the puja articles so that they are purified.

BHUTOCHATANA
To drive away evil spirits, repeat the following mantra and clap your hands over your head three times on the word 'PHAT':

>ASPASARPANTUTAE BHUTA YEBHUTA BHUVI SAMSTITAHA
>YEBHUTA VIGHNAKARTARASTAE GACHANTU SHIVAJNAYA
>(ITI SHIVAM SAMPRAARTHYA) OM NAMO ASTRAAYA PHAT
>
>O evil spirits, trying to settle here on earth and trying to disrupt our worship to God, in the name of Lord Shiva, at His mandate, I command you to immediately get out of this place (thus praying to Shiva). Salutations to Lord Shiva. May His sharp arrow strike, strike, strike. *(Clap on the word, 'strike.')*

GHANTANAADAHA—Worship of the Bell
Repeat the following mantra while ringing the bell:

>GHANTAAGRAE BRAHMADAIVATYAM MUKUTAE GARUDASTATHA
>NAADAE SARASWATI VINDYANNAALAE NAAGAADHIDAIVATAM
>
>At the top of the bell we invoke Brahma (creator); at the top of the handle, we invoke Garuda (eagle); we invoke Saraswati in the sound of the bell and the serpent god at the root of the bell. (When the bell is played with mantra, snakes and evil spirits run away and angels will manifest.)

KALASHA PUJA—Preparation of the *puja* vessel with the coconut
Fill the kalasha with water. Offer sandalwood powder, flowers and tulasi to decorate it. Place a coconut on top of the vessel and put your palms over the top of it while chanting the following mantras:

>KALASHASYA MUKHAE VISHNUHU KANTAE RUDRAHA
>SAMAASHRITAHA
>MULAE TATRA STHITHO BRAHMA MADHYAE MAATRAGANAHA
>SMRITAHA
>
>We worship the *kalasha* (vessel above which the coconut is placed) invoking Mahavishnu at the mouth of the vessel. We invoke Lord Rudra (an aspect of Shiva) at the neck of the *kalasha* and Brahma at the base of the vessel. We invoke the Universal Mother Goddess and Her retinue in the midst of the *kalasha*. Thus the male and female trinities are invoked. Salutations!

>KUKSHOUTU SAAGARATSARVAE SAPTADVIPA VASUNDHARAA
>RIGVEDOTHA YAJURVEDAHA SAAMAVEDO ATHARVANAHA
>ANGAISCHA SAHITAHA SARVAE KALASHAAMBU SAMAASHRITAHA

LORD GANESHA

In the belly of the *kalasha* is hidden all oceans, seven islands and Mother Earth, along with the four *Vedas* known as *Rig Veda, Yajur Veda, Sama Veda* and *Atharva Veda*; and also the limbs of the *Vedas* like grammar, meter, astrology, herb medicine, etc.

Now continue to worship the holy waters in the vessel by invoking the sacred rivers. Ring bell throughout the chanting:

**GANGAECHA YAMUNAE CHAIVA GODAAVARI SARASWATI
NARMADAE SINDHU KAAVERI JALESMIN SANNIDHIM KURU**
  O bless us with thy presence, O Divine Rivers Ganges, Jamuna, Godavari, Saraswathi, Narmada, Sindhu and Kaveri.

**OM IMAM MAE GANGAE YAMUNAE SARASWATI SHUTUDRI
STHOMUM SACHATA PARUSHNYA
ASIKNYA MARUDVRIDHAE VITASTHAYAARJEEKEEYAE SHRINUHYAA
SUSHOMAYAA**
  We invoke with devotion the presiding deities over the rivers Ganges, Jamuna and Saraswathi. These rivers are manifest in the *kalasha* as we pour the holy waters into the vessel. These rivers are the flowing mercy of God. May the holy waters of the *kalasha* protect all of us. OM. Salutations.

**SITAASITAE SARITAE YATRA SANGATHAE TATRAA PLUTAASO
DIVAMUTPATANTI
EVAITANVA VISRAJANTIDHIRAASTHE JANAASO AMRITATVAM
BHAJANTAE**
  Where the confluence of all the holy rivers take place, that is where the divine nectar flows, partaking which a bold meditator attains immortality.

**KALASHADEVATAABHYO NAMAHA
GANDHA PUSHPAKSHATAAN SAMARPAYAMI**
  Salutations to the presiding deity over the *kalasha*. With devotion I offer sandalwood paste, flowers and red rice to the deity.

The symbology behind this is to invoke all knowledge, presiding deities and the whole cosmos in the vessel. What a powerful way to worship the Lord!

PANCHAMRITA PUJA—Puja of the Five Nectars
Pour the five nectars—milk, yogurt, ghee, honey and sugar—into five bowls as shown in the diagram below:

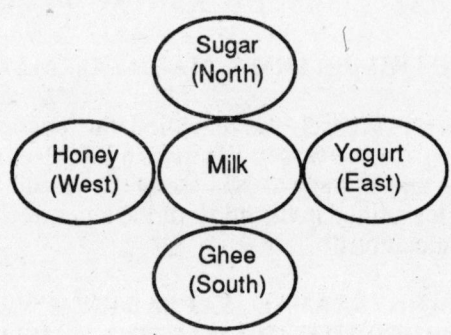

Sri Ganesha Puja

KSHIRAE GOVINDAAYA NAMAHA
DHADHINI VAMANAAYA NAMAHA
GHRITE VISHNAVAE NAMAHA
MADHUNI MADHUSUDANAAYA NAMAHA
SHARKARAYAM ACHYUTAAYA NAMAHA
  I offer milk to Govinda. Salutations! I offer curds (yogurt) to Vamana. Salutations! I offer *ghee* to Vishnu. Salutations! I offer honey to Madhusudana. Salutations! I offer sugar to Achyuta. Salutations!

Saying the following mantras, offer flowers and water to the five bowls:

PANCHAMRITA DEVATAABHYO NAMAHA TULASIDALAM
SAMARPAYAAMI
  Salutations to the presiding deity over the five nectars. I offer *tulasi* (basil leaves) to the deity.

MANTAPA PUJA—Worship of the Altar
Perform the altar puja, offering sandalwood powder, flowers and red rice while you chant the following mantras:

SUVARNA MANTAPAAYA NAMAHA
YOGA MANTAPAAYA NAMAHA
BHOGA MANTAPAAYA NAMAHA
RATNA MANTAPAAYA NAMAHA
VAJRA MANTAPAAYA NAMAHA
HEMAPRAKAARAAYA NAMAHA
RATNASOPAANAAYA NAMAHA
SUVARNAVEDIKAAYAI NAMAHA
  Salutations to the golden altar. Salutations to the yoga altar. Salutations to the altar of bliss. Salutations to the altar of jewels. Salutations to the altar of diamonds. Salutations to the golden circle. Salutations to the steps made of gems. Salutations to the golden platform!

DHYANAM—Meditation

UTAPOJVALA KAANCHANAENA RACHITAM
TUNGAANGARANGASTHALAM
SHUDDHA SPAT KA BHITIKA VILASITAISTHUMBHAISCHA HEMAIHI
SHUBHAIHI

MUKTAJALA VILAMBAMANTAPAYUTAM VAJRAISCHA
SOPAANAKAIHI
NAANAARATNA VIRAJITAISCHA KALASHAIRATYANTA
SHOBHAVAHAM

DVAARAISCHAAMARA RATNARAAJA KHACHITAIHI SHOBHAVAHAM
MANTAPAM
RATNAGRAIRAPI SHANKHACHAKRA DHAVALAIHI PRABHRAAJITAM
SVASTIKAIHI
MAINKYOJVALA DIPADIPTI VILASALAKSHMI VILAASAPADAM
DHYAENMANTAPA ARCHANESHU SAKALESHVEVAM VIDHUM
SADHAKAHA

LORD GANESHA

I meditate on Ganesha whose radiance eclipses millions of suns and moons. The platform and throne, shining like molten gold, contain the aura of vermilion (blood red) color. The Lord is shining in the crystal altar.

In front of the altar and the platform is a shining lake containing the waters of immortality. The steps to the lake are made up of diamonds. The gates of the altar are all decked with nine gems, the beauty of which is beyond description.

The symbols of conch, disc, swastika and other mystical symbols are decorated on the celestial doors. Flames and lights are shining continuously in the glasses and plates of emerald. Thus, I meditate on that altar and seat of Lord Ganesha which brings fulfillment to His devotees.

DWARA PUJA—Worship of the Doors of the Altar
Offer flowers and red rice to the doors of the altar while you chant the following mantras:

PURVADVAARAE SHRIYAI NAMAHA
JAYAAYA NAMAHA
VIJAYAAYA NAMAHA
I invoke Mahalakshmi on the eastern door. Salutations! She is accompanied by Jaya and Vijaya. To them also I offer my salutations.

DAKSHINADVAARAE SHRIYAI NAMAHA
BALAAYA NAMAHA
PRABALAAYA NAMAHA
Now I invoke Mahalakshmi on the southern door. Salutations! Also, I offer salutations to the strange gatekeepers there called Bala and Prabala.

PASCHIMADVAARAE SHRIYAI NAMAHA
BHADRAAYA NAMAHA
SUBHADRAAYA NAMAHA
I invoke Mahalakshmi on the western door. Salutations! And also, to the two gatekeepers there called Bhadra and Subhadra, I offer my salutations.

UTTARADVAARAE SHRIYAI NAMAHA
CHANDAAYA NAMAHA
PRACHANDAAYA NAMAHA
I invoke Mahalakshmi on the northern door. Salutations! I offer my salutations to the two gatekeepers there called Chanda and Prachanda.

INDRAADYASTA LOKAPAALAKEBHYO NAMAHA
I offer my salutations to the eight guardian angels, including Indra.

DIKPALAKAS—Salutations to the Guardian Deities
Salute the eight guardian deities by folding your hands and inclining your head toward each of the directions over which the deities preside:

OM INDRAAYA NAMAHA	East	Salutations to Indra, lord of the celestials
OM AGNAYAE NAMAHA	Southeast	Salutations to Agni, lord of fire
OM YAMAAYA NAMAHA	South	Salutations to Yama, god of death
OM NIRATIYAE NAMAHA	Southwest	Salutations to Nirati, the shining angel

Sri Ganesha Puja

OM VARUNAAYA NAMAHA	West	Salutations to Varuna, god of waters
OM VAAYUVAE NAMAHA	Northwest	Salutations to Vaayu, the life breath
OM KUBERAAYA NAMAHA	North	Salutations to Kubera, the lord of wealth
OM ISHAANAAYA NAMAHA	Northeast	Salutations to Ishaana, an aspect of Shiva

ITI DIKPAALAKA PUJAAM SAMARPAYAAMI
Salutations to the guardian deities of the eight principal directions.

PEETA PUJA (AASANA PUJA)—Worship of the Seat of the Lord
Offer flowers and red rice onto the aasana while chanting the following mantras:

NAVARATNA SIMHASANAAYA NAMAHA
Salutations to the throne of nine gems.

ARUNAASANAAYA NAMAHA
Salutations to the throne of crimson color.

KAMALAASANAAYA NAMAHA
Salutations to the lotus seat of the Lord.

PADMAASANAAYA NAMAHA
Salutations to the lotus posture of the Lord.

TANMADHYAE ADHAARASHAKTAI NAMAHA
In the middle of the seat, I invoke Adharashakti, the all-supportive energy. Salutations!

MULAPRAKRATIYAE NAMAHA
Salutations to the primordial energy.

KURMAAYA NAMAHA
Salutations to the tortoise energy which upholds the universe.

VARAAHAAYA NAMAHA
Salutations to the divine boar energy that restored the earth.

ANANTAAYA NAMAHA
Salutations to the infinite energy.

PRATHIVYAE NAMAHA
Salutations Mother Earth.

SKANDAAYA NAMAHA
Salutations to Skanda Subramanya, the son of Shiva.

PATRAEBHYO NAMAHA
Salutations to all of the sacred leaves to be offered to God.

DALAEBHYO NAMAHA
Salutations to the flower petals.

BIJAEBHYO NAMAHA
Salutations to the seeds, nuts and grains to be offered to God.

KESARAEBHYO NAMAHA
Salutations to the saffron to be offered to God.

LORD GANESHA

ASHTADALA PADMAAYA NAMAHA
Salutations to the eight-petalled lotus.

MAHAAPANNAGA PEETAAYA NAMAHA
Salutations to the great serpent seat (the symbol of Kundalini Shakti).

DIVYA SIMHASANAAYA NAMAHA
Salutations to the divine throne.

MADHYAE SRI SIDDHI VINAAYAKAAYA NAMAHA
Salutations to Sri Siddhi Vinaayakaaya.

PEETA PUJAAM SAMARPAYAAMI
Thus I offer worship of the seat of the Lord.

PRAANA PRATISHTA—Installation of the Murti with the Living Energy of God
Holding in your palms flowers and red rice, touch the heart center of the image and chant the following mantra:

**ASYA SRI SIDDHI VINAAYAKA PRAANA PRATISHTAA MANTRASYA
BRAHMA . . . VISHNU . . . MAHESHVARA RUSHAYAHA
RIGYAJUSAAMA ATHARVANI CHANDAAMSI
PARAA PRAANASHAKTI DEVATAA
AAM BIJAM
HREEM SHAKTIHI
KRAUM KEELAKAM
ASYAM MURTHOU PRAANAPRATISHTAAPANAE VINIYOGAHA
OM, AAM, HREEM, KRAUM, AM, YAM, RAM, LAM, VAM, SHAM,
SHHAM, SAM, HAM, LAM, KSHAM, AHA
ASYAM MURTHOU SARVENDRIYAANI PRAANAJIVAAS THISHTANTU
ASYEI PRAANAHA PRATISHTANTU ASYEIHI PRAANAHA
KSHARANTUCHA
ASYEI DEVAATVAM ARCHYEI MAAMAHETI CHA KASCHANA**
For invoking the energy of God in the image, Brahma, Vishnu and Shiva themselves are the sages. The four *Vedas* are the meters. The transcendental energy of God is the *prana shakti* and all the mystical words like HRAM are the seed syllables; KREEM is the cosmic energy invoked; HROOM is the key through which the door of the energy is opened. Thus, the ritual of the installation that is offered to God.

Now we offer several mystical sounds at the feet of the Lord. May these mantras invoke *prana* in all the limbs of the image so that the image becomes the Living Image of God. May the Lord accept my worship and bless me and the devotees.

DHYANAM—Meditation

**RAKTAAMBODHIS TAPOTOLLASADARUNA SAROJADHIRUDAA
KARABJEIHI PAASHAM KODANDAM IKSHOODBHAVA GUNAMALI
ANKUSHAM PUSHPA BAANAAN**

**BIBRAANAA SRAKKAPALAM TRINAYANAVPUSHA PEENAVAKSHORU
HAADYA
DEVI BAALAARKAVARNAA BHAVATU SUKHAKARI PRAANASHAKTIHI
PRASANNA**
I meditate on Lord Ganesha sitting on the red, full-blossomed lotus. His body is shining completely with the vermilion color. In His lotus hands, He is holding a noose

Sri Ganesha Puja

and a bowl of sugar cane with five flower arrows. He is holding the goad and a skull. The three-eyed Lord is shining with broad shoulders and a large chest befitting His divine form. The color of His energy is like the rising young sun.

OM GANANAM TVA GANAPATIM HAVAMAHAE KAVIM KAVEENA
MUPAMASHRA VASTHAMAM
JYESTARAAJAM BRAHMANAAM BRAHMANASPATA AANAHA
SHRANVANNUTIBHIHI SEEDA SAADANAM

O Lord Ganesha, You are appointed by the Trinity as the supreme head of all the *ganas* or divine species: angels, archangels, semi-gods, demi-gods and the presiding deities of all the planets. All the saints and poets meditate on You for their perfection in expressing or writing Your glory. You are considered the first to be adored, worshipped and saluted. Your blessings bring the fruit of all the *sadhanas* or spiritual practices of the seekers of Brahman. O Lord Ganesha, remove the obstacles from us and bless us to receive this *puja* by Your presence.

OM ATMAADEVAANAAM BHUVANASYA GARBHO
YATHA VASHAMCHARATI DEVA AESHAHA
GHOSHAA IDASYA SHRANVIRAE NA RUPAM
TASMAI VAATAAYA HAVISHA VIDHAEMA

ASUNITAE PUNARASMAASU CHAKSHUHU PUNAHA
PRAANAMIHAMO DHEHI BHOGAM
JYOKPASHYAEMA SURYA MUCHHARANTA
MANUMATAE MRALAYAANA NAHA SVASTI

TADASTU MITRA VARUNAA TADAGNESHAM
YORASMABHYAMIDAMASTU SHASTAM
ASHEEMAHI GAADHAMUTA PRATISHTAAM
NAMO DIVAE BRAHATAE SAADHANAAYA

GRAHAA VAI PRATISHTAA SUKTUM TATPRATISHTITA TAMAYAA
VACHASHAMSTAVYAM TASMADYADYAPI DOORA IVA
PASHUMLABHATAE
GRAHAANEVAI NAANAA JIGAMISHATI GRAHAAHI PASHUNAAM
PRATISHTAA PRATISHTAA

Lord Ganesha is our *Atma* (the great Self). He is the womb of the entire creation. All the *devas* move by His will. The wind blows at His will. Sun, moon and stars shine at His will. He is the Light of all the lights. May His blessings be always with us. Sun god, Varuna (the god of waters), Agni (the fire god), and other deities are present when we install the *murti* of Ganesha. Thus we have recited the hymn of installation to proclaim to the world that God is present. God is present in the Living Image.

Chant the following mantra and offer flowers and red rice to take the evil eye from Lord Ganesha:

OM TACHAKSHURDEVAHITAM SHUKRAMUCHARAT
PASHYEMA SHARADAHA SHATAM JIVAEMA SHARADAHA SHATAM

O Lord Ganesha, let no one dare to cast an evil eye on You. You are the protector of all. We, Your devotees, want You to bless us with our full span of life of one hundred years.

LORD GANESHA

Chant the following mantra and offer flowers and red rice:

**CHATURBHUJAIR GAJADANTA AKSHAMALA PARASHU MODAKA DHAARINAE
TAPTA KAANCHANAVARNAAYA SHURPAKARNAAYA GAJANANAAYA LAMBODHARAAYA
SARPAYAJNOPAVITINAE VYAGHRAACHARMA AMBARA DHARAAYA
SARVAABHARANA BHUSHITAAYA MUSHIKOPARI SAMSTITAAYA
OM NAMO BHAGAVATAE SAKALAGUNAATMANAE
SAKALASHAKTIYUTAAYA MAHAAYOGAPEETASTHAAYA**

I invoke and invite Lord Ganesha for this *puja*. I invoke Him who has four arms, an elephant face with one tusk, One whose neck is decked with the divine rosary; One who is holding a hatchet in one hand and a vessel containing the divine porridge; One whose body is shining like molten gold; One who is of cosmic belly and One who has the serpent as the sacred thread, clad with the skin of the tiger, decked with all the divine ornaments and who is mounted upon a mouse. Salutations, Lord Ganesha, again and again!

OM SRI SIDDHI VINAAYAKAAYA NAMAHA AVAHAYAAMI

I invoke and invite Lord Ganesha, also known as Siddhi Vinaayaka, who is installed in the seat of great yoga (the kingdom of Ganesha), who is all-powerful and the abode of divine virtues. Salutations unto Him!

DHYANAM—Meditation

Hold flowers in your palms and meditate on Ganesha while chanting the following mantra:

**EKADANTAM SHURPAKARNAM GAJAVAKTRAM CHATURBHUJAM
PAASHAMKUSHADHARAM DEVAM DHYAAYET SIDDHI VINAAYAKAM**

I meditate on Siddhi Vinaayaka who has four arms, holding the noose, goad, and who displays the fear-not gesture and the gesture of bestowing boons. His face is that of an elephant with one tusk and large ears.

**OM SRI SIDDHI VINAAYAKAAYA NAMAHA
DHYAANAM SAMARPAYAAMI**

Salutations to Siddhi Vinaayaka to whom I dedicate this meditation.

Now offer the flowers and red rice.

AAVAAHANAM—Inviting the Lord

**AAVAAHAYAAMI VIGHESHAM SURARAAJARCHITESHVARAM
ANATHANAATHAM SARVAJNAM PUJAARTHAM GANAANAAYAKAM**

O Lord Ganesha, we welcome You to accept our humble worship. You are the all-knowing Lord of the forlorn worshipped by the head of the celestials.

**OM SRI SIDDHI VINAAYAKAAYA NAMAHA
AAVAAHANAM SAMARPAYAAMI**

Salutations to Siddhi Vinaayaka. Thus we offer our invitation.

Offer flowers and red rice.

Sri Ganesha Puja

AASANAM—Offering the Seat to the Lord

>   VICHITRA RATNA KACHITAM DIVYAASTARANA SAMYUTAM
>   SWARNA SIMHAASANAM CHAARU GRAHAANA SURAPUJITA
>> O Lord Ganesha, always worshipped by the *devas*, we offer You the golden throne decked with wonderful gems and other divine ornamentation. Kindly be seated.

>   OM SRI SIDDHI VINAAYAKAAYA NAMAHA
>   AASANAM SAMARPAYAAMI
>> Salutations to Siddhi Vinaayaka. Thus the seat is offered.

PAADYAM—Offering Water to Wash the Feet of the Lord

>   SARVA TIRTHA SAMAANEETAM PAADYAM GANDHAADI SAMYUTAM
>   VIGHNA RAAJA GRAHAANEDAM BHAGAVAN BHAGAVATSALA
>> O Bhagavan Ganesha, kind to Your devotees, remover of obstacles, here is the holy water from all the sacred rivers mixed with sandalwood paste. Kindly accept it and bless us.

>   OM SRI SIDDHI VINAAYAKAAYA NAMAHA
>   PAADYAM SAMARPAYAAMI
>> Salutations to Siddhi Vinaayaka. Thus the water is offered for washing the feet.

Offer a spoonful of water to the ground as well as flowers and red rice.

ARGHYAM—Offering Water to Wash the Hands of the Lord

>   ARGHYAAMCHA PHALASAMYUKTAM
>   GANDHAPUSHPAAKSHATAIRYUTAM
>   GANAADHYAKSHA NAMASTESTU GRAHAANA KARUNAANIDHAE
>> O Ocean of Mercy, Lord of the world, kindly accept water to Your hands and the fruits, flowers and red rice.

>   OM SRI SIDDHI VINAAYAKAAYA NAMAHA
>   ARGHYAM SAMARPAAYAMI
>> Salutations to Siddhi Vinaayaka. Thus we offer water for washing the hands of God.

Offer a spoonful of water to the ground as well as flowers and red rice.

AACHAMANAM—Offering Water to Drink

>   SURASINDHI RAJAHA PAATRAM KOTISURYA SAMAPRABHAM
>   SUMYAGACHAMANAAM DEVA SVEEKURUSHVA VINAAYAKA
>> O Lord Vinaayaka, shining like millions of suns, accept this holy water from all the sacred rivers.

>   OM SRI SIDDHI VINAAYAKAAYA NAMAHA
>   AACHAMANAM SAMARPAYAAMI
>> Salutations to Siddhi Vinaayaka. Thus we offer water to the Lord for drinking.

Offer three spoonfuls of water to the ground and chant ACHAMANA three times while offering flowers and red rice.

LORD GANESHA

MADHUPARKAAM—Offering Honey and Fruit

**VIGHNESVARA VISHAALAAKSHA SAPTAARNAVA VINAAYAKA
MADHUPARKAM GRAHAANATVAM MAYAA SAMPRAARTHITO BHAVA**
 O Lord Ganesha, we offer honey and fruits. O lotus-eyed Lord, consider this as seven oceans of milk and honey and all fruits and receive it.

**OM SRI SIDDHI VINAAYAKAAYA NAMAHA
MADHUPARKAM SAMARPAYAAMI**
 Salutations to Siddhi Vinaayaka. Thus we offer honey and fruits to the Lord.

Offer red rice.

MALAAPAKARSYA SNAANAM—Bathing for Purification

**GANGAADI SARVATIRTHEBHYA AANEETAM TOYAMUTTAMAM
BHAKTYAA SAMARPITAM TUBHYAM SNAANAYAA ABHISHTA
DAAYAKA**
 O Lord Ganesha, we offer You the holy waters of the Ganges and all the sacred rivers for Your bathing. Kindly wash away our karma. O Fulfiller of wishes, thus we offer the water.

**OM SRI SIDDHI VINAAYAKAAYA NAMAHA
MALAAPAKARSHA SNAANAM SMARPAYAAMI**
 Salutations to Siddhi Vinaayaka. Thus we have offered water for bathing.

Offer a spoonful of water to the ground.

ATHA PANCHAAMRITA ABHISHEKAHA—Bathing with Five Nectars
While chanting the following six mantras, offer the five nectars—milk, yogurt, ghee, honey and sugar—along with coconut water and bathe the deities in each. Ring the bell while chanting each of the mantras.

KSHEERA SNAANAM (PAYAHA SNAANAM)—Bathing the Deity with Milk

**KAAMADHENU SAMADBHUTAM PARAMAM PAAVANAM PAYAHA
TAENA SNAANAM KURUSHVA TVAM HAERAMBA GANANAAYAKA**
 O Lord Ganesha, pure milk from the dripping udders of the cow of plenty we offer unto Thee. Please accept it and bless us with abundance.

**OM AAPAAYASVA SAMAETUTAE VISHVATAHA SOMA VRISHNYAM
BHAVAA VAAJASYA SANGATHAE**
 O Lord Ganesha, this is the pure milk from the ocean of milk. This is the nectar dripping from the full moon. As we bathe You with the milk, may You bathe our soul with the nectar of immortality.

**OM SRI SIDDHI VINAAYAKAAYA NAMAHA
KSHEERA SNAANAM SAMARPAYAAMI**
 Salutations to Siddhi Vinaayaka. Thus we have offered the milk.

DADHI SNAANAM—Bathing the Deity with Yogurt

**CHANDRA MANDALA SANKAASHAM SARVA DEVA PRIYAM DADHI
SNAANARTHAM TAE PRAYACHHAAMI GRAHAANA GANANAAYAKA**

Sri Ganesha Puja

O Lord Ganesha, here is the vessel filled with curds which are white as the circle of the moon. Kindly accept this and bless us.

OM DADHI KRAAVNO AKAARISHAM JISHNORASHVASYA VAAJINAHA
SURABHINO MUKAAKARAT PRANA AAYUMSHITAARISHAT
 O Lord Ganesha, we have prepared special curds to offer to You in bathing. This is prepared by the divine milk of the cow of plenty. Kindly accept this.

OM SRI SIDDHI VINAAYAKAAYA NAMAHA
DADHI SNAANAM SMARPAYAAMI
 Salutations to Siddhi Vinaayaka. Thus we have offered yogurt.

GHRITA SNAANAM—Bathing the Deity with Ghee

AAJAM SURANAAM AAHAARAM AAJYAM YAAJNAE PRATISHTITAM
AAJYAM PAVITRAM PARAMAM SNAANARTHAM PRATI
GRAHYATAAM
 Oblations with *ghee* is the food for the *devas*. *Yajna* or fire sacrifice is established by oblations. Oblations are supremely sacred, O Lord Ganesha. Kindly accept oblations of *ghee* for Your bathing.

OM GHRITAM MIMKSHAE GHRITAMASYA YONIRGHRITAE SHRITO
GHRITAMVASYA DHAAMA
ANUSHVADHAMAAVAHA MAADYASVA SWAAHAAKRITAM
VRISHABHA VAKSHI HAVYAM
 O Lord Ganesha, this *ghee* is prepared with the greatest devotion. It is prepared from the milk of the wish-fulfilling cow called Kaamadhenu. This *ghee* is especially offered in the great *yajnas* or fire sacrifices.

OM SRI SIDDHI VINAAYAKAAYA NAMAHA
GHRITA SNAANAM SAMARPAYAAMI
 Salutations to Siddhi Vinaayaka. Thus have we offered the *ghee*.

MADHU SNAANAM—Bathing the Deity with Honey

SARVOUSHADHI SAMUDBHUTAM PIYUSHA MADHURAM MADHU
SNAANAARTHAM TAE PRAYCHHAAMI GRAHAANA GIRIJAASUTA
 O Lord, son of Shakti, such a sweet honey from all the nectar of flowers and herbs we offer for Your bathing. Accept it and bless us.

OM MADHUVAATA RITAAYATAE MADHU KSHARANTI SINDHAVAHA
MADVEERNAHA SANTVOSHADHEEHI
MADHU NAKTAMUTOSHASO MADHUMAT PAARTHIVAM RAJAHA
MADHU DYAURASTU NAHA PITAA
MADHUMAANNO VANASPATIR
MADHUMAA ASTU SURYAHA
MAADHVEERGAAVO BHAVANTU NAHA
 O Lord Ganesha, may the winds be sweet to us. May the seasons be sweet to us. May the oceans be sweet to us. May the herbs be sweet to us. May the starry heavens be sweet to us. May Mother Earth be sweet to us. May the atmospheric regions be sweet to us. May the ancestral world be sweet to us.

LORD GANESHA

May the plant kingdom be sweet to us. May the solar deity be sweet to us. May the cosmos bless us with sweet milk. O Lord Ganesha, we bathe You with the honey so that our lives may become sweet, which means filled with health, wealth, peace and prosperity.

**OM SRI SIDDHI VINAAYAKAAYA NAMAHA
MADHU SNAANAM SAMARPAYAAMI**
Salutations to Lord Vinaayaka. Thus have we offered the honey.

SHARKARA SNAANAM—Bathing the Deity with Sugar

**IKSHUDANDA SAMUDBHUTAM DIVYA SHARKARAYAA TVAHAM
SNAAPAYAAMI MAHAA BHAKTYAA PRITO BHAAVA SHIVAATMAJA**
O Lord Ganesha, O son of Shiva, here we have the divine sugar prepared especially from sugar canes. This we offer unto Thee. Please accept it.

**OM SVAADHUH PAVASYA DIVYAAYA JANMANAE
SVAADURINDRAAYA SUHAVEETU NAAMNAE
SVAADUR MITRAAYA VARUNAAYA VAAYAVAE BRIHASPATAYAE
MADHUMA ADAABHYAHA**
O Lord Ganesha, from the wonderful sugar cane the juice is converted into sugar. This tasty sugar we apply to Your celestial body. May the milk and food build our bodies with perfect health. May the sun god, god of waters, god of air, the celestial guru Brihaspati, and all the nature forms and angels be propitious to us.

**OM SRI SIDDHI VINAAYAKAAYA NAMAHA
SHARKARA SNAANAM SAMARPAYAAMI**
Salutations to Siddhi Vinaayaka. Thus we have offered the sugar.

NARIKELODAKA SNAANAM—Bathing the Deity with Coconut Water

**SVACHHAIR NAANAAVIDHAIR DIVYAI GRAHAANA
STHAAPANODAKAIHI
SARVA TIRTHA SAMAANITAM PAYAHA PRIYA PRASIDAMAE**
O Lord Ganesha, from different coconut trees the fresh nectarian water is ready for Your bathing. Please accept it and bless us.

**OM SUYAVASAAD BHAGAVATIHI BHUYAA ATHO VAYAM
BHAGAVANTA SYAAMA
ADHITRANAMAGNYAE VISHWA DAANEEM PIBA SHUDDHAAMUDAKA
MAACHARANTEE**
Pure is this water. Kindly partake of it, O Lord Ganesha. O mystic fire and O divine Mother Shakti, may all of You be pleased as we offer this coconut water to Lord Ganesha.

**OM SRI SIDDHI VINAAYAKAAYA NAMAHA
NARIKELODAKA SNAANAM SAMARPAYAAMI**
Salutations to Siddhi Vinaayaka. Thus we have offered the coconut water.

**SNAANAM PANCHAAMRITAM DIVYAM KSHEERO DADHI, GHRITAM,
MADHU, SHARKARAAMCHA GRAHAANTVAM INDRAADYAIRABHI
PUJITA**

Sri Ganesha Puja

O Lord Ganesha, propitiated by Indra and other celestials, here we offer unto Thee the five nectars in the form of milk, curds, *ghee*, honey and sugar. Kindly accept it for Your showers and bless us with abundance.

OM SRI SIDDHI VINAAYAKAAYA NAMAHA
PANCHAAMRITA SNAANAM SAMARPAYAAMI
Salutations to Siddhi Vinaayaka. Thus have we offered the five nectars with coconut water.

ANGODVARTANAM—Smearing the Paste of Tumeric and Kum Kum

ANGODVARTANAKAM DEVA KASTURYAA DIVI MISHRITAM
LEPANAARTHAM GRAHAANAEDAM HARIDRAA KUMKUMAIRYUTAM
O Lord Ganesha, here we offer tumeric powder and red powder mixed with musk to apply to Your celestial body. Kindly accept this and bless us.

OM SRI SIDDHI VINAAYAKAAYA NAMAHA
ANGODVARTANAM SAMARPAYAAMI
Salutations to Siddhi Vinaayaka. Thus we have offered the paste of tumeric and kum kum.

Offer a spoonful of water into the plate.

USHNODAKA SNAANAM—Bathing the Deity with Warm Water

NAANAA TIRTHAA HRITAM YATNAATTOYAMUSHNAM MAYAA KRITAM
SNAANAARTHAM TAE PRAYACHHAAMI SVEEKURUSHVA DAYAANIDHAE
O Lord Ganesha, here we have prepared holy waters from the sacred rivers which is made warm for Your bathing. Kindly accept this water and bless us, O Ocean of Mercy.

OM SRI SIDDHI VINAAYAKAAYA NAMAHA
USHNODAKA SNAANAM SAMARPAYAAMI
Salutations to Siddhi Vinaayaka. Thus we have offered warm water for bathing.

Offer a spoonful of water into the plate.

GANDHODAKA SNAANAM—Bathing the Deity with Water Mixed with Sandalwood Powder and Camphor

CHANDANAAGARU KARPURA SURABHI SVAADU SHEETALAM
GANDHODAKAM GANAADHYAKSHA SNAANAARTHAM PRATIGRAHYATAAM
O Lord Ganesha, here is the pure water mixed with sandalwood powder, camphor and other perfumes. Kindly accept this for Your bathing and bless us.

OM SRI SIDDHI VINAAYAKAAYA NAMAHA
GANDHODAKA SNAANAM SAMARPAYAAMI
Salutations to Siddhi Vinaayaka. Thus we have offered water mixed with sandalwood powder and camphor.

Offer a spoonful of water into the plate.

LORD GANESHA

PURUSHA SUKTA—Mantras to the Supreme Person

Now chant the mantra of the Purusha Sukta and bathe the deity:

HARI OM
SAHASRA SHEERSHA PURUSHAHA
SAHASRAKSHAHA SAHASRAPAT SA BHUMIM VISHWATO VRITVAA
ATVATISTA DASHAANGULAM
   OM. The Primal Person has a thousand heads, a thousand eyes, a thousand feet. Pervading the entire universe, He transcends everything. (He is twenty finger widths above, which means transcendental; the number thousand means infinite.)

OM PURUSHA AEVADAM SARVAM
YADBHUTAM YACCHA BHAVYAM UTAAMRITATVASYESHAANAHA
YADANNENAATIROHATI
   All this is that Supreme Person—that which was, that which will be. He is the Lord of immortality. When embodied, He shows as if He grows by the food (whereas He is the essence).

OM ETAAVAANASYA MAHIMA
ATO JYAAYAAMSCHA PURUSHAHA
PAADOSYA VISHWAA BHUTAANI
TRIPAADASYAAMRITAM DIVI
   The glory of this Primeval Person is manifested in this universe which is His creation. He is infinitely greater than this universe. This whole universe with all animate and inanimate objects is only one-quarter of this Supreme Person. Three-fourths of His power and manifestation is shining above in the transcendental spheres which are indestructible.

OM TRIPAADURDHVA UDAITPURUSHAHA
PADOSYEHAABHAVATPUNAHA TATO
VISHWA VYAKRAAMAT
SAASHANAANASHANAE ABHI
   The invisible three-fourths effulgence of this Cosmic Reality is established in spheres of light. Only His one-fourth effulgence appears and disappears here. In this manifested one-fourth power, this Primal Person is pervading all the living animals (those who manifest hunger and thirst), and all the inert matter, too, with various names and forms.

OM TASMAADVIRADAJAAYATA
VIRAAJO ADHI PURUSHAHA
SAJAATO ATYARICHYATA
PASCHAADBHUMI MATHO PURAHA
   The universe of varied forms emerged from this Primal Person. Holding this cosmos as His body, the Supreme Person manifested. He created the celestials, animals, human beings and the earth by His own power, even though He was always transcendental.

OM YATPURUSHENA HAVISHAA
DEVAA YAJNA MATANVATA
VASANTO ASYAASEEDAAJYAM
GREESHMA IDHMA SHARADDHAVIHI
   Later, to propitiate this Cosmic Truth, the celestials made a symbolic mental fire sacrifice. To this fire sacrifice, spring became the oblation, summer became the holy grass, rainy season became the main offering.

Sri Ganesha Puja

OM SAPTAASHYA SANPARIDHYAYAHA
TRISAPTA SAMIDHAHA KRITAAHA
DEEVAA YADYAJNAM TANVAANAAHA
ABADHNAN PURUSHAM PASHAM

For this sacrifice, seven meters are the boundaries. Twenty-one principles are the oblations. To this sacrificial pillar, gods bound the Cosmic Truth Itself by the cord of mantra for their realization.

OM TAM YAJNAM BARHISHI PROUKSHAN
PURUSHAM JAATAMAGRATAHA
TENA DEVAA AYAJANTHA
SAADHYA RISHAYASCHAYAE

They installed the Cosmic Person over the holy grass and invoked Him there, the One who was before the creation and the object of the great fire sacrifice. Thus the celestials and the perfected beings, joining together, performed the mental fire sacrifice, the great meditation, keeping Him as the main oblation.

MAHAABHISHEKAHA—The Great Ceremonial Bathing
Bathe the deity with water while chanting the following mantras:

OM APOHISTA MAYO BHUVAHA
O water gods, you always confer happiness on those who meditate on you.

OM TAANA OORJAE DADHAATANA
Bless us with strength to be able to do everlasting, noble deeds.

OM MAHAERANAAYA CHAKSHASAE
Bless us to attain the highest wisdom.

OM YOVAHA SHIVATAMO RASAHA
Bless us with the essence of bliss.

OM TASYA BHAAJAYATAE HANAHA
Bless us to grow in this world by giving us the essence of Truth.

OM USHATEERIVA MATARAHA
Even as mothers feed their children with the milk from their bosoms, you protect us and make us grow.

OM TASMA ARANGA MAMAVAHA
O water spirits, we obey you in every way.

OM YASYA KSHAYAAYA JINVATHA
Expiate our sins and bless us to expand.

OM APO JANAYATHA CHA NAHA
Bless us with spiritual children and grandchildren to continue this spiritual line.

OM GANANAM TVA GANAPATIM HAVAMAHAE KAVIM KAVEENA
MUPAMASHRA-VASTHAMAM
JYESTARAAJAM BRAHMANAAM BRAHMANASPATA AANAHA
SHRAVANNUTIBHIHI SEEDA SAADANAM

O Lord Ganesha, You are appointed by the Trinity as the supreme head of all the *ganas* or divine species: angels, archangels, semi-gods, demi-gods and the presiding deities of all the planets. All the saints and poets meditate on You for their perfection in expressing or writing Your glory. You are considered the first to be adored, worshipped and saluted. Your blessings bring the fruit of all the *sadhanas* or spiritual practices of the seekers of Brahman. O Lord Ganesha, remove the obstacles from us and bless us to receive this *puja* by Your presence.

ITYAADYATHARVA SHIRHSA SUKTAENACHA ABHISHEKAM KURYAAT
Thus one has to conduct the ceremonial bathing by reciting the *sukta* or the hymn from the holy text of Atharva Sheersha.

**OM SRI SIDDHI VINAAYAKAAYA NAMAHA
SHUDDHODAKA SNAANAM SAMARPAYAAMI**
Salutations to Siddhi Vinaayaka. Thus we have offered pure water for bathing.

**OM SRI SIDDHI VINAAYAKAAYA NAMAHA
AACHAMANAM SAMARPAYAAMI**
Salutations to Siddhi Vinaayaka. Thus we have offered pure water for drinking.

Offer three spoonfuls of water to the plate.

VASTRAM—Offering Clothes to the Deity
Offer clothes to the deity while chanting the following mantra:

**RAKTA VASTRA YUGAM DEVA DEVAANGA SADRASHAM NAVAM
MAYAA DATTAM GRAHAANEEDAM SARVAPRADA NAMOSTUTAE**
O Lord Ganesha, here we offer two red cloths for *dhoti* and shawl which are fresh and new. Kindly accept this and bless us.

**OM SRI SIDDHI VINAAYAKAAYA NAMAHA
VASTRAYUGMAM SAMARPAYAAMI**
Salutations to Siddhi Vinaayaka. Thus we have offered clothes.

YAJNOPAVITAM—Offering the Sacred Thread to the Deity
Offer the sacred thread to the deity while chanting the following mantra:

**RAAJATAM BRAHMASUTRAMCHA KAANCHANAM CHATTARIYAKAM
GRAHAANA CHAARU SARVAJNA BHAKTAABHISHTA PRADAAYAKA**
O Lord Ganesha, One who fulfills the wishes of Your votaries; O omniscient Lord, here we offer the sacred thread of Brahma for You to wear.

**OM SRI SIDDHI VINAAYAKAAYA NAMAHA
YAJNOPAVITAM SAMARPAYAAMI**
Salutations to Lord Ganesha. Thus we have offered the sacred thread.

ABHARANAM—Offering Ornaments to the Deity
Offer jewels to the deity while chanting the following mantra:

**ANAEKA RATNA KHACHITAM SARVAABHARANA BHUSHITAM
GRAHAANA BHUSHANAM DEVA BHAKTAPRIYA NAMOSTUTAE**
O Lord Ganesha, the beloved of Your devotees, here are the precious ornaments of gold and gems for Your decoration. Kindly accept them and bless us.

**OM SRI SIDDHI VINAAYAKAAYA NAMAHA
ABHARANAM SAMARPAYAAMI**
Salutations to Lord Ganesha. Thus we have offered the ornaments for Your decoration.

Sri Ganesha Puja

GANDHAM—Offering Sandalwood Powder
Offer sandalwood powder to the deity while chanting the following mantra:

GANDHA KARPURA SAMYUKTAM DIVYA CHANDANA MUTTAMAM
VILEPANAM SURASHRESTHA PRIRTYARTHAM PRATI GRAHYATAAM
O Lord Ganesha, divine is the sandalwood paste mixed with camphor and other perfumes for applying to Your transcendental body. O God of gods, kindly accept this and bless us.

OM SRI SIDDHI VINAAYAKAAYA NAMAHA
GANDHAM SAMARPAYAAMI
Salutations to Siddhi Vinaayaka. Thus we have offered the sandalwood powder.

AKSHATAA—Offering Red Rice
Offer red rice while chanting the following mantra:

RAKTAAKSHATAAMSCHA DEVESHA GRAHAANA DVIRADAANANA
LALAATA PATALAE CHANDRAHA TASYOPARI VIDHAARYATAM
O Lord Ganesha, even as You have decked the moon on Your forehead, deck Your head with red rice, O Supreme God of elephant head.

OM SRI SIDDHI VINAAYAKAAYA NAMAHA
AKSHATAM SAMARPAYAAMI
Salutations to Siddhi Vinaayaka. Thus we have offered the red rice.

SINDURAM—Offering Kum Kum
Offer red powder to the deity while chanting the following mantra:

UDYAD BHAASKARA SANKAASHAM SANDHYAA VARUNAM PRABHO
VEERAALANKARANAM DIVYAM SINDURAM PRATI GRAHYATAAM
O Lord Ganesha, this divine red powder is applied always by the most powerful. As You are the almighty Lord, apply this red powder to Your body which will shine like the sky during dawn and dusk with crimson color.

OM SRI SIDDHI VINAAYAKAAYA NAMAHA
SINDURAM SAMARPAYAMI
Salutations to Siddhi Vinaayaka. Thus we have offered the red powder.

PARIMALADRAVYAM—Offering Scented Water
Offer scented water to the deity while chanting the following mantra:

KASTURYAADYEIR VIMISHRAMCHA NAANAA CHURNAIHI
SUGANDHIBHIHI
PREETYARTHAM TAE GRAHAANAEDAM PARIMALADRAVYAM
GANESHVARA
O Lord Ganesha, to please You we have prepared several kinds of perfume. Some are powder, some are paste mixed with musk. Kindly accept this and apply to Your body according to Your will.

OM SRI SIDDHI VINAAYAKAAYA NAMAHA
PARIMALADRAVYAANI SAMARPAYAAMI
Salutations to Siddhi Vinaayaka. Thus we have offered the perfumed water.

LORD GANESHA

PUSHPA—Offering Flowers
Offer flowers while chanting the following mantra:

**NAMASTAE VIGHNARAAJAAYA SARVA VIGHNAHARO BHAVA
SUVARNAPUSHPA ABHARANAM HARASOONO NAMOSTUTAE**
   O Lord Ganesha, son of Shiva, remover of obstacles, here we offer the golden flowers at Your lotus feet. Kindly bless us.

**OM SRI VINAAYAKAAYA NAMAHA
PUSHPANI SAMARPAYAAMI**
   Salutations to Siddhi Vinaayaka. Thus we have offered flowers.

AYUDHA—Offering of Weapons
Offer weapons to the deity while chanting the following mantra:

**AYUDHAANICHA TEEVRAANI DAITYA SANGAATAKAANICHA
MAMA VIGHNA VINAASHAAYA DHARAAYA SRI GAJAANANA
ANKUSHAM PARASHUM PAASHAM DANTAM DHARAAYA
BAAHUBHIHI
ABHEESHTAM KURUMAE DEVA SARVA SHATROON VIMARDAYA**
   O Lord Ganesha, here are the sharp weapons for the destruction of demons and for removing our troubles. Here is the goad, hatchet, noose and a tusk for You to hold in Your hand for the destruction of all enemies of Truth. Kindly accept them and bless us with peace.

**OM SRI SIDDHI VINAAYAKAAYA NAMAHA
AYUDHAANI SAMARPAYAAMI**
   Salutations to Siddhi Vinaayaka. Thus we have offered weapons.

AEKAVISHANTI NAMA PUJA—Salutations to the Lord
While chanting the twenty-one names of Ganesha, offer flowers and red rice with each mantra:

1. **VIGHNARAAJAAYA NAMAHA**
   Salutations to the Lord who removes obstacles.

2. **GAJAANANAAYA NAMAHA**
   Salutations to the elephant-headed god.

3. **LAMBODARAAYA NAMAHA**
   Salutations to the cosmic-bellied one.

4. **SHIVAATMAJAAYA NAMAHA**
   Salutations to the son of Shiva.

5. **VAKRATUNDAAYA NAMAHA**
   Salutations to the curve-faced one.

6. **SHURPAKARNAAYA NAMAHA**
   Salutations to the Lord of elephant ears.

7. **GANESHVARAAYA NAMAHA**
   Salutations to the Lord of the *ganas*.

8. **VIGHNANASHINAE NAMAHA**
   Salutations to the Lord who destroys trouble.

Sri Ganesha Puja

9. **VIKATAAYA NAMAHA**
   Salutations to the terrible Lord.

10. **VAAMANAAYA NAMAHA**
    Salutations to the dwarf incarnation.

11. **SARVADEVAAYA NAMAHA**
    Salutations to the embodiment of all gods.

12. **SARVADUKHAVINAASHINAE NAMAHA**
    Salutations to the destroyer of all miseries.

13. **VIGHNARHARTRAE NAMAHA**
    Salutations to the remover of impediments.

14. **DHUMRAAYA NAMAHA**
    Salutations to the Lord who has a brown-colored banner.

15. **SARVADEVAADHIDEVAAYA NAMAHA**
    Salutations to the primal God of all the gods.

16. **AEKADANTAAYA NAMAHA**
    Salutations to the Lord of one tusk.

17. **KRISHNAPINGALAAYA NAMAHA**
    Salutations to the Lord of black and blue color.

18. **PHAALACHANDRAAYA NAMAHA**
    Salutations to the Lord whose forehead is decked with the crescent moon.

19. **GANANAATHAAYA NAMAHA**
    Salutations to the supreme head of all the *ganas*.

20. **SHANKARASUNAVAE NAMAHA**
    Salutations to the son of Shankara.

21. **ANANGAPUJITAAYA NAMAHA**
    Salutations to the formless Lord.

OM SRI SIDDHI VINAAYAKAAYA NAMAHA
NAAMA PUJAANI SAMARPAYAAMI
Salutations to Siddhi Vinaayaka. Thus the *puja* with holy names if offered.

AAVARANA PUJA—Puja of the Circles
Offer red rice when you chant the "namaha" of each of the following mantras:

1. **GANANAATHAAYA NAMAHA**
   Salutations to the Lord of the *ganas*.

2. **HERUMBAAYA NAMAHA**
   Salutations to the Lord who is the first to be worshipped.

3. **IBHAVAKTRAAYA NAMAHA**
   Salutations to the elephant-faced one.

4. **MOOSHAKAVAAHANAAYA NAMAHA**
   Salutations to the Lord who has the mouse as His vehicle.

5. **SHIVAPRIYAAYA NAMAHA**
   Salutations to Ganesha who is very dear to Lord Shiva.

LORD GANESHA

6. **UMAAPUTRAAYA NAMAHA**
   Salutations to the son of Uma Parvati.

**DAYAABDHAE TRAAHI SAMSAARA SARPAANMAAM SHARANAAGATAM
BHAKTYAA SAMARPAYAE TUBHYAM PRATHAMAAVARANA ARCHANAM**
Lord Ganesha, here we offer the worship to the first circle of the altar with devotion. Protect us, those who have come in total surrender to Thee, from the poisonous cobra of karma and rebirth. O Ocean of Mercy, protect, protect.

**OM SRI SIDDHI VINAAYAKAAYA NAMAHA
PRATHAMAAVARANA PUJAAM SAMARPAYAAMI**
Salutations to Siddhi Vinaayaka. Thus we offer worship to the first circle.

1. **VARAGANAPATAYAE NAMAHA**
   Salutations to Ganapati, the bestower of boons.

2. **SURAGANAPATAYAE NAMAHA**
   Salutations to Ganapati who is worshipped by the *devas*.

3. **CHANDAGANAPATAYAE NAMAHA**
   Salutations to Ganapati who is all-powerful.

4. **IBHAVAKTRAGANAPATAYAE NAMAHA**
   Salutations to Ganapati who has an elephant face.

5. **KSHIPRAGANAPATAYAE NAMAHA**
   Salutations to Ganapati who blesses His devotee instantaneously.

6. **PRASAADAGANAPATAYAE NAMAHA**
   Salutations to Ganapati who blesses the devotee with placidity of mind.

7. **LAMBODARAGANAPATAYAE NAMAHA**
   Salutations to Ganapati of cosmic belly.

**DAYAABDHAE TRAAHI SAMSAARA SARPAANMAAM SHARANAAGATAM
BHAKTYAA SAMARPAYAE TUBHYAM DWITEEYAAVARANA ARCHANAM**
Lord Ganesha, here we offer the worship to the second circle of the altar with devotion. Protect us, those who have come in total surrender to Thee, from the poisonous cobra of karma and rebirth. O Ocean of Mercy, protect, protect.

**OM SRI SIDDHI VINAAYAKAAYA NAMAHA
DWITEEYAAVARANA PUJAAM SAMARPAYAAMI**
Salutations to Siddhi Vinaayaka. Thus we offer worship to the second circle.

1. **INDRAAYA NAMAHA**
   Salutations to Indra, the lord of the celestials.

2. **AGNAYAE NAMAHA**
   Salutations to Agni, the lord of fire.

3. **YAMAAYA NAMAHA**
   Salutations to Yama, the god of death.

Sri Ganesha Puja

4. **NIRATIYAE NAMAHA**
   Salutations to Nirati, the shining angel.

5. **VARUNAAYA NAMAHA**
   Salutations to Varuna, the god of waters.

6. **VAAYUVAE NAMAHA**
   Salutations to Vaayu, the lord of the life breath.

7. **KUBERAAYA NAMAHA**
   Salutations to Kubera, the lord of wealth.

8. **ISHAANAAYA NAMAHA**
   Salutations to Ishaanaa (an aspect of Shiva).

DAYAABDHAE TRAAHI SAMSAARA SARPAANMAAM SHARANAAGATAM
BHAKTYAA SAMARPAYAE TUBHYAM TRITEEYAAVARANA ARCHANAM
   Lord Ganesha, here we offer the worship to the third circle of the altar with devotion. Protect us, those who have come in total surrender to Thee, from the poisonous cobra of karma and rebirth. O Ocean of Mercy, protect, protect.

OM SRI SIDDHI VINAAYAKAAYA NAMAHA
TRITEEYAAVARANA PUJAAM SAMARPAYAAMI
   Salutations to Siddhi Vinaayaka. Thus we offer worship to the third circle.

1. **VINAAYAKAAYA NAMAHA**
   Salutations to Vinaayaka, the supreme Lord.

2. **DWAIMAATURAAYA NAMAHA**
   Salutations to Lord Ganesha who has two mothers (Ganga and Parvati).

3. **VIGHNARAAYAAYA NAMAHA**
   Salutations to Ganesha who is the remover of obstacles.

4. **GANAADHIPAAYA NAMAHA**
   Salutations to Ganesha who is the emperor of the *ganas*.

5. **HERAMBAAYA NAMAHA**
   Salutations to Ganesha who is the first to be worshipped.

6. **AEKADANTAAYA NAMAHA**
   Salutations to Ganesha who has one tusk.

7. **LAMBODHARAAYA NAMAHA**
   Salutations to Ganesha of cosmic belly.

DAYAABDHAE TRAAHI SAMSAARA SARPAANMAAM SHARANAAGATAM
BHAKTYAA SAMARPAYAE TUBHYAM CHATURTHAAVARANA ARCHANAM
   Lord Ganesha, here we offer the worship to the fourth circle of the altar with devotion. Protect us, those who have come in total surrender to Thee, from the poisonous cobra of karma and rebirth. O Ocean of Mercy, protect, protect.

LORD GANESHA

OM SRI SIDDHI VINAAYAKAAYA NAMAHA
CHATURTHAAVARANA PUJAM SAMARPAYAAMI
   Salutations to Siddhi Vinaayaka. Thus we offer worship to the fourth circle.

1. **TEESHNA DAMSHTRAAYA NAMAHA**
   Salutations to Ganesha of sharp, pointed tusks.

2. **SUTARUPAAYA NAMAHA**
   Salutations to Ganesha who is the all-pervading one, holding all the pearls.

3. **GAJASYAAYA NAMAHA**
   Salutations to Ganesha of elephant face.

4. **TRINETRAAYA NAMAHA**
   Salutations to Ganesha of three eyes.

5. **RAKTAPRIYAAYA NAMAHA**
   Salutations to Ganesha who loves the red color.

6. **BRAHADUDARAAYA NAMAHA**
   Salutations to Ganesha of big belly.

7. **SURAVANDYAAYA NAMAHA**
   Salutations to Ganesha who is propitiated by the celestials.

8. **SHIVASUTAAYA NAMAHA**
   Salutations to Ganesha, the son of Shiva.

DAYAABDHAE TRAAHI SAMSAARA SARPAANMAAM
SHARANAAGATAM
BHAKTYAA SAMARPAYAE TUBHYAM PANCHAMAAVARANA
ARCHANAM
   Lord Ganesha, here we offer the worship to the fifth circle of the altar with devotion. Protect us, those who have come in total surrender to Thee, from the poisonous cobra of karma and rebirth. O Ocean of Mercy, protect, protect.

OM SRI SIDDHI VINAAYAKAAYA NAMAHA
PANCHAMAAVARANA PUJAM SAMARPAYAAMI
   Salutations to Siddhi Vinaayaka. Thus we offer worship to the fifth circle.

1. **BHADRAKAALINAE NAMAHA**
   Salutations to Ganesha who is terrifying to the demons.

2. **BHAIRAVAAYA NAMAHA**
   Salutations to Ganesha who is of colossal size.

3. **SHESHAAYA NAMAHA**
   Salutations to Ganesha who is the all-pervading energy.

4. **VARUNAAYA NAMAHA**
   Salutations to Ganesha who is Varuna, the god of waters.

5. **SATAAMPATAYAE NAMAHA**
   Salutations to Ganesha who is the Lord of Truth.

6. **SAMVATSARAAYA NAMAHA**
   Salutations to Ganesha who is the Lord of the ear (the throat here is worshipped).

Sri Ganesha Puja

7. **SHAANTAAYA NAMAHA**
   Salutations to Ganesha who is the abode of peace.

DAYAABDHAE TRAAHI SAMSAARA SARPAANMAAM SHARANAAGATAM
BHAKTYAA SAMARPAYAE TUBHYAM SHASHTAAMAAVARANA ARCHANAM
   Lord Ganesha, here we offer the worship to the sixth circle of the altar with devotion. Protect us, those who have come in total surrender to Thee, from the poisonous cobra of karma and rebirth. O Ocean of Mercy, protect, protect.

OM SRI SIDDHI VINAAYAKAAYA NAMAHA
SHASHTAAMAAVARANA PUJAM SAMARPAYAAMI
   Salutations to Siddhi Vinaayaka. Thus we offer worship to the sixth circle.

Note: Also in the sixth circle, Bhadrakali (Parvati) and Bhairava, the angry aspect of Shiva; the serpent god Shesha; Varuna, the god of waters and other deities are worshipped. Similarly, in the seventh circle, different aspects of gods and goddesses are worshipped.

1. **SARASWATYAE NAMAHA**
   Salutations to Saraswati.

2. **LAKSHMYAE NAMAHA**
   Salutations to Lakshmi.

3. **BHAARATYAE NAMAHA**
   Salutations to Bharati.

4. **BRAHMANAE NAMAHA**
   Salutations to Brahma.

5. **VISHNAVAE NAMAHA**
   Salutations to Vishnu.

6. **RUDRAAYA NAMAHA**
   Salutations to Rudra.

7. **AAKASHAAYA NAMAHA**
   Salutations to the sky.

8. **VEDAAYA NAMAHA**
   Salutations to the *Vedas*.

9. **VAASTUPURUSHAAYA NAMAHA**
   Salutations to the Lord of sight.

DAYAABDHAE TRAAHI SAMSAARA SARPAANMAAM SHARANAAGATAM
BHAKTYAA SAMARPAYAE TUBHYAM SAPTAAMAAVARANA ARCHANAM
   Lord Ganesha, here we offer the worship to the seventh circle of the altar with devotion. Protect us, those who have come in total surrender to Thee, from the poisonous cobra of karma and rebirth. O Ocean of Mercy, protect, protect.

OM SRI SIDDHI VINAAYAKAAYA NAMAHA
SAPTAAMAAVARANA PUJAM SAMARPAYAAMI
   Salutations to Siddhi Vinaayaka. Thus we offer worship to the seventh circle.

LORD GANESHA

After chanting the above mantras, do three achamanas (sip water three times from the right hand), three pranayamas (three alternate nostril breaths) and the sankalpa or decision to offer 108 salutations to Lord Ganesha.

While holding flowers, red rice and the holy grass (if available) in your palm, chant the following mantra. Afterwards, offer the articles to Lord Ganesha.

> OM ASYA SRI GANESHAA ASHTOTTRA MANTRASYA
> GRATSAMADA RISHIHI
> GANAPATHI DEVATAA
> ANUSHTUP CHANDAHA
>> As per the will of Lord Vishnu, to please Him and to please Lord Ganesha who is Siddhi Vinaayaka, we offer 108 salutations in this worship along with holy grass, red rice and flower petals.
>
> GAM BIJAM
> NAM SHAKTIHI
> MAM KEELAKAM
> OM SRI SIDDHI VINAAYAKAA PREERTYARTHAE JAPAE VINIYOGAHA
>> In these mantras offering 108 salutations to Ganesha, we remember the seer of this mantra, Sage Gritsamada. Lord Ganapati Himself is the presiding deity. The meter is *anustup*. The seed syllable is **GAM**. Shakti is **NAM**. *Keelaka* (key) is **MAM**. We offer this *japa* or discipline of repeating the mantra to Lord Ganesha.

DHYAANAM—Meditation

> GAJAANANAM BHUTA GANAADI SEVITAM
> KAPITTHA JAMBU PHALASAARA BHAKSHITAM
> UMAASUTAM SHOKA VINAASHA KAARANAM
> NAMAAM VIGHNESHVARA PAADA PANKAJAM
>> I salute the lotus feet of Ganesha known as Vighneshwara who is propitiated by five cosmic elements and all the *ganas* (attendants of Shiva). To the one who enjoys the fruits and fruit juices, to the son of Uma Parvati, to the reliever of all grief and pain, to Gajaanana, the elephant-faced god, I offer salutations.

Offer flowers and red rice to the deity.

SRI GANESHA ASHTOTTARA SHATA NAAMAAVALIHI—Salutations to Ganesha with 108 Names

Offer red rice with each "namaha" of the following mantras:

1. **OM VINAAYAKAAYA NAMAHA**
   Salutations to Ganesha, the supreme Lord of all the denizens of heaven

2. **OM VIGHNARAAJAAYA NAMAHA**
   Salutations to Ganesha, the remover of obstacles

3. **OM GAURIPUTRAAYA NAMAHA**
   Salutations to Ganesha, the son of the white goddess, Gauri

4. **OM GANESHVARAAYA NAMAHA**
   Salutations to Ganesha, the head of the *ganas*

Sri Ganesha Puja

5. **OM SKANDAANUJAAYA NAMAHA**
   Salutations to Ganesha, the elder brother of Skanda (Subrahmanya)

6. **OM AVYAYAAYA NAMAHA**
   Salutations to Ganesha, the formless and indestructible Lord

7. **OM POOTAAYA NAMAHA**
   Salutations to Ganesha, the pure consciousness

8. **OM DAKSHAADHYAKSHAAYA NAMAHA**
   Salutations to Ganesha, the Lord of Daksha and other progenitors

9. **OM DWIJAPRIYAAYA NAMAHA**
   Salutations to Ganesha, the lover of the twice-born

10. **OM AGNIGARVACHHIDAE NAMAHA**
    Salutations to Ganesha who destroyed the ego of Agni, the fire god

11. **OM INDRA SRIPRADAAYA NAMAHA**
    Salutations to Ganesha who restored the wealth of Indra

12. **OM VANIBALAPRADAAYA NAMAHA**
    Salutations to Ganesha, the bestower of perfect speech

13. **OM SARVA SIDDHIPRADAAYAKAAYA NAMAHA**
    Salutations to Ganesha who bestows all supernatural powers

14. **OM SHARVATANAYAAYA NAMAHA**
    Salutations to Ganesha, the son of Shiva

15. **OM SHARVARIPRIYAAYA NAMAHA**
    Salutations to Ganesha, the son of Shakti who is the spouse of Shiva

16. **OM SARVATMAKAAYA NAMAHA**
    Salutations to Ganesha, the great Self of everyone

17. **OM SRISHTIKARTRAE NAMAHA**
    Salutations to Ganesha, the creator of the universe

18. **OM DEVAANIKAARCHITAAYA NAMAHA**
    Salutations to Ganesha who is worshipped by the *devas*

19. **OM SHIVAAYA NAMAHA**
    Salutations to Ganesha who is Shiva Himself

20. **OM SHUDDHABUDDHIPRIYAAYA NAMAHA**
    Salutations to Ganesha who blesses the devotee with pure intellect

21. **OM SHAANTAAYA NAMAHA**
    Salutations to Ganesha who is the peaceful one

22. **OM BRAHMACHARINAE NAMAHA**
    Salutations to Ganesha, the celibate

LORD GANESHA

23. OM GAJAANAAYA NAMAHA
    Salutations to Ganesha of the elephant face

24. OM DWAIMAATURAAYA NAMAHA
    Salutations to Ganesha, the son of two mothers

25. OM MUNISTUTYAAYA NAMAHA
    Salutations to Ganesha who is propitiated by the sages

26. OM BHAKTAVIGHNAVINAASHINAE NAMAHA
    Salutations to Ganesha, the destroyer of the troubles of His devotees

27. OM AEKADANTAAYA NAMAHA
    Salutations to Ganesha of one tusk

28. OM CHATURBAAHAVAE NAMAHA
    Salutations to Ganesha with four arms

29. OM SHAKTISAMYUTAAYA NAMAHA
    Salutations to Ganesha, the one who is filled with energy

30. OM CHATURAAYA NAMAHA
    Salutations to Ganesha who is intelligent and clever

31. OM LAMBODARAAYA NAMAHA
    Salutations to Ganesha of cosmic belly

32. OM SHURPAKARNAAYA NAMAHA
    Salutations to Ganesha of big ears

33. OM HERAMBAAYA NAMAHA
    Salutations to Ganesha who is the first to be worshipped

34. OM BRAHMAVITTAMAAYA NAMAHA
    Salutations to Ganesha, the knower of Brahman

35. OM LEELAAYA NAMAHA
    Salutations to Ganesha of divine sports

36. OM GRAHAPATAYAE NAMAHA
    Salutations to Ganesha who is the head of the planets

37. OM KAAMINAE NAMAHA
    Salutations to Ganesha, God of love

38. OM SOMASURYAAGNI LOCHANAAYA NAMAHA
    Salutations to Ganesha whose three eyes are the sun, moon and fire

39. OM PAASHAANKUSHADHARAAYA NAMAHA
    Salutations to Ganesha, the holder of the noose and the goad

40. OM CHANDAAYA NAMAHA
    Salutations to Ganesha, the powerful one

41. OM GUNAATITAAYA NAMAHA
    Salutations to Ganesha who is beyond the three *gunas* (three qualities of nature)

42. OM NIRANJANAAYA NAMAHA
    Salutations to Ganesha, the attributeless one

43. OM AKALMASHAAYA NAMAHA
    Salutations to Ganesha who is free from blemish

44. OM SWAYAMSIDDHAARCHITA PADAAYA NAMAHA
    Salutations to Ganesha whose feet are worshipped by the perfected beings

45. OM BIJAPURAKAAYA NAMAHA
    Salutations to Ganesha, the seed of the universe

46. OM AVYAKTAAYA NAMAHA
    Salutations to Ganesha, the unmanifested

47. OM VARADAAYA NAMAHA
    Salutations to Ganesha, the bestower of boons

48. OM SHASHWATAAYA NAMAHA
    Salutations to Ganesha, the eternal one

49. OM KRITINAE NAMAHA
    Salutations to Ganesha, the creative intelligence

50. OM VIDVATPRIYAAYA NAMAHA
    Salutations to Ganesha, the lover of wisdom

51. OM VITABHAYAAYA NAMAHA
    Salutations to Ganesha who is free from fear

52. OM GADINAE NAMAHA
    Salutations to Ganesha who holds the mace

53. OM CHAKRINAE NAMAHA
    Salutations to Ganesha who hold the disc

54. OM IKSHUCHAAPADHARAAYA NAMAHA
    Salutations to Ganesha who holds the sugarcane bow

55. OM ABJOTPALAKARAAYA NAMAHA
    Salutations to Ganesha of lotus-like hands

56. OM SHRISHAAYA NAMAHA
    Salutations to Ganesha, the lord of wealth

57. OM SRIPATAAYAE NAMAHA
    Salutations to Ganesha who is Vishnu Himself

58. OM STUTIHARSHITAAYA NAMAHA
    Salutations to Ganesha who is pleased with praise

59. **OM KULADRIBHETRAE NAMAHA**
    Salutations to Ganesha who is like a formidable mountain

60. **OM JATINAE NAMAHA**
    Salutations to Ganesha, the matted-locked one

61. **OM CHANDRACHUDAAYA NAMAHA**
    Salutations to Ganesha whose forehead is adorned with the crescent moon

62. **OM AMARESHWARAAYA NAMAHA**
    Salutations to Ganesha, the Lord of divine beings

63. **OM NAGAYAJNOPAVITINAE NAMAHA**
    Salutations to Ganesha who has the serpent as His sacred thread

64. **OM SRIKANTAAYA NAMAHA**
    Salutations to Ganesha of beautiful neck (or voice)

65. **OM RAMAARCHITAPADAAYA NAMAHA**
    Salutations to Ganesha whose feet are worshipped by Sri Rama

66. **OM VRITANAE NAMAHA**
    Salutations to Ganesha of strict vows

67. **OM STULAKANTAAYA NAMAHA**
    Salutations to Ganesha of elephant neck

68. **OM TRAYIKARTRAE NAMAHA**
    Salutations to Ganesha, the creator of the three worlds

69. **OM KAVAYAE NAMAHA**
    Salutations to Ganesha, the great poet

70. **OM SAAMAGHOSHAPRIYAAYA NAMAHA**
    Salutations to Ganesha, the lover of songs and Vedic chanting

71. **OM PURUSHOTAMAAYA NAMAHA**
    Salutations to Ganesha, the Supreme Being

72. **OM STHULATANDAAYA NAMAHA**
    Salutations to Ganesha of big mouth (or elephant face)

73. **OM AGRAGANYAAYA NAMAHA**
    Salutations to Ganesha, the Supreme

74. **OM GRAAMANYAI NAMAHA**
    Salutations to Ganesha who is worshipped in all religions

75. **OM GANAPAAYA NAMAHA**
    Salutations to Ganesha, the head of the *ganas*

76. **OM STHIRAAYA NAMAHA**
    Salutations to Ganesha, the permanent one

77. OM VRIDDHIDAAYAKAAYA NAMAHA
    Salutations to Ganesha who blesses us with prosperity

78. OM SUBHAGAAYA NAMAHA
    Salutations to Ganesha, the beautiful one

79. OM SHURAAYA NAMAHA
    Salutations to Ganesha, the Lord of great valor

80. OM VAGISHAAYA NAMAHA
    Salutations to Ganesha, the bestower of best speech

81. OM SIDDHIDAAYAKAAYA NAMAHA
    Salutations to Ganesha, the bestower of *siddhis*

82. OM DURVAABILVAPRIYAAYA NAMAHA
    Salutations to Ganesha, the lover of *bilva* leaves and *kusha* grass

83. OM KAANTAAYA NAMAHA
    Salutations to Ganesha who is our Lord

84. OM PAAPAHAARINAE NAMAHA
    Salutations to Ganesha, the destroyer of sins

85. OM KRITAAGAMAAYA NAMAHA
    Salutations to Ganesha, the one who restores lost health or wealth

86. OM SAMAAHITAAYA NAMAHA
    Salutations to Ganesha, the well-wisher of everyone

87. OM VAKRATUNDAAYA NAMAHA
    Salutations to Ganesha, the curve-faced one

88. OM SRIPRADAAYA NAMAHA
    Salutations to Ganesha, the bestower of wealth

89. OM SAUMYAAYA NAMAHA
    Salutations to Ganesha, the peaceful one

90. OM BHAKTAKAANKSHITADAAYA NAMAHA
    Salutations to Ganesha, the fulfiller of wishes of His devotees

91. OM ACHYUTAAYA NAMAHA
    Salutations to Ganesha, the invincible one

92. OM KAIVALYAAYA NAMAHA
    Salutations to Ganesha, the abode of freedom

93. OM SIDDHAAYA NAMAHA
    Salutations to Ganesha, the perfect one

94. OM SACHIDAANANDAVIGRAHAAYA NAMAHA
    Salutations to Ganesha, the embodiment of truth, consciousness and bliss

LORD GANESHA

95. OM JNAANINAE NAMAHA
    Salutations to Ganesha, the great wisdom

96. OM MAAYAAYUKTAAYA NAMAHA
    Salutations to Ganesha who is acting as if He is with *maya*, the illusory power

97. OM DAANTAAYA NAMAHA
    Salutations to Ganesha, the sublime Lord

98. OM BRAHMADWESHA VIVARJITAAYA NAMAHA
    Salutations to Ganesha who is free of hatred

99. OM PRAMATTA DAITYABHAYADAAYA NAMAHA
    Salutations to Ganesha who is the terror of the demons

100. OM VYAKTAMURTAYE NAMAHA
     Salutations to Ganesha who is the revealing truth

101. OM AMURTAKAAYA NAMAHA
     Salutations to Ganesha, the formless one

102. OM SARVATOMUKHAAYA NAMAHA
     Salutations to Ganesha whose face is everywhere

103. OM PARVATISHANKAROTSANGA KHELANOTSAVAAYA NAMAHA
     Salutations to Ganesha whose play is a festival of Shiva and Shakti

104. OM SAMASTA JAGADAADHAARAAYA NAMAHA
     Salutations to Ganesha, the support of the whole universe

105. OM VARAMUSHAKA VAAHANAAYA NAMAHA
     Salutations to Ganesha whose vehicle is the mouse

106. OM HRISHTA CHITTAAYA NAMAHA
     Salutations to Ganesha who is always happy

107. OM PRASANNAATMANAE NAMAHA
     Salutations to Ganesha who is blissful

108. OM SRI SARVASIDDHIPRADAAYAKAAYA NAMAHA
     Salutations to Ganesha who is the bestower of all supernatural powers

OM SRI SIDDHI VINAAYAKAAYA NAMAHA
Salutations to Siddhi Vinaayaka.

While chanting the following mantra, offer a spoonful of water into the plate along with flowers:

ANAENA SRI GANESHA ASHTOTRA SHATANAAMABHIHI
GAJAANANAAYA PUSHPA DURVA AKSHATA SAMARPANAENA
BHAGAVAAN GANESHAMURTIHI PREEYATAAM PREETO BHAVATU
    Thus we have offered with 108 Names the 108 salutations to the elephant-headed Ganesha with flowers, holy grass and red rice. May this please our Lord Ganesha and may He shower His supreme blessings.

Sri Ganesha Puja

DHUPA—Offering of the Incense
Light the incense and offer it to the deity while chanting the following mantra:

**DASHAANGAM GUGGULAM DHUPAM SUGANDHAMCHA MANOHARAM
BHAKTYAA DATTAM GRAHAANAEDAM LAMBODARA HARAATMAJA**
O Lord Ganesha, son of Shiva, with devotion we are offering incense of wonderful fragrance. Kindly accept this and bless us.

**OM SRI SIDDHI VINAAYAKAAYA NAMAHA
DHUPAM SAMARPAYAAMI**
Salutations to Siddhi Vinaayaka. Thus we have offered the incense.

DEEPA—Offering of the Light
Wave the wick light before the deity while chanting the following mantra:

**GRAHAANA MANGALAM DEVA GHRITAVARTI SAMANVITAM
DEEPAM JNAANAPRADAM DEVA RUDRAPRIYA NAMOSTUTAE**
Salutations unto Thee, O Lord Ganesha who is dear to Rudra. Here we offer the auspicious wick light filled with ghee. Salutations.

NAIVEDYAM—Offering of the Food
Offer the food to the deity while chanting the following mantra:

**OM BHUR BHUVAHA SWAHA SATYAM TWARTAENA
PARISHINCHAAMI**
For the realization of Truth and for purification, I sprinkle this water.

Sprinkle water on the offered food.

Offer a spoonful of water into the plate while chanting the following mantra:

**OM SRI SIDDHI VINAAYAKAAYA NAMAHA
APOSHANAARTHAE UDAKAM SAMARPAYAAMI**
Salutations to Siddhi Vinaayaka. For the purification of the mouth I offer the water.

Before chanting the following mantras, offer water through the conch into the plate five times. While chanting each mantra, offer a flower:

**OM PRANAAYA SWAAHA
OM APAANAAYA SWAAHA
OM VYAANAAYA SWAAHA
OM UDAANAAYA SWAAHA
OM SAMAANAAYA SWAAHA**
To the five pranas or vital breaths of the whole universe, I offer the divine food.

Offer water, flowers and red rice while chanting the following mantras:

**LADDUKAA NAARIKELAMCHA PHALAANI VIVIDHAANICHA
PAAYASAM GHRITASAMYUKTAM NAIVEDYAM PRATIGRAHYATAAM
NAANAAKHAADYAMIDAM DIVYAM TUSHTYATHAM TAE NIVEDITAM
MAYAA BHAKTYAA SHIVAAPUTRA GRAHAANA GANANAAYAKA**
O Lord Ganesha, son of Parvati, with devotion we offer sugar balls, tender coconut and varieties of fruits. We offer unto Thee a variety of divine porridge mixed with *ghee*.

LORD GANESHA

We have prepared several kinds of dishes for Your joy. Kindly partake this food and bless us with abundance.

**OM SRI SIDDHI VINAAYAKAAYA NAMAHA
NAANAABHAKSHYA NAIVEDYAM SAMARPAYAAMI**
Salutations to Siddhi Vinaayaka. Thus several varieties of food are offered.

PAANEEYAM—Offering of Drinking Water
Offer water to the deities while chanting the following mantra:

**AELOSHEERA LAVANGAADI KARPURA PARIVAASITAM
PRAASHANAARTHAM KRITAM TOYAM GRAHAANA GANANAAYAKA**
O Lord Ganesha, this pure water contains cardamom, cloves and camphor. Partake this water and bless us.

**OM SRI SIDDHI VINAAYAKAAYA NAMAHA
PAANEEYAM SAMARPAYAAMI**
Salutations to Siddhi Vinaayaka. Thus we have offered scented water for drinking.

Offer one spoonful of water into the plate while chanting the following mantra:

**AMRITAPIDHAANAMASI SWAAHA
OM SRI SIDDHI VINAAYAKAAYA NAMAHA
UTTARA APOSHANAARTHAE UDAKAM SAMARPAYAAMI**
Nectarian food is offered. Salutations to Siddhi Vinaayaka. Water is offered for washing the hands.

HASTAPRAKSHYAALANAM—Offering Water to Wash the Hands
Offer one spoonful of water into the plate while chanting the following mantra:

**USHNODAKAM SHUDDHAKARAM SHEETALAM JALAMUTTAMAM
HASTAPRAKSHYAALANAMIDAM PRITYARTHAM PRATIGRAHYATAAM**
O Lord Ganesha, for washing Your hands, here is pure water, both warm and cold. Kindly wash Your hands.

**OM SRI SIDDHI VINAAYAKAAYA NAMAHA
HASTAPRAKSHYAALANAM SAMARPAYAAMI**
Salutations to Siddhi Vinaayaka. Water for washing the hands is offered.

Offer a spoonful of water into the plate while chanting the following mantra:

**OM SRI SIDDHI VINAAYAKAAYA NAMAHA
GANDUSHAARTHAE UDAKAM SAMARPAYAAMI**
Salutations to Siddhi Vinaayaka. For rinsing the mouth, water is offered.

PUNARAACHAMANAM—Sipping the Water Three Times
Take three sips of water using the palm of the right hand as a conch; then offer two spoonsful of water to the ground.

**GANGAAJALA SAMAANEETAM SUVARNA KALASHAE STHITAM
ACHAMYATAAM UMAASOONO PUNARAACHAMANAM SMRATAM**
O Lord Ganesha, son of Uma, for sipping the water again, we have kept a golden vessel containing the pure Ganges water.

Sri Ganesha Puja

OM SRI SIDDHI VINAAYAKAAYA NAMAHA
PUNARAACHAMANAM SAMARPAYAAMI
   Salutations to Siddhi Vinaayaka. Again, water is offered for sipping.

KARODVARTANAM—Offering Sandalwood Paste to the Hands
While chanting the following mantra, offer sandalwood powder or paste to the deity:

MALAYAACHALA SAMBHUTAM KARPURAENA SAMANVITAM
KARODWARTANAKAM CHAARU GRAHYATAAM JAGATAHA PATAE
   O Lord Ganesha, Lord of the universe and of divine fragrance, apply this chandan or sandalwood paste prepared from a special sandalwood brought from Mount Malaya of the Himalayas and mixed with camphor.

OM SRI SIDDHI VINAAYAKAAYA NAMAHA
KARODWAARTHANARTHAE CHANDANAM SAMARPAYAAMI
   Salutations to Siddhi Vinaayaka. Sandalwood paste is offered for the hands of God.

PHALAA—Offering of Fruits
Offer fruit while chanting the following mantra:

NAARIKELAMCHA KADALI DRAAKSHA PANASAMEVACHA
KHARJURAENACHA SAMYUKTAM PHALAMTU PRATIGRAHYATAAM
   O Lord Ganesha, we have tender coconut, bananas, grapes, jackfruit, dates and other fruits. Kindly partake the fruit and bless us with the fruit of wisdom.

OM SRI SIDDHI VINAAYAKAAYA NAMAHA
PHALAANI SAMARPAYAAMI
   Salutations to Siddhi Vinaayaka. Thus we have offered the fruit.

MODAKAHA—Offering of Nectarian Porridge
Offer porridge to the deity while chanting the following mantra:

AEKAVISHATI SANKHYAAKAAN MODAKAAN GHRITAPAACHITAAN
NAIVEDYAM SAPHALAM DADYAAM NAMASTAE VIGHNANAASHINAE
   O Lord Ganesha, we have prepared twenty-one kinds of porridge mixed with pure *ghee*. We offer our salutations for the removal of obstacles. Kindly partake this food.

OM SRI SIDDHI VINAAYAKAAYA NAMAHA
AEKAVISHATI MODAKAAN SAMARPAYAAMI
   Salutations to Siddhi Vinaayaka. We have offered twenty-one kinds of porridge.

TAAMBULAM—Offering of Beetlenuts and Beetle Leaves
While chanting the following mantra, offer beetlenuts and leaves to the deity:

PUGIPHALAM MAHAADIVYAM NAAGAVALYAA SAMANVITAM
KARPURAELADI SAMYUKTAM TAAMBULAM PRATIGRAHYATAAM
   O Lord Ganesha, we have brought the special beetle leaves and beetlenuts mixed with camphor and cardamom. Kindly accept this to freshen the mouth.

OM SRI SIDDHI VINAAYAKAAYA NAMAHA
TAAMBULAM SAMARPAYAAMI
   Salutations to Siddhi Vinaayaka. Thus the beetlenuts and beetle leaves are offered.

LORD GANESHA

DAKSHINA—Offering of Coins
Offer coins to the plate while chanting the following mantra:

**PUJAAPHALA PRASIDHYARTHAM TAVAAGRAE DEVA DAKSHINAAM
HIRANYAGARBHA GARBHASTAM HEMABIJAM VIVHAAYASOHO
ANANTAPUNYA PHALADAM ATAHA SHAANTIM PRAYACHHAMAE**
 O Lord Ganesha, for the fulfillment of the *puja* we offer a few coins as dakshina or reverential offering. Let this be the seed of gold coming from Brahma, the golden-bellied one. May this bring us wealth and prosperity and the blessings of peace.

**OM SRI SIDDHI VINAAYAKAAYA NAMAHA
HIRANYA DAKSHINAAM SAMARPAYAAMI**
 Salutations to Siddhi Vinaayaka. Coins are offered, mentally feeling that gold is offered.

MANGALAARATI—Offering of the Light
Wave the light before the deity while chanting the following mantras:

**CHANDRADITYAUCHA DHARANI VIDYUDAGNI STHATHAIVACHA
TWAMEVA SARVAJYOTHIMSHI ARTIKYAM PRATIGRAPHYATAAM**
 O Lord Ganesha, we invoke the light of the moon, sun, lightning and mystic fire in this wick lamp which we are waving before You. May it please You.

**OM SHRIYA JAATAHA SHRIYA ANIREEYAAYA SHRIYAM VAYO
JARITRABHYO DADAATI
SHRIYAM VASAANA AMRITATTWAMAAYAN BHAVANTI SATYAA
SAMITHAA MITADRAU**
 O Lord Ganesha, we invoke Mahalakshmi, the goddes of prosperity, in our midst. Wherever You are, there Mother Shree (Lakshmi) is present. Wealth creates more wealth and to use the wealth to serve God is to attain immortality.

**OM SRI SIDDHI VINAAYAKAAYA NAMAHA
MANGALANIRAAJINAM SAMARPAAYAMI**
 Salutations to Siddhi Vinaayaka. Thus the auspicious light is offered to Ganesha and Lakshmi.

MANTRAPUSHPAANJALI—Offering of Flowers as Mantra
Hold flowers and red rice in your hands while chanting the following mantras. Afterwards, offer them to the deity.

**MAALATI MALLIKA PUSHPAIRVIVIDHAISCHA SAMANVITAM
PUSHPAANJALIM GRAHAANEDAM PAADAAMBUJA YUGAARPITAM**
 O Lord Ganesha, kindly accept these beautiful flowers—lotus, jasmine and other flowers—which we offer to Your lotus feet.

**OM GANANAM TWA GANAPATIM HAVAMAHAE KAVIM KAVEENA
MUPAMASHRA VASTHAMAM
JYESTARAAJAM BRAHMANAAM BRAHMANASPATA AANAHA
SHRANVANNUTIBHIHI SEEDA SAADANAM**
 O Lord Ganesha, You are appointed by the Trinity as the supreme head of all the ganas or divine species—angels, archangels, semi-gods, demi-gods and the presiding deities of all the planets. All the saints and poets meditate on You for their perfection in expressing or writing Your glory. You are considered the first to be adored,

Sri Ganesha Puja

worshipped and saluted. Your blessings bring the fruit of all the sadhanas or spiritual practices of the seekers of Brahman. O Lord Ganesha, remove the obstacles from us and bless us to receive this *puja* by Your presence.

OM SRI SIDDHI VINAAYAKAAYA NAMAHA
MANTRAPUSHPAM SAMARPAYAAMI
Salutations to Siddhi Vinaayaka. Flowers as mantra are offered.

PRADAKSHINA—Perambulation
Turn clockwise three times while chanting the following:

PRADAKSHINATRAYAM DEVA PRAYATNAENA MAYA KRITAM
TAENA PAAPAANI SARVAANI VYAPOHATU GANESHVARA
O Lord Ganesha, I perambulate and circumnavigate around Thee thrice for getting rid of all my sins and bad karma. Please absolve me of all my karma and bless me, O Lord Ganesha.

OM SRI SIDDHI VINAAYAKAAYA NAMAHA
PRADAKSHINAAN SAMARPAYAAMI
Salutatons to Siddhi Vinaayaka. Thus we offer perambulation and circumnavigation.

NAMASKAARA—Offering Salutations
With joined palms, offer prostrations while chanting the following:

NAMASTAE VIGHNASAMHARTRAE NAMO BHAKTAEPSITAPRADA
NAMASTAE DEVADEVESHA NAMASTAE GANANAAYAKA
Salutations, O Lord of *ganas*, God of gods, fulfiller of the wishes of Your devotees. Remover of obstacles, salutations again and again.

PRAARTHANA—Offering of Prayers
Now offer your prayers to the deity:

NAMASTAE VIGHNANAASHAAYA SARVAVIGHNAHARO BHAVA
SHEEGHRAM MAMA VARAM DEHI NAMASTAE BHAKTAVATSALA
YANMAYA CHARITAM DEVA VRITAMAETAT SUDURLABHAM
GANESHA TWAM PRASANNAHA SAN SAPHALAM KURU SARVADAA

VINAAYAKAESHAPUTRA TWAM GANARAAJA SUROTTAMA
DEHIMAE SAKALAAN KAAMAAN VANDAE SIDDHIVINAAYAKA
VINAAYAKA GANESHAANA SARVADEVA NAMASKRITA
PAARVATIPRIYA VIGHNESHA MAMA VIGHNAA NIVAARAYA
O Lord Ganesha, protector of Your devotees, shower on us Your grace and bless us with divine boons. Relieve us of all troubles, O Lord, the destroyer of obstacles. This worship vow which is so difficult to obtain, we obtain through Your grace. Let this *puja* be fruitful in pleasing you, my Lord. Hey, Siddhi Vinaayaka, consider us as Your sons, O supreme among gods, and fulfill all of our wishes. Salutations!

O Lord Ganesha, saluted by all denizens of heaven; O dear son of Parvati, remove all that is blocking our way to attain prosperity and peace.

OM SRI SIDDHI VINAAYAKAAYA NAMAHA
PRAARTHANAAM SAMARPAYAAMI
Salutations to Siddhi Vinaayaka. Thus we have offered our prayers.

LORD GANESHA

After chanting the above mantras, offer flowers and red rice to the deity.

PRASAADAGRAHANAM—Mantras for Purifying the Food
Chant the following mantras to purify the food which has been offered:

    VAKRATUNDA MAHAAKAAYA KOTISURYA SAMAPRABHAA
    NIRVIGHNAM KURUMAE DEVA
    SARVA KAARYAESHU SARVADAA
      O Lord Ganesha of huge body and elephant head, shining like billions of suns, remove, O God, all obstacles from our endeavors.

    AGAJAANAN PADMARKAM GAJAANANAM AHARNISHAM
    ANAEKADANTAM BHAKTAANAAM AEKADANTAMUPASMAHAE

    GAJAANANAM BHUTAGANAADI SEVITAM
    KAPITTHA JAMBU PHALASAARA BHAKSHITAM
    UMASUTAM SHOKAVINAASHA KAARANAM
    NAMAAMI VIGHNESHWARA PAADA PANKAJAM
      I meditate on Aekadanta, Lord of one tusk who blesses His votaries in many bold ways. I meditate on the elephant-faced one night and day. He is like the sun to make the lotus-like face of His Mother Shakti, the mountain daughter, to blossom. Salutations! I salute the lotus feet of Vighneshwara, the remover of all grief, the son of Uma, one who likes to partake the essence of good fruits, propitiated by attendants of Shiva. Salutations again and again to the elephant-faced one!

KRISHNAARPANAM—Complete Offering
With the following, everything is offered to Krishna-Ganesha.

    OM TAT SAT SRI KRISHNA ARPANAMASTU
      Everything is offered to Lord Sri Krishna who is Ganesha.

    TWAMAEVA MATACHA PITA TWAMAEVA
    TWAMAEVA BANDHUSCHA SAKHA TWAMAEVA
    TWAMAEVA VIDYA DRAVINAM TWAMAEVA
    TWAMAEVA SARVAM MAMADEVADEVA
      Thou art my mother, father Thou art. Thou art my relative, friend Thou art. Thou art my wisdom, my wealth Thou art. Thou art my everything, O God of gods.

    KAAYAENA VAACHA MANASENDRIYAIRVA
    BUDDHYATMANAAVAA PRIKRITI SWABHAAVAT
    KAROMI YADYAT SAKALAMPARASMAI
    NARAAYANA YETI SAMARPAYAAMI
      O Lord Narayana, I offer all that I have done through thought, word and body (deed), consciously or unconsciously, by the force of habit or pull of *maya* and karma. Kindly forgive me and protect me.

    OM ASATHOMAA SADGAMAYA
    TAMASOMAA JYOTHIRGAMAYA
    MRITYORMAA AMRITAM GAMAYA
    OM SHANTIHI SHANTIHI SHANTIHI
      Lord, lead us from untruth toward the truth; from darkness toward the Light; from death toward immortality. OM, peace, peace, peace.

Sri Ganesha Sahasra Naamavali

1. OM GANESHWARAAYA NAMAHA
   Salutations to Lord Ganesha who is the Lord of the *ganas*

2. OM GANADHYAKSHAAYA NAMAHA
   Salutations to Lord Ganesha who is the supervisor of the *ganas*

3. OM GANARAADHYAAYA NAMAHA
   Salutations to Lord Ganesha who is worshipped by the *ganas*

4. OM GANAPRIYAAYA NAMAHA
   Salutations to Lord Ganesha who is dear to the *ganas*

5. OM GANANAATHAAYA NAMAHA
   Salutations to Lord Ganesha who is the authority over the *ganas*

6. OM GANASWAAMINAE NAMAHA
   Salutations to Lord Ganesha who is Master of the *ganas*

7. OM GANESHAAYA NAMAHA
   Salutations to Lord Ganesha who is the refuge of the *ganas*

8. OM GANANAAYAKAAYA NAMAHA
   Salutations to Lord Ganesha who is the leader of the *ganas*

9. OM GANAMOORTAYAE NAMAHA
   Salutations to Lord Ganesha who is the head of the *ganas*

10. OM GANAPATAYAE NAMAHA
    Salutations to Lord Ganesha who is the boss of the *ganas*

11. OM GANATRAATRAE NAMAHA
    Salutations to Lord Ganesha who is the protector of the *ganas*

12. OM GANANJAYAAYA NAMAHA
    Salutations to Lord Ganesha who brings victory to the *ganas*

13. OM GANAPAAYA NAMAHA
    Salutations to Lord Ganesha who is greatest among the *ganas*

14. OM GANAKRIDAAYA NAMAHA
    Salutations to Lord Ganesha who plays with the *ganas*

15. OM GANADAEVAAYA NAMAHA
    Salutations to Lord Ganesha who is God of the *ganas*

16. OM GANAADHIPAAYA NAMAHA
    Salutations to Lord Ganesha who is emperor among the *ganas*

17. OM GANAJESHTAAYA NAMAHA
    Salutations to Lord Ganesha who is eldest among the *ganas*

18. OM GANASHRAESHTHAAYA NAMAHA
    Salutations to Lord Ganesha who is the abode of the *ganas*

LORD GANESHA

19. OM GANADHI RAAJAE NAMAHA
    Salutations to Lord Ganesha who is king among the *ganas*

20. OM GANA RAAJAE NAMAHA
    Salutations to Lord Ganesha who is prince among the *ganas*

21. OM GANA GOPTRAE NAMAHA
    Salutations to Lord Ganesha who is the mysterious truth of the *ganas*

22. OM GANAANGAAYA NAMAHA
    Salutations to Lord Ganesha who is the body of the *ganas*

23. OM GANADAIVATAAYA NAMAHA
    Salutations to Lord Ganesha who is the presiding deity over the *ganas*

24. OM GANA BANDHAVAE NAMAHA
    Salutations to Lord Ganesha who is the true relative of the *ganas*

25. OM GANA SUHRUDAE NAMAHA
    Salutations to Lord Ganesha who is the friend of the *ganas*

26. OM GANAADHEESHAAYA NAMAHA
    Salutations to Lord Ganesha who is the monarch among the *ganas*

27. OM GANA PRAMATHAAYA NAMAHA
    Salutations to Lord Ganesha who is first among the *ganas*

28. OM GANA PRIYA SAKHAAYA NAMAHA
    Salutations to Lord Ganesha who is the dear comrade of the *ganas*

29. OM GANA PRIYA SUHRUDAE NAMAHA
    Salutations to Lord Ganesha who is the dear counselor of the *ganas*

30. OM GANA NITYA PRIYA RATAAYA NAMAHA
    Salutations to Lord Ganesha who is beloved of the *ganas*

31. OM GANAPREETIVIVARDHANAAYA NAMAHA
    Salutations to Lord Ganesha who expands the love of the *ganas*

32. OM GANAMANDALA MADHYASTHAAYA NAMAHA
    Salutations to Lord Ganesha who is the central figure in the circle of the *ganas*

33. OM GANAKAELIPARAAYANAAYA NAMAHA
    Salutations to Lord Ganesha who is engaged in sports with the *ganas*

34. OM GATAAGRANYAE NAMAHA
    Salutations to Lord Ganesha who is ancient among the *ganas*

35. OM GANESHAANAAYA NAMAHA
    Salutations to Lord Ganesha who is the face of the *ganas*

36. OM GANAGEETAAYA NAMAHA
    Salutations to Lord Ganesha who is the song of the *ganas*

37. OM GANOCHHRAYAAYA NAMAHA
    Salutations to Lord Ganesha who is the eloquence of the *ganas*

38. OM GANYAAYA NAMAHA
    Salutations to Lord Ganesha who is the supreme *gana* Himself

39. OM GANAHITAAYA NAMAHA
    Salutations to Lord Ganesha who is the well-wisher of the *ganas*

40. OM GARJADGANASAENAAYA NAMAHA
    Salutations to Lord Ganesha who is the inspiring roar to the troupe of the *ganas*

41. OM GANODYATAAYA NAMAHA
    Salutations to Lord Ganesha who is the inspirer of the *ganas*

42. OM GANAAPREETIPRAMATHANAAYA NAMAHA
    Salutations to Lord Ganesha who is the supreme test of the true love of the *ganas*

43. OM GANABHEETYAPAHAARAKAAYA NAMAHA
    Salutations to Lord Ganesha who is the remover of the fear of the *ganas*

44. OM GANAARHANAAYA NAMAHA
    Salutations to Lord Ganesha who is the deserving teacher of the *ganas*

45. OM GANAPROUDHAAYA NAMAHA
    Salutations to Lord Ganesha who is unequalled among the *ganas*

46. OM GANABARTRAE NAMAHA
    Salutations to Lord Ganesha who is the support of the *ganas*

47. OM GANAPRABHAVAE NAMAHA
    Salutations to Lord Ganesha who is the light of the *ganas*

48. OM GANASENAAYA NAMAHA
    Salutations to Lord Ganesha who is the commander-in-chief of the *ganas*

49. OM GANCHARAAYA NAMAHA
    Salutations to Lord Ganesha who is the moving spirit of the *ganas*

50. OM GANAPRAAJNAAYA NAMAHA
    Salutations to Lord Ganesha who is the wisdom of the *ganas*

51. OM GANAIKARAAJAE NAMAHA
    Salutations to Lord Ganesha who is the one ruler of the *ganas*

52. OM GANAAGYRAAYA NAMAHA
    Salutations to Lord Ganesha who is eldest among the *ganas*

53. OM GANYANAAMNAE NAMAHA
    Salutations to Lord Ganesha who is the proud name among the *ganas*

54. OM GANAPAALANATATPARAAYA NAMAHA
    Salutations to Lord Ganesha who is engaged in protecting the *ganas*

55. OM GANAJITAE NAMAHA
    Salutations to Lord Ganesha who is the victory of the *ganas*

56. OM GANAGARBHASTHAAYA NAMAHA
    Salutations to Lord Ganesha who is the womb of the *ganas*

57. OM GANAPRAVANAMAANASAAYA NAMAHA
    Salutations to Lord Ganesha who is the meditation of the *ganas*

LORD GANESHA

58. OM GANAGARVAPAREEHARTRAE NAMAHA
    Salutations to Lord Ganesha who is the humbler of the pride of the *ganas*

59. OM GANAAYA NAMAHA
    Salutations to Lord Ganesha who is number one among the *ganas*

60. OM GANA NAMASKRUTAAYA NAMAHA
    Salutations to Lord Ganesha who is the creator of the name "*gana*"

61. OM GARNAARCHITAANGHRIYUGALAAYA NAMAHA
    Salutations to Lord Ganesha whose lotus feet are worshipped by the *ganas*

62. OM GANARAKSHANA KRUTPRABHAVAE NAMAHA
    Salutations to Lord Ganesha who is the supporter of the *ganas*

63. OM GANADHYAATAAYA NAMAHA
    Salutations to Lord Ganesha who is the goal of the *ganas*

64. OM GANA GURUVAE NAMAHA
    Salutations to Lord Ganesha who is the guru of the *ganas*

65. OM GANAPRAANAYA TATPARAAYA NAMAHA
    Salutations to Lord Ganesha who is affectionate to the *ganas*

66. OM GANA AGANA PARITRAATRAE NAMAHA
    Salutations to Lord Ganesha who is the shelter for the *ganas* and non-*ganas*

67. OM GANAADHIPA HARANODDHARAAYA NAMAHA
    Salutations to Lord Ganesha who is the protector of the spirit of the *ganas*

68. OM GANASAETAVAE NAMAHA
    Salutations to Lord Ganesha who is the bridge among the *ganas*

69. OM GANANAATAAYA NAMAHA
    Salutations to Lord Ganesha who is the Soul of the *ganas*

70. OM GANAKAETUVAE NAMAHA
    Salutations to Lord Ganesha who is the banner of the *ganas*

71. OM GANAAGRAGAAYA NAMAHA
    Salutations to Lord Ganesha who is top among the *ganas*

72. OM GANAHAETUVAE NAMAHA
    Salutations to Lord Ganesha who is the cause of the *ganas*

73. OM GANAGRAAHINAE NAMAHA
    Salutations to Lord Ganesha who is the abode of the *ganas*

74. OM GANAANUGRAHAKAARAKAAYA NAMAHA
    Salutations to Lord Ganesha who showers the grace upon the *ganas*

75. OM GANA AGANAANUGRAHABHAVAE NAMAHA
    Salutations to Lord Ganesha who is the source of the *ganas* and non-*ganas*

76. OM GANAAGANA VARAPRADAAYA NAMAHA
    Salutations to Lord Ganesha who is the bestower of boons to the *ganas*

77. OM GANASTUTAAYA NAMAHA
    Salutations to Lord Ganesha who is praised by the *ganas*

Sri Ganesha Sahasra Naamavali

78. OM GANAPRAANAAYA NAMAHA
    Salutations to Lord Ganesha who is the life of the *ganas*

79. OM GUNASARVA SVADAAYAKAAYA NAMAHA
    Salutations to Lord Ganesha who upholds the virtues of the *ganas*

80. OM GANA VALLABHA MOORTAYE NAMAHA
    Salutations to Lord Ganesha who is the worshipful *murti* (living image) of the *ganas*

81. OM GANA BHOOTAYE NAMAHA
    Salutations to Lord Ganesha who is the bestower of *gana*-ship

82. OM GANESHTADAAYA NAMAHA
    Salutations to Lord Ganesha who is compassionate to the *ganas*

83. OM GANASOUKHYA PRADAATRE NAMAHA
    Salutations to Lord Ganesha who is the bestower of happiness to the *ganas*

84. OM GANADUKHAPRANAASHANAAYA NAMAHA
    Salutations to Lord Ganesha who is the remover of the afflictions of the *ganas*

85. OM GANAPRATHITANAAMNE NAMAHA
    Salutations to Lord Ganesha who is the imperishable name among the *ganas*

86. OM GANAABHEESHTAKARAAYA NAMAHA
    Salutations to Lord Ganesha who is the fulfiller of the wishes of the *ganas*

87. OM GANAMAANYAAYA NAMAHA
    Salutations to Lord Ganesha who is highly respected among the *ganas*

88. OM GANAKHYAATAAYA NAMAHA
    Salutations to Lord Ganesha who is famous among the *ganas*

89. OM GANAVEETAAYA NAMAHA
    Salutations to Lord Ganesha who is prudent among the *ganas*

90. OM GANOTKATAAYA NAMAHA
    Salutations to Lord Ganesha who is great among the *ganas*

91. OM GANAPAALAAYA NAMAHA
    Salutations to Lord Ganesha who is the guardian of the *ganas*

92. OM GANAVARAAYA NAMAHA
    Salutations to Lord Ganesha who is paramount among the *ganas*

93. OM GANAGAURAVADAAYA NAMAHA
    Salutations to Lord Ganesha who brings honor to the *ganas*

94. OM GANA GARJITA SANTUSHTAAYA NAMAHA
    Salutations to Lord Ganesha who is pleased with the praise of the *ganas*

95. OM GANASVACHHANDA GAYANAAYA NAMAHA
    Salutations to Lord Ganesha who freely moves among the *ganas*

96. OM GANAARAAJAAYA NAMAHA
    Salutations to Lord Ganesha who is the incomparable Lord of the *ganas*

LORD GANESHA

97. OM GANASHREEDAYA NAMAHA
    Salutations to Lord Ganesha who is the bestower of wealth to the *ganas*

98. OM GANABHEETIHARAAYA NAMAHA
    Salutations to Lord Ganesha who makes the *ganas* fearless

99. OM GANAMOORDHAABHISHIKTAAYA NAMAHA
    Salutations to Lord Ganesha who is who coronated by the *ganas*

100. OM GANASAINYA PURASARAAYA NAMAHA
     Salutations to Lord Ganesha who is honored by the *ganas*

101. OM GUNAATEETAAYA NAMAHA
     Salutations to Lord Ganesha who is beyond the *gunas* (qualities of nature)

102. OM GUNAMAYAAYA NAMAHA
     Salutations to Lord Ganesha who is the embodiment of the *gunas*

103. OM GUNATRAYAVIBHAAGA KRITAE NAMAHA
     Salutations to Lord Ganesha who divides the *gunas* into three, i.e., *sattva*, *rajas* and *tamas*

104. OM GUNINAE NAMAHA
     Salutations to Lord Ganesha who is the abode of virtues

105. OM GUNAAKRUTIDHARAAYA NAMAHA
     Salutations to Lord Ganesha who has taken the form of the *gunas*

106. OM GUNASHAALIHAE NAMAHA
     Salutations to Lord Ganesha who is good

107. OM GUNAPRIYAAYA NAMAHA
     Salutations to Lord Ganesha who loves the *gunas*

108. OM GUNAPOORNAAYA NAMAHA
     Salutations to Lord Ganesha who is of perfect virtue

109. OM GUNAAMABODHAYAE NAMAHA
     Salutations to Lord Ganesha who is the ocean of virtue

110. OM GUNABHAAJAE NAMAHA
     Salutations to Lord Ganesha who is virtuous

111. OM GUNADOORAGAAYA NAMAHA
     Salutations to Lord Ganesha whom the qualities of nature cannot touch

112. OM GUNAAGUNAVAPUSHAE NAMAHA
     Salutations to Lord Ganesha who is the source of virtue and non-virtue

113. OM GOUNASHAREERAAYA NAMAHA
     Salutations to Lord Ganesha who is the embodiment of virtue

114. OM GUNAMANDITAAYA NAMAHA
     Salutations to Lord Ganesha who is the expression of virtue

115. OM GUNASHRASTAE NAMAHA
     Salutations to Lord Ganesha who is the creator of virtue

Sri Ganesha Sahasra Naamavali

116. OM GUNESHAANAAYA NAMAHA
     Salutations to Lord Ganesha who is the Lord of virtue

117. OM GUNESHAAYA NAMAHA
     Salutations to Lord Ganesha who is the house of virtue

118. OM GUNESHVARAAYA NAMAHA
     Salutations to Lord Ganesha who is the God of virtue

119. OM GUNASHRUSHTA JAGATSANGHAAYA NAMAHA
     Salutations to Lord Ganesha who has created everything in the world by the power of *gunas*

120. OM GUNAMUKHYAAYA NAMAHA
     Salutations to Lord Ganesha who is the Lord of infinite virtue

121. OM GUNAIKARAAJAE NAMAHA
     Salutations to Lord Ganesha who is incomparable in virtue

122. OM GUNAPRAVISHTAAYA NAMAHA
     Salutations to Lord Ganesha who is the spirit of virtue

123. OM GUNABHUVAE NAMAHA
     Salutations to Lord Ganesha who is filled with virtue

124. OM GUNEEKRUTACHARAAYA NAMAHA
     Salutations to Lord Ganesha who has fixed the moveable and immovable in the universe by the power of the *gunas*

125. OM GUNAPRAVANASAANTUSHTAAYA NAMAHA
     Salutations to Lord Ganesha who is the happy inspirer of virtue

126. OM GUNAHEENAPARAANMUKHAAYA NAMAHA
     Salutations to Lord Ganesha who is the opponent of the non-virtuous

127. OM GUNAIKABHUVAE NAMAHA
     Salutations to Lord Ganesha who is the one Lord of the virtuous

128. OM GUNASHRESHTHAAYA NAMAHA
     Salutations to Lord Ganesha who is highly virtuous

129. OM GUNAJESHTHAAYA
     Salutations to Lord Ganesha who is the eldest brother of the virtuous

130. OM GUNAPRABHAVAE NAMAHA
     Salutations to Lord Ganesha who is the promoter of the virtuous

131. OM GUNAGNAAYA NAMAHA
     Salutations to Lord Ganesha who is the knower of virtue

132. OM GUNASAMPOOJYAAYA NAMAHA
     Salutations to Lord Ganesha who is worshipped by the virtuous

133. OM GUNAPRAVARARAKSHAKAAYA NAMAHA
     Salutations to Lord Ganesha who is the protector of the virtuous

134. OM GUNAPRAANATAPADAABJAAYA NAMAHA
     Salutations to Lord Ganesha whose lotus feet is the refuge of the virtuous

LORD GANESHA

135. OM GUNAGEETAAYA NAMAHA
Salutations to Lord Ganesha whose glory is sung by the virtuous

136. OM GUNAJVALAAYA NAMAHA
Salutations to Lord Ganesha who is the light of the virtuous

137. OM GUNAVATAE NAMAHA
Salutations to Lord Ganesha who is the personification of virtue

138. OM GUNASAMPANNAAYA NAMAHA
Salutations to Lord Ganesha who is wealthy among the virtuous

139. OM GUNAANANDITA MAANASAAYA NAMAHA
Salutations to Lord Ganesha who is the blissful mind of the virtuous

140. OM GUNASANCHAARA CHATURAAYA NAMAHA
Salutations to Lord Ganesha who intelligently moves through virtue

141. OM GUNA SANCHAYA SUNDARAAYA NAMAHA
Salutations to Lord Ganesha who is the beautiful storehouse of virtue

142. OM GUNA GOURAAYA NAMAHA
Salutations to Lord Ganesha who is honored by the virtuous

143. OM GUNA DHAARAAYA NAMAHA
Salutations to Lord Ganesha who is the support of virtue

144. OM GUNA SAMVEETACHAETANAAYA NAMAHA
Salutations to Lord Ganesha who is the spirit of virtue

145. OM GUNAKRITAE NAMAHA
Salutations to Lord Ganesha who is the living image of virtue

146. OM GUNABHRUTAE NAMAHA
Salutations to Lord Ganesha who is the fulfillment of virtue

147. OM GUNYAAYA NAMAHA
Salutations to Lord Ganesha who is the goal of the virtuous

148. OM GUNAAGRYAAYA NAMAHA
Salutations to Lord Ganesha who is first among the virtuous

149. OM GUNAPAARADRISHAE NAMAHA
Salutations to Lord Ganesha who is the crystal among the virtuous

150. OM GUNAPRACHAARINAE NAMAHA
Salutations to Lord Ganesha who is the preacher of virtue

151. OM GUNAYUJAE NAMAHA
Salutations to Lord Ganesha who is nothing but virtue

152. OM GUNAA GUNA VIVAEKAKRITAE NAMAHA
Salutations to Lord Ganesha who is the discriminating light teaching the difference between virtue and non-virtue

153. OM GUNAAKARAAYA NAMAHA
Salutations to Lord Ganesha who is the bestower of virtue

Sri Ganesha Sahasra Naamavali

154. OM GUNA KARAAYA NAMAHA
    Salutations to Lord Ganesha who is the source of virtue

155. OM GUNAPRAVANAVARDHANAAYA NAMAHA
    Salutations to Lord Ganesha who is the expander of virtue

156. OM GUNAGOODHA CHARAAYA NAMAHA
    Salutations to Lord Ganesha who is the mystic secret of virtue

157. OM GOUNASARVA SAMSAARA CHAESHTITAAYA NAMAHA
    Salutations to Lord Ganesha who plays with the duality of the world

158. OM GUNADAKSHINA SOUHARDAAYA NAMAHA
    Salutations to Lord Ganesha who is satisfied with the donation of virtue

159. OM GUNALAKSHANATATTVAVIDAE NAMAHA
    Salutations to Lord Ganesha who is the revealer of Truth to the virtuous

160. OM GUNAHAARINAE NAMAHA
    Salutations to Lord Ganesha who is the destroyer of evil

161. OM GUNAKALAAYA NAMAHA
    Salutations to Lord Ganesha who is the radiance of virtue

162. OM GUNA SANGHA SAKHAAYA NAMAHA
    Salutations to Lord Ganesha who is the befriender of the society of the virtuous

163. OM GUNA SAMSKRITA SAMSAARAAYA NAMAHA
    Salutations to Lord Ganesha who is the family of the virtuous

164. OM GUNATATTVA VIVAECHAKAAYA NAMAHA
    Salutations to Lord Ganesha who has the discriminating light to understand the philosophy of virtue

165. OM GUNA GARVADHARAAYA NAMAHA
    Salutations to Lord Ganesha who is proud of His virtue

166. OM GOUNASUKHADUKHODAYAAYA NAMAHA
    Salutations to Lord Ganesha who is the source of the troubles of duality (misery and happiness)

167. OM GUNAAYA NAMAHA
    Salutations to Lord Ganesha who is the triple modes of nature

168. OM GUNAADHEESHAAYA NAMAHA
    Salutations to Lord Ganesha who is the supreme Master of virtue

169. OM GUNALAYAAYA NAMAHA
    Salutations to Lord Ganesha who is the home of virtue

170. OM GUNAVEEKSHANALAALASAAYA NAMAHA
    Salutations to Lord Ganesha who is the witness consciousness of the triple qualities of nature

171. OM GUNA GAURAVADAATRAE NAMAHA
    Salutations to Lord Ganesha who gives honor to virtue

172. OM GUNADAATRAE NAMAHA
    Salutations to Lord Ganesha who is the benevolent giver of divine virtue

LORD GANESHA

173. OM GUNAPRABHAVAE NAMAHA
Salutations to Lord Ganesha who is the light of virtue

174. OM GUNAKRITAE NAMAHA
Salutations to Lord Ganesha who is the creator of virtue

175. OM GUNA SAMBHODHAAYA NAMAHA
Salutations to Lord Ganesha who is the revealer of virtue

176. OM GUNABHUJAE NAMAHA
Salutations to Lord Ganesha who is the support of virtue

177. OM GUNABANDHANAAYA NAMAHA
Salutations to Lord Ganesha who is bound by virtue

178. OM GUNAHRIDYAAYA NAMAHA
Salutations to Lord Ganesha who is the heart of virtue

179. OM GUNASTHAYINAE NAMAHA
Salutations to Lord Ganesha who is established in virtue

180. OM GUNADAAYINAE NAMAHA
Salutations to Lord Ganesha who is the vouchsafer of virtue

181. OM GUNOTKATAAYA NAMAHA
Salutations to Lord Ganesha who is highly virtuous

182. OM GUNACHAKRACHARAAYA NAMAHA
Salutations to Lord Ganesha who set the wheel of creation in motion

183. OM GOUNAAVATAARAAYA NAMAHA
Salutations to Lord Ganesha who is the incarnation of virtue

184. OM GUNABAANDHAVAAYA NAMAHA
Salutations to Lord Ganesha who is the relative of the virtuous

185. OM GUNABANDHAVAE NAMAHA
Salutations to Lord Ganesha who binds us with divine virtue

186. OM GUNAPRAJNAAYA NAMAHA
Salutations to Lord Ganesha who is the wisdom of the virtuous

187. OM GUNAPRAAGNAAYA NAMAHA
Salutations to Lord Ganesha who is wise among the virtuous

188. OM GUNAALAYAAYA NAMAHA
Salutations to Lord Ganesha who is the treasure house of virtue

189. OM GUNADHAATRAE NAMAHA
Salutations to Lord Ganesha who is the foundation of virtue

190. OM GUNAPRAANAAYA NAMAHA
Salutations to Lord Ganesha who is the life of virtue

191. OM GUNAGOPAAYA NAMAHA
Salutations to Lord Ganesha who is the secret of the virtuous

192. OM GUNAASHRAYAAYA NAMAHA
Salutations to Lord Ganesha who is the refuge of virtue

Sri Ganesha Sahasra Naamavali

193. OM GUNAYAAYINAE NAMAHA
     Salutations to Lord Ganesha who is the giver of virtue

194. OM GUNADHAYINAE NAMAHA
     Salutations to Lord Ganesha who is the munificent giver of virtue

195. OM GUNAPAAYA NAMAHA
     Salutations to Lord Ganesha who is the personification of virtue

196. OM GUNAPAALAKAAYA NAMAHA
     Salutations to Lord Ganesha who is the protector of virtue

197. OM GUNAAHRITATANAVAE NAMAHA
     Salutations to Lord Ganesha whose body is free from the triple qualities of nature

198. OM GAUNAAYA NAMAHA
     Salutations to Lord Ganesha who is the great one

199. OM GEERVAANAAYA NAMAHA
     Salutations to Lord Ganesha who is the bestower of eloquence

200. OM GUNAGAURAVAAYA NAMAHA
     Salutations to Lord Ganesha who is honored for His virtue

201. OM GUNAGATPOOJITAPADAAYA NAMAHA
     Salutations to Lord Ganesha whose lotus feet are worshipped by the great ones

202. OM GUNAVATPRITIDAAYAKAAYA NAMAHA
     Salutations to Lord Ganesha who is loved by the virtuous

203. OM GUNAVADGEETA KIRTAYAE NAMAHA
     Salutations to Lord Ganesha whose glories are sung by the great ones

204. OM GUNABADDHA SOUHRIDAAYA NAMAHA
     Salutations to Lord Ganesha who is the staunch friend of the virtuous

205. OM GUNAVADVARADAAYA NAMAHA
     Salutations to Lord Ganesha who is blessing the virtuous

206. OM GUNAVATPRATI PAALAKAAYA NAMAHA
     Salutations to Lord Ganesha who gives loving protection to the good

207. OM GUNA VADGUNA SANTUSHTAAYA NAMAHA
     Salutations to Lord Ganesha who is pleased with the good devotees

208. OM GUNAVADRACHITASTAVAAYA NAMAHA
     Salutations to Lord Ganesha who is propitiated by the great hymns

209. OM GUNA VADRAKSHANAPARAAYA NAMAHA
     Salutations to Lord Ganesha who is constantly engaged in protecting devotees

210. OM GUNAVATPRANA PRIYAYA NAMAHA
     Salutations to Lord Ganesha who has taken the pledge to protect His votaries

211. OM GUNAVACHHAKRA SAMSAARAAYA NAMAHA
     Salutations to Lord Ganesha who protects devotees from the cycle of rebirth

212. OM GUNAVATKEERTI VARDHANAAYA NAMAHA
     Salutations to Lord Ganesha who blesses His devotees with great fame

213. OM GUNAVADGANA CHITTASTHAAYA NAMAHA
    Salutations to Lord Ganesha who is dwelling in the minds of His votaries

214. OM GUNAVADGUNA RAKSHANAAYA NAMAHA
    Salutations to Lord Ganesha who is protecting the virtue of the good

215. OM GUNAVATPOSHANA KARAAYA NAMAHA
    Salutations to Lord Ganesha who protects the virtuous

216. OM GUNAVACHHATRUSOODANAAYA NAMAHA
    Salutations to Lord Ganesha who destroys the enemies of the good

217. OM GUNAVATSIDDHI DAATRAE NAMAHA
    Salutations to Lord Ganesha who blesses with supernatural powers

218. OM GUNAVADGAURAVA PRADAAYA NAMAHA
    Salutations to Lord Ganesha who blesses His devotees with great honor

219. OM GUNAVATPRANAVASVAANTAAYA NAMAHA
    Salutations to Lord Ganesha who is pleased with the chanting of "OM"

220. OM GUNAVADGUNABHOOSHANAAYA NAMAHA
    Salutations to Lord Ganesha whose ornament is virtue

221. OM GUNAVATKULAVIDVESHI VINAASHAKARANA KSHAMAAYA NAMAHA
    Salutations to Lord Ganesha who forgives the wrongs of His votaries

222. OM GUNASTUTA GANAAYA NAMAHA
    Salutations to Lord Ganesha who is praised by the *ganas*

223. OM GARJATPRALAYAAMBUDA NISWANAAYA NAMAHA
    Salutations to Lord Ganesha whose roar brings cataclysm to the world

224. OM GAJAAYA NAMAHA
    Salutations to Lord Ganesha who is elephant-faced

225. OM GAJJAPATAYAE NAMAHA
    Salutations to Lord Ganesha who is the Lord of the elephants

226. OM GARJADGAJAYUDDHA VISHAARADAAYA NAMAHA
    Salutations to Lord Ganesha who bellows like an elephant during battle with His enemies

227. OM GAJAASYAAYA NAMAHA
    Salutations to Lord Ganesha whose face is like an elephant

228. OM GAJAKARNAAYA NAMAHA
    Salutations to Lord Ganesha whose ears are like that of an elephant

229. OM GAJARAAJAAYA NAMAHA
    Salutations to Lord Ganesha who is the king of elephants

230. OM GAJAANANAAYA NAMAHA
    Salutations to Lord Ganesha who has an elephant face

Sri Ganesha Sahasra Naamavali

231. **OM GAJAROOPADHARAAYA NAMAHA**
    Salutations to Lord Ganesha who has assumed the form of an elephant

232. **OM GARJATAE NAMAHA**
    Salutations to Lord Ganesha who roars at times

233. **OM GAJAYODHODDHURADHVANAYAE NAMAHA**
    Salutations to Lord Ganesha who defeats enemies of elephant strength

234. **OM GANAADHEESHAAYA NAMAHA**
    Salutations to Lord Ganesha who is greatest among elephants

235. **OM GAJAADHARAAYA NAMAHA**
    Salutations to Lord Ganesha who is the holder of elephant face on the trunk

236. **OM GAJAASURAYODDHURAAYA NAMAHA**
    Salutations to Lord Ganesha who is the destroyer of Gajaasura

237. **OM GAJADANTAAYA NAMAHA**
    Salutations to Lord Ganesha who has the tusk of an elephant

238. **OM GAJAVARAAYA NAMAHA**
    Salutations to Lord Ganesha who is supreme among the elephants

239. **OM GAJAKUMBHAAYA NAMAHA**
    Salutations to Lord Ganesha who is the elephant-trunked one

240. **OM GAJADHVANAVAE NAMAHA**
    Salutations to Lord Ganesha whose voice is like that of an elephant

241. **OM GAJAMAAYAAYA NAMAHA**
    Salutations to Lord Ganesha who is the creator of delusions with the mask of an elephant face

242. **OM GAJAMAYAAYA NAMAHA**
    Salutations to Lord Ganesha who is filled with elephant "OM" consciousness

243. **OM GAJASHREEYAE NAMAHA**
    Salutations to Lord Ganesha who is the wealth-giving elephant

244. **OM GAJAGHARJITAAYA NAMAHA**
    Salutations to Lord Ganesha who bellows like an elephant

245. **OM GAJAAMAYAHARAAYA NAMAHA**
    Salutations to Lord Ganesha who is the destroyer of the elephant ego

246. **OM GAJAPUSHTIPRADAAYAKAAYA NAMAHA**
    Salutations to Lord Ganesha who is the giver of plenty

247. **OM GAJOTPATAYAE NAMAHA**
    Salutations to Lord Ganesha who is the source of creation

248. **OM GAJATRATRAE NAMAHA**
    Salutations to Lord Ganesha who the support of the universe

249. **OM GAJAHAETAVAE NAMAHA**
    Salutations to Lord Ganesha who is the cause of the origin of the universe

LORD GANESHA

250. OM GAJAADHIPAAYA NAMAHA
    Salutations to Lord Ganesha who is the head of creation

251. OM GAJAMUKHYAAYA NAMAHA
    Salutations to Lord Ganesha who is supreme among the celestials

252. OM GAJAKULAPRAVARAAYA NAMAHA
    Salutations to Lord Ganesha who is the origin of the race of celestials

253. OM GAJADAITYAGHNAE NAMAHA
    Salutations to Lord Ganesha who is the destroyer of ignorance

254. OM GAJAKAETAVAE NAMAHA
    Salutations to Lord Ganesha who has the banner of an elephant

255. OM GAJAADHYAKSHAAYA NAMAHA
    Salutations to Lord Ganesha who is the presiding deity over all the celestials

256. OM GAJASAETAVAE NAMAHA
    Salutations to Lord Ganesha who is the bridge between earth and heaven

257. OM GAJAKRUTAYAE NAMAHA
    Salutations to Lord Ganesha who assumed the form of an elephant

258. OM GAJAVANDYAAYA NAMAHA
    Salutations to Lord Ganesha who is worshipped by the angels

259. OM GAJAPRAANAAYA NAMAHA
    Salutations to Lord Ganesha who is the life of the *devas*

260. OM GAJASAEVYAAYA NAMAHA
    Salutations to Lord Ganesha who is served by the *devas*

261. OM GAJAPRABHAVAE NAMAHA
    Salutations to Lord Ganesha who is Lord of the *devas*

262. OM GAJAMATTAAYA NAMAHA
    Salutations to Lord Ganesha who intoxicates with the truth

263. OM GAJESHAANAAYA NAMAHA
    Salutations to Lord Ganesha who is the supreme deity of the *devas*

264. OM GAJESHAAYA NAMAHA
    Salutations to Lord Ganesha who is Almighty God

265. OM GAJAPUNGAVAAYA NAMAHA
    Salutations to Lord Ganesha who blesses with prudence

266. OM GAJADANTADHARAAYA NAMAHA
    Salutations to Lord Ganesha who holds one tusk, showing oneness

267. OM GUNJANMADHUPAAYA NAMAHA
    Salutations to Lord Ganesha who is the nectar of immortality

268. OM GAJAVESHABHRUTAE NAMAHA
    Salutations to Lord Ganesha who assumes the elephant form, the symbol of the macrocosm

Sri Ganesha Sahasra Naamavali

269. OM GAJACHHADMANAE NAMAHA
     Salutations to Lord Ganesha who has the elephant mask

270. OM GAJAAGRASTHAAYA NAMAHA
     Salutations to Lord Ganesha who is ancient among the *devas*

271. OM GAJAYAAYINAE NAMAHA
     Salutations to Lord Ganesha who is the origin of the *devas*

272. OM GAJAAJAYAAYA NAMAHA
     Salutations to Lord Ganesha who brings victory to the *devas*

273. OM GAJARAAJAE NAMAHA
     Salutations to Lord Ganesha who is prince of the *devas*

274. OM GAJAYOODHASTHAAYA NAMAHA
     Salutations to Lord Ganesha who is mighty energy

275. OM GAJAGANJAKABHANJAKAAYA NAMAHA
     Salutations to Lord Ganesha who is the destroyer of the enemies of the *devas*

276. OM GARJITOJJITADAITYASAVAE NAMAHA
     Salutations to Lord Ganesha whose roar frightens the demons

277. OM GARJITATRAATAVISHTAPAAYA NAMAHA
     Salutations to Lord Ganesha whose roar brings an end to the demons

278. OM GAANAJNANAAYA NAMAHA
     Salutations to Lord Ganesha whose roar brings the dissolution of the universe

279. OM GAANAKUSHALAAYA NAMAHA
     Salutations to Lord Ganesha who has knowledge of music

280. OM GAANATATTVAVIVAECHAKAAYA NAMAHA
     Salutations to Lord Ganesha who is excellent in music

281. OM GAANASHLAGHINAE NAMAHA
     Salutations to Lord Ganesha who knows the philosophy of sound

282. OM GAANARASAAYA NAMAHA
     Salutations to Lord Ganesha who appreciates music

283. OM GAANAJNANA PARAAYANAAYA NAMAHA
     Salutations to Lord Ganesha who is the nectar of music

284. OM GAANAAGAMAJNAAYA NAMAHA
     Salutations to Lord Ganesha who is always enjoyed in music

285. OM GAANAANGAAYA NAMAHA
     Salutations to Lord Ganesha who is revealed through music

286. OM GAANAPRAVANACHAETANAAYA NAMAHA
     Salutations to Lord Ganesha whose body is filled with music

287. OM GAANADHYAEYAAYA NAMAHA
     Salutations to Lord Ganesha who is the spirit of music

LORD GANESHA

288. OM GAANAGAMYAAYA NAMAHA
     Salutations to Lord Ganesha who is the goal of music

289. OM GAANADHYANA PARAAYANAAYA NAMAHA
     Salutations to Lord Ganesha who meditates on sound

290. OM GAANAKRUTAE NAMAHA
     Salutations to Lord Ganesha who has composed music

291. OM GAANACHATURAAYA NAMAHA
     Salutations to Lord Ganesha who is clever in music

292. OM GAANAVIDYAVISHARADAAYA NAMAHA
     Salutations to Lord Ganesha who is unequaled in music

293. OM GAANABHUYAE NAMAHA
     Salutations to Lord Ganesha who is the origin of music

294. OM GAANASHEELAAYA NAMAHA
     Salutations to Lord Ganesha who always enjoys music

295. OM GAANASHAALINAE NAMAHA
     Salutations to Lord Ganesha who sings music

296. OM GATASHRAMAAYA NAMAHA
     Salutations to Lord Ganesha who is always relaxed

297. OM GAANAVIJNAANA SAMPANNAAYA NAMAHA
     Salutations to Lord Ganesha who adores the wealth of music

298. OM GAANA SHRAVANALAALASAAYA NAMAHA
     Salutations to Lord Ganesha who always likes to hear His praise through music

299. OM GAANAAYATTAAYA NAMAHA
     Salutations to Lord Ganesha who is the energy of music

300. OM GAANAMAYAAYA NAMAHA
     Salutations to Lord Ganesha who is filled with music

301. OM GAANAPRANAYAVATAE NAMAHA
     Salutations to Lord Ganesha who is "OM", the sound of creation

302. OM GAANADHYAATRAE NAMAHA
     Salutations to Lord Ganesha who meditates on musical sounds

303. OM GAANABUDDHIYAE NAMAHA
     Salutations to Lord Ganesha who is the bestower of intelligence to know the sounds

304. OM GAANOTSUKAMANASAE NAMAHA
     Salutations to Lord Ganesha who is very eager to sing

305. OM GAANOTSUKAAYA NAMAHA
     Salutations to Lord Ganesha who is the inspiration to sing

306. OM GAANABHOOMAYAE NAMAHA
     Salutations to Lord Ganesha who is the source of singing

307. OM GAANASEEMNAE NAMAHA
   Salutations to Lord Ganesha who is the limit of the limitless sound

308. OM GUNOJJWALAAYA NAMAHA
   Salutations to Lord Ganesha who is the shining gem

309. OM GAANAJNA JNAANAVATAE NAMAHA
   Salutations to Lord Ganesha who is filled with the knowledge of sounds

310. OM GAANA MAANAVATAE NAMAHA
   Salutations to Lord Ganesha who respects singers

311. OM GAANAPAESHALAAYA NAMAHA
   Salutations to Lord Ganesha who bestows the gift of singing

312. OM GAANAVATPRANAYAAYA NAMAHA
   Salutations to Lord Ganesha who bestows the love of music

313. OM GAANASAMUDRAAYA NAMAHA
   Salutations to Lord Ganesha who is the ocean of music

314. OM GAANABHOOSHANAAYA NAMAHA
   Salutations to Lord Ganesha who is decked with the ornament of music

315. OM GAANASINDHAVAE NAMAHA
   Salutations to Lord Ganesha who is the sea of sounds

316. OM GAANAPARAAYA NAMAHA
   Salutations to Lord Ganesha who merged in music

317. OM GAANAPRAANAAYA NAMAHA
   Salutations to Lord Ganesha who is the life of music

318. OM GANAASHRAYAAYA NAMAHA
   Salutations to Lord Ganesha who is the abode of the *ganas*

319. OM GAANAIKABHUVAE NAMAHA
   Salutations to Lord Ganesha who is One without a second in music

320. OM GAANAHRUSHTAAYA NAMAHA
   Salutations to Lord Ganesha who enjoys devotional music

321. OM GAANACHAKSHUSHAE NAMAHA
   Salutations to Lord Ganesha who is the intuition of music

322. OM GANAIKADRUSHAE NAMAHA
   Salutations to Lord Ganesha who is visible only to the *ganas*

323. OM GAANAMATTAAYA NAMAHA
   Salutations to Lord Ganesha who is intoxicated with music

324. OM GAANARUCHAYAE NAMAHA
   Salutations to Lord Ganesha who bestows taste for inner sound

325. OM GAANAVIDAE NAMAHA
   Salutations to Lord Ganesha who is supreme among celestial singers

LORD GANESHA

326. OM GAANAVITPRIYAAYA NAMAHA
    Salutations to Lord Ganesha who loves the cosmic sound

327. OM GAANAANTARAATMANAE NAMAHA
    Salutations to Lord Ganesha who is the inner spirit of music

328. OM GAANAADHYAAYA NAMAHA
    Salutations to Lord Ganesha who is expert in spiritual music

329. OM GAANABHRAAJATSWABHAAVAKAAYA NAMAHA
    Salutations to Lord Ganesha who reveals Himself through devotional music

330. OM GAANA MAAYAAYA NAMAHA
    Salutations to Lord Ganesha who enchants through music

331. OM GANADHARAAYA NAMAHA
    Salutations to Lord Ganesha who is the upholder of music

332. OM GAANA VIDYAVISHODHAKAAYA NAMAHA
    Salutations to Lord Ganesha who is the bestows insight into the science of music

333. OM GAANAAHITA JNAAYA NAMAHA
    Salutations to Lord Ganesha who is the well-wisher of the science of sounds

334. OM GAANENDRAAYA NAMAHA
    Salutations to Lord Ganesha who is unequal in the art of music

335. OM GAANALEENAAYA NAMAHA
    Salutations to Lord Ganesha who is merged in music

336. OM GATIPRIYAAYA NAMAHA
    Salutations to Lord Ganesha who loves the rhythm of music

337. OM GAANAADHEESHAAYA NAMAHA
    Salutations to Lord Ganesha who is God among singers

338. OM GAANALAYAAYA NAMAHA
    Salutations to Lord Ganesha who loses Himself in the music

339. OM GAANAADHAARAAYA NAMAHA
    Salutations to Lord Ganesha who is the support of celestial music

340. OM GATEESHWARAAYA NAMAHA
    Salutations to Lord Ganesha who is the master of musical rhythms

341. OM GAANAVANMANADAAYA NAMAHA
    Salutations to Lord Ganesha who is well known for his music

342. OM GAANABHUTAYAE NAMAHA
    Salutations to Lord Ganesha who is God of music

343. OM GAANAIKABHOOTIMATAE NAMAHA
    Salutations to Lord Ganesha who is One without a second in music

344. OM GAANATAANARATAAYA NAMAHA
    Salutations to Lord Ganesha who forgets Himself when He sings

Sri Ganesha Sahasra Naamavali

345. OM GAANATAANADAANA VIMOHITAAYA NAMAHA
Salutations to Lord Ganesha who loves those who are gifted with music

346. OM GURAVAE NAMAHA
Salutations to Lord Ganesha who is Lord of the gurus

347. OM GURUDARASHRONAYAE NAMAHA
Salutations to Lord Ganesha who is great among the gurus

348. OM GURUTATTVAARTHA DARSHANAAYA NAMAHA
Salutations to Lord Ganesha who reveals the philosophy of the guru

349. OM GURUSTUTAAYA NAMAHA
Salutations to Lord Ganesha who is praised by the gurus

350. OM GURUGUNAAYA NAMAHA
Salutations to Lord Ganesha who is propitiated by the gurus

351. OM GURUMAAYAYA NAMAHA
Salutations to Lord Ganesha who is the bestower of energy to the gurus

352. OM GURUPRIYAAYA NAMAHA
Salutations to Lord Ganesha who is loved by the gurus

353. OM GURUKIRTAYAE NAMAHA
Salutations to Lord Ganesha who is extolled by the gurus

354. OM GURUBHUJAAYA NAMAHA
Salutations to Lord Ganesha who is the refuge of the gurus

355. OM GURUVAKSHASAE NAMAHA
Salutations to Lord Ganesha who stays in the heart of the gurus

356. OM GURUPRABHAAYA NAMAHA
Salutations to Lord Ganesha who is the light to the gurus

357. OM GURULAKSHANA SAMPANNAAYA NAMAHA
Salutations to Lord Ganesha who is filled with the virtues of the great guru

358. OM GURUDROHAPARAGMUKHAAYA NAMAHA
Salutations to Lord Ganesha who stays away from those who insult the guru

359. OM GURUVIDYAAYA NAMAHA
Salutations to Lord Ganesha who is the wisdom of the gurus

360. OM GURUPRAANAAYA NAMAHA
Salutations to Lord Ganesha who is the life of the gurus

361. OM GURUBAAHUBALOCCHHRAYAAYA NAMAHA
Salutations to Lord Ganesha who is the strength of the gurus

362. OM GURUDAITYA PRAANAHARAAYA NAMAHA
Salutations to Lord Ganesha who is the destroyer of demons who hurt the gurus

363. OM GURUDAITYAA PAHAARAKAAYA NAMAHA
Salutations to Lord Ganesha who takes away the demonical qualities

364. OM GURUGARVAHARAAYA NAMAHA
Salutations to Lord Ganesha who takes away the pride of the proud

365. OM GUHYA PRAVARAAYA NAMAHA
Salutations to Lord Ganesha who is the secret origin of races

366. OM GURUDARPAGHNAE NAMAHA
Salutations to Lord Ganesha who is the dispeller of arrogance

367. OM GURUGAURAVADAAYINAE NAMAHA
Salutations to Lord Ganesha who honors the real preceptors

368. OM GURUBHEETYA PAHAARAKAAYA NAMAHA
Salutations to Lord Ganesha who removes the fear of the gurus

369. OM GURUSHUNDAAYA NAMAHA
Salutations to Lord Ganesha who has the big trunk of an elephant

370. OM GURUSKANDHAAYA NAMAHA
Salutations to Lord Ganesha who has broad shoulders

371. OM GURUJANGHAAYA NAMAHAHt
Salutations to Lord Ganesha who has mighty thighs

372. OM GURUPRAMATHAAYA NAMAHA
Salutations to Lord Ganesha who has a strong body

373. OM GURUPAALAAYA NAMAHA
Salutations to Lord Ganesha who has a broad forehead

374. OM GURUGALAAYA NAMAHA
Salutations to Lord Ganesha who has a huge neck

375. OM GURUSHREEYAE NAMAHA
Salutations to Lord Ganesha who has immense wealth

376. OM GURUGARVANUDAE NAMAHA
Salutations to Lord Ganesha who is the destroyer of ego

377. OM GUROORAVAE NAMAHA
Salutations to Lord Ganesha who is the preceptor

378. OM GURUPEENAAMSAAYA NAMAHA
Salutations to Lord Ganesha who has a broad chest

379. OM GURUPRANAYA LAALASAAYA NAMAHA
Salutations to Lord Ganesha who loves to play with His *shakti*

380. OM GURUMUKHYAAYA NAMAHA
Salutations to Lord Ganesha who is the head of the gurus

381. OM GURUKULSTHAAYINAE NAMAHA
Salutations to Lord Ganesha who is the protector of "*Guru-Kula*" traditions

382. OM GUNAGURUVAE NAMAHA
Salutations to Lord Ganesha who is the guru of great virtues

Sri Ganesha Sahasra Naamavali

383. OM GURUSAMSHAYABHAETRAE NAMAHA
Salutations to Lord Ganesha who is the dispeller of doubts of the gurus

384. OM GURUMAANYA PRADAAYAKAAYA NAMAHA
Salutations to Lord Ganesha who protects the honor of the gurus

385. OM GURUDHARMASADAARAADHYAAYA NAMAHA
Salutations to Lord Ganesha who is the worshipper of the *dharma* of the gurus

386. OM GURUDHAARMIKA KETANAAYA NAMAHA
Salutations to Lord Ganesha who is the abode of *guru-dharma*

387. OM GURUDAITYAGALACHHETRAE NAMAHA
Salutations to Lord Ganesha who is the destroyer of great demons

388. OM GURUSAINYAAYA NAMAHA
Salutations to Lord Ganesha who has the military of *ganas*

389. OM GURUDYUTAYAE NAMAHA
Salutations to Lord Ganesha who is God of great effulgence

390. OM GURUDHARMAGRA GANYAAYA NAMAHA
Salutations to Lord Ganesha who is supreme among those who practice *dharma*

391. OM GURUDHARMADHURANDHARAAYA NAMAHA
Salutations to Lord Ganesha who has committed Himself to protect *dharma*

392. OM GARISHTHAAYA NAMAHA
Salutations to Lord Ganesha who is greater than the greatest

393. OM GURUSANTAAPASHAMANAAYA NAMAHA
Salutations to Lord Ganesha who is relieved of great afflictions

394. OM GURUPOOJITAAYA NAMAHA
Salutations to Lord Ganesha who is worshipped by the gurus

395. OM GURUDHARMAADHARAAYA NAMAHA
Salutations to Lord Ganesha who is the supporter of *guru-dharma*

396. OM GAURADHARMAADHARAAYA NAMAHA
Salutations to Lord Ganesha who is the protector of the ancient *dharma*

397. OM GADAAPAHAAYA NAMAHA
Salutations to Lord Ganesha who is the revolver of the mace

398. OM GURUSHASTRAYVICHAARAJNAAYA NAMAHA
Salutations to Lord Ganesha who is revealed through the holy scriptures

399. OM GURUSHAASTRAKRUTODYAMAAYA NAMAHA
Salutations to Lord Ganesha who gave the great scriptures to the world

400. OM GURUSHAASTRAARTHANILAYAAYA NAMAHA
Salutations to Lord Ganesha who is the abode of the spirit of the scriptures

401. OM GURU SHAASTRA AALAYAAYA NAMAHA
Salutations to Lord Ganesha who is the embodiment of the holy scriptures

LORD GANESHA

402. OM GURUMANTRAAYA NAMAHA
Salutations to Lord Ganesha who is the guru-mantra Himself

403. OM GURUSHRAESTAAYA NAMAHA
Salutations to Lord Ganesha who is supreme among the teachers

404. OM GURUMANTRAPHALAPRADAAYA NAMAHA
Salutations to Lord Ganesha who is the bestower of fruits of guru-mantra

405. OM GURUPAATAKASANDOHA PRAAYASHCHITTAYITAARCHANAAYA NAMAHA
Salutations to Lord Ganesha who is the forgiver of vicious sins

406. OM GURU SAMSAARASUKHADAAYA NAMAHA
Salutations to Lord Ganesha who is the bestower of happiness to the family

407. OM GURUSAMSARADUKHABHIDAE NAMAHA
Salutations to Lord Ganesha who is the remover of grief of the family

408. OM GURU SHLAAGHAAPARAAYA NAMAHA
Salutations to Lord Ganesha who praises His devotees

409. OM GAURABHANUKHANDAVATAMSABHRITAE NAMAHA
Salutations to Lord Ganesha who shines with the effulgence of a thousand suns

410. OM GURUPRASANNA MOORTAYAE NAMAHA
Salutations to Lord Ganesha who is the embodiment of supreme happiness

411. OM GURUSHAAPAVIMOCHAKAAYA NAMAHA
Salutations to Lord Ganesha who is the remover of curses

412. OM GURUKANTAYAE NAMAHA
Salutations to Lord Ganesha who shines with divine halo

413. OM GURUMAHATAE NAMAHA
Salutations to Lord Ganesha who is the embodiment of cosmic consciousness

414. OM GURUSHAASANA PAALAKAAYA NAMAHA
Salutations to Lord Ganesha who is the protector of divine law

415. OM GURUTANTRAAYA NAMAHA
Salutations to Lord Ganesha who is the tantra-bodied one

416. OM GURUPRAJNAAYA NAMAHA
Salutations to Lord Ganesha who is wisdom embodied

417. OM GURUBHAAYA NAMAHA
Salutations to Lord Ganesha who is the light of the gurus

418. OM GURUDAIVATAAYA NAMAHA
Salutations to Lord Ganesha who is God, the Guru

419. OM GURUVIKRAMASANCHAARAAYA NAMAHA
Salutations to Lord Ganesha who is the power of the guru

420. OM GURUDRISHAE NAMAHA
Salutations to Lord Ganesha who is the revealer of truth

Sri Ganesha Sahasra Naamavali

421. **OM GURUVIKRAMAAYA NAMAHA**
   Salutations to Lord Ganesha who is the bestower of courage

422. **OM GURUKRAMAAYA NAMAHA**
   Salutations to Lord Ganesha who is the discipline of the guru

423. **OM GURUPRESHTAAYA NAMAHA**
   Salutations to Lord Ganesha who is the host of the gurus

424. **OM GURUPAASHANDA KHANDAKAAYA NAMAHA**
   Salutations to Lord Ganesha who is the destroyer of the unrighteous

425. **OM GURUGARJITA SAMPOORNA BRAHMANDAAYA NAMAHA**
   Salutations to Lord Ganesha who is the sound of the entire creation

426. **OM GURUGARJITAAYA NAMAHA**
   Salutations to Lord Ganesha whose roar is "OM"

427. **OM GURUPUTRA PRIYA SAKHAAYA NAMAHA**
   Salutations to Lord Ganesha who is a good friend to the family of the guru

428. **OM GURUPUTRABHAYAAPAHAAYA NAMAHA**
   Salutations to Lord Ganesha who is the remover of fear of the guru's family

429. **OM GURUPUTRA PARITRATRAE NAMAHA**
   Salutations to Lord Ganesha who is the protector of the preceptor's children

430. **OM GURUPUTRAVARAPRADAAYA NAMAHA**
   Salutations to Lord Ganesha who is the bestower of boons to the devoted children of the guru

431. **OM GURUPUTRAARTI SHAMANAAYA NAMAHA**
   Salutations to Lord Ganesha who is the remover of afflictions from the family of the guru

432. **OM GURUPUTRAADHI NAASHANAAYA NAMAHA**
   Salutations to Lord Ganesha who is the destroyer of ailments of the family of His devotees

433. **OM GURUPUTRAPRAANADAATRAE NAMAHA**
   Salutations to Lord Ganesha who is the giver of life to the family and children of the guru

434. **OM GURU BHAKTIPARAAYANAAYA NAMAHA**
   Salutations to Lord Ganesha who has special grace for His devotees

435. **OM GURUVIJNAANA VIBHAVAAYA NAMAHA**
   Salutations to Lord Ganesha who glorifies the wisdom of the gurus

436. **OM GAURABHAANUVARAPRADAAYA NAMAHA**
   Salutations to Lord Ganesha who is the bestower of blessings to Gaurabhaanu, His devotee

437. **OM GAURABHAANUSTUTAAYA NAMAHA**
   Salutations to Lord Ganesha who assumed the form of a son to Gaurabhaanu

LORD GANESHA

438. OM GAURABHAANUTRAASAAPAHAARAKAAYA NAMAHA
Salutations to Lord Ganesha who removed the afflictions of Gaurabhaanu

439. OM GAURABHAANUPRIYAAYA NAMAHA
Salutations to Lord Ganesha who is dear to Gaurabhaanu

440. OM GAURABHAANAVAE NAMAHA
Salutations to Lord Ganesha who is the shining light of His votaries

441. OM GAURAVARDHANAAYA NAMAHA
Salutations to Lord Ganesha whose blessings bring great fame

442. OM GAURABHAANUPARITRAATRAE NAMAHA
Salutations to Lord Ganesha who always protects Gaurabhaanu

443. OM GAURABHAANUSAKHAAYA NAMAHA
Salutations to Lord Ganesha who is the friend and guard of Gaurabhaanu

444. OM GAURABHAANU PRABHAVAE NAMAHA
Salutations to Lord Ganesha who is Lord of Gaurabhaanu

445. OM GAURABHAANU BHEETIPRANAASHANAAYA NAMAHA
Salutations to Lord Ganesha who is healer of the sickness of Gaurabhaanu

446. OM GAURITAEJASAMUTPANNAAYA NAMAHA
Salutations to Lord Ganesha who is born of the radiance of the White Goddess, Gauri

447. OM GAURIHRIDAYA NANDANAAYA NAMAHA
Salutations to Lord Ganesha who is the darling son of Gauri

448. OM GAURISTANAMDHAYAAYA NAMAHA
Salutations to Lord Ganesha who drank milk from the breast of Gauri

449. OM GAURIMANOVAANCCHITASIDDHIKRITAE NAMAHA
Salutations to Lord Ganesha who fulfills Mother Gauri's wishes

450. OM GAURAAYA NAMAHA
Salutations to Lord Ganesha who is white as light

451. OM GAURAGUNAAYA NAMAHA
Salutations to Lord Ganesha who is of great virtue and valor

452. OM GAURAPRAKAASHAAYA NAMAHA
Salutations to Lord Ganesha who is filled with the halo of light

453. OM GAURABHAIRAVAAYA NAMAHA
Salutations to Lord Ganesha who is Bhairava, the destroyer of dark power

454. OM GAURISHANANDANAAYA NAMAHA
Salutations to Lord Ganesha who is the son of Shiva, the spouse of Gauri

455. OM GAURIPRIYAPUTRAAYA NAMAHA
Salutations to Lord Ganesha who is the very dear son of Gauri

456. OM GADAADHARAAYA NAMAHA
Salutations to Lord Ganesha who is the wielder of the mace

Sri Ganesha Sahasra Naamavali

457. OM GAURIVARAPRADAAYA NAMAHA
    Salutations to Lord Ganesha who is the bestower of boons to Mother Gauri

458. OM GAURIPRANAYAAYA NAMAHA
    Salutations to Lord Ganesha who is the beloved son of Gauri

459. OM GAURA SACCHAVAYAE NAMAHA
    Salutations to Lord Ganesha who is filled with white halo

460. OM GAURIGANESHWARAAYA NAMAHA
    Salutations to Lord Ganesha who is Lord of the *ganas* and worshipped together with his mother, Gauri

461. OM GAURIPRAVANAAYA NAMAHA
    Salutations to Lord Ganesha who brings joy to Mother Gauri

462. OM GAURABHAAVANAAYA NAMAHA
    Salutations to Lord Ganesha who feels for His devotees

463. OM GAURAATMANAE NAMAHA
    Salutations to Lord Ganesha who is the soul of the universe

464. OM GAURAKEERTAYAE NAMAHA
    Salutations to Lord Ganesha who is the well-known God of the universe

465. OM GAURABHAAVAAYA NAMAHA
    Salutations to Lord Ganesha who is the bestower of divine feeling

466. OM GARISTAADRISHAE NAMAHA
    Salutations to Lord Ganesha who is difficult of *darshan* to the non-believers

467. OM GAUTAMAAYA NAMAHA
    Salutations to Lord Ganesha who is the head of the lineage of sages

468. OM GAUTAMEENAATAAYA NAMAHA
    Salutations to Lord Ganesha who is the Lord of supernatural powers

469. OM GAUTAMEEPRAANA VALLABHAAYA NAMAHA
    Salutations to Lord Ganesha who is the spouse of Gautami, the Goddess of Siddhi

470. OM GAUTAMAABHEESHTAVARADAAYA NAMAHA
    Salutations to Lord Ganesha who has fulfilled the wishes of Sage Gautama

471. OM GAUTAMAABHAYADAAYAKAAYA NAMAHA
    Salutations to Lord Ganesha who made Sage Gautama fearless with His blessings

472. OM GAUTAMA PRANAYA PRAHVAAYA NAMAHA
    Salutations to Lord Ganesha who removed the ignorance of Gautama

473. OM GAUTAMAASHRAMA DUKHAGHNAE NAMAHA
    Salutations to Lord Ganesha who cooled the scorching fire of grief in the *ashrama* of Gautama

474. OM GAUTAMEETEERA SANCHAARINAE NAMAHA
    Salutations to Lord Ganesha who wanders 'round the bank of Gautami river

LORD GANESHA

475. OM GAUTAMEETEERTHA DAAYAKAAYA NAMAHA
Salutations to Lord Ganesha who made the Gautami river very holy

476. OM GAUTAMAAPAT PARIHARAAYA NAMAHA
Salutations to Lord Ganesha who removed the danger from Gautama's life

477. OM GAUTAMADHI VINAASHANAAYA NAMAHA
Salutations to Lord Ganesha who healed the sickness of Sage Gautama

478. OM GOPATAYAE NAMAHA
Salutations to Lord Ganesha who is Lord of the gopas

479. OM GODHANAAYA NAMAHA
Salutations to Lord Ganesha who has the cow as wealth
(The ignorant masses are considered as cattle. God is the cowherd. This is similar to the sheep/shepherd mysticism in Christianity.)

480. OM GOPAAYA NAMAHA
Salutations to Lord Ganesha who is the cowherd Himself.

481. OM GOPALAPRIYADARSHANAAYA NAMAHA
Salutations to Lord Ganesha who loves the cowherds

482. OM GOPALAAYA NAMAHA
Salutations to Lord Ganesha who takes care of the cattle

483. OM GOGANAADHEESHAAYA NAMAHA
Salutations to Lord Ganesha who is Lord of cattle and the divine species

484. OM GOKASHMALA NIVARTAKAAYA NAMAHA
Salutations to Lord Ganesha who is the remover of the dirt of ignorance from the herd of humanity

485. OM GOSAHASRAAYA NAMAHA
Salutations to Lord Ganesha who is God of the multitudes

486. OM GOPAVARAAYA NAMAHA
Salutations to Lord Ganesha who is best among the cowherds of protectors

487. OM GOPA GOPI SUKHAAVAHAAYA NAMAHA
Salutations to Lord Ganesha who gives the greatest happiness to cowherds and milkmaids

488. OM GOVARDHANAAYA NAMAHA
Salutations to Lord Ganesha who enhances the happiness of humanity

489. OM GOPA GOPAAYA NAMAHA
Salutations to Lord Ganesha who out of mercy acts as a human being

490. OM GOMATAE NAMAHA
Salutations to Lord Ganesha who is the protector of cows

491. OM GOKULA VARDHANAAYA NAMAHA
Salutations to Lord Ganesha who blesses the progress of the cattle wealth

492. OM GOCHARAAYA NAMAHA
Salutations to Lord Ganesha who is visible to the inner eye

Sri Ganesha Sahasra Naamavali

493. OM GOCHARA PREETI VRIDDHI KRITAE NAMAHA
    Salutations to Lord Ganesha who is the bestower of mytic vision

494. OM GOCHARAARAADHYAAYA NAMAHA
    Salutations to Lord Ganesha who makes our devotion for Him grow

495. OM GOMINAE NAMAHA
    Salutations to Lord Ganesha who is the Great Self of humanity

496. OM GOKASHTA SANTRAATRAE NAMAHA
    Salutations to Lord Ganesha who is the destroyer of misery of humanity

497. OM GOSANTAAPA NIVARTAKAAYA NAMAHA
    Salutations to Lord Ganesha who is the dispeller of the agony of humanity

498. OM GOSHTAAYA NAMAHA
    Salutations to Lord Ganesha who is the refuge of humanity

499. OM GOSHTAASHRAYAAYA NAMAHA
    Salutations to Lord Ganesha who is the shelter of His devotees

500. OM GOSHTAPATAYE NAMAHA
    Salutations to Lord Ganesha who is the supreme God of humanity

501. OM GODHANA VARDHANAAYA NAMAHA
    Salutations to Lord Ganesha who blesses us for the growth of humanity

502. OM GOSHTA PRIYAAYA NAMAHA
    Salutations to Lord Ganesha who loves humanity

503. OM GOSHTAMAYAAYA NAMAHA
    Salutations to Lord Ganesha who manifests in the consciousness of humanity

504. OM GOSHTAMAYA NIVARTAKAAYA NAMAHA
    Salutations to Lord Ganesha who is the dispeller of the ignorance of humanity

505. OM GOLOKAAYA NAMAHA
    Salutations to Lord Ganesha who is Goloka, the transcendental heaven

506. OM GOLAKAAYA NAMAHA
    Salutations to Lord Ganesha who is the seven circles of the seven upper regions

507. OM GOBHRITAE NAMAHA
    Salutations to Lord Ganesha who is the source of humanity

508. OM GOBHARTRAE NAMAHA
    Salutations to Lord Ganesha who is the supporter of humanity

509. OM GOSUKHAAVAHAAYA NAMAHA
    Salutations to Lord Ganesha who is the giver of happiness to humanity

510. OM GODUHAE NAMAHA
    Salutations to Lord Ganesha who is the milk of wisdom

511. OM GODUGGANA PRESHTAAYA NAMAHA
    Salutations to Lord Ganesha who loves cow's milk

LORD GANESHA

512. **OM GODUGDRAE NAMAHA**
Salutations to Lord Ganesha who pervades humanity

513. **OM GOPAYAHA PRIYAAYA NAMAHA**
Salutations to Lord Ganesha who is dear to the upholders of *dharma*

514. **OM GOTRAAYA NAMAHA**
Salutations to Lord Ganesha who is the origin of lineage

515. **OM GOTRAPATAYAE NAMAHA**
Salutations to Lord Ganesha who is the head of lineage

516. **OM GOTRAPRABHAVAE NAMAHA**
Salutations to Lord Ganesha who is the progenitor of lineage

517. **OM GOTRA BHAYAAVAHAAYA NAMAHA**
Salutations to Lord Ganesha who dispels the fear of His lineage

518. **OM GOTRAVRIDDHI KARAAYA NAMAHA**
Salutations to Lord Ganesha who blesses with expansion of lineage

519. **OM GOTRA PRIYAAYA NAMAHA**
Salutations to Lord Ganesha who is the lover of lineage

520. **OM GOTRARTINAASHANAAYA NAMAHA**
Salutations to Lord Ganesha who is the remover of grief from lineage

521. **OM GOTRADDHAARA PARAAYA NAMAHA**
Salutations to Lord Ganesha who is engaged in lifting soul from its lineage

522. **OM GOTRADAIVATAAYA NAMAHA**
Salutations to Lord Ganesha who is the light of lineage

523. **OM GOTRAVIKHYAATA NAAMNAE NAMAHA**
Salutations to Lord Ganesha who is the presiding deity over lineage

524. **OM GOTRINAE NAMAHA**
Salutations to Lord Ganesha who is famous in His lineage

525. **OM GOTRAPRAPAALAKAAYA NAMAHA**
Salutations to Lord Ganesha who is the lineage

526. **OM GOTRASETAVAE NAMAHA**
Salutations to Lord Ganesha who is the supreme protector of lineage

527. **OM GOTRAKETAVAE NAMAHA**
Salutations to Lord Ganesha who is the banner of lineage

528. **OM GOTRAHETAVAE NAMAHA**
Salutations to Lord Ganesha who the prime cause of lineage

529. **OM GATAKLAMAAYA NAMAHA**
Salutations to Lord Ganesha who is the ancient principle of lineage

Sri Ganesha Sahasra Naamavali

530. OM GOTRATRAANA KARAAYA NAMAHA
    Salutations to Lord Ganesha who is the strength of lineage

531. OM GOTRAPATAYE NAMAHA
    Salutations to Lord Ganesha who is the prime deity of lineage

532. OM GOTRAESHA POOJITAAYA NAMAHA
    Salutations to Lord Ganesha who is worshipped by lineage

533. OM GOTRAVIDAE NAMAHA
    Salutations to Lord Ganesha who is the wisdom of lineage

534. OM GOTRABHITRAATRAE NAMAHA
    Salutations to Lord Ganesha who is the uplifter of lineage

535. OM GOTRABHIDVARADAAYAKAAYA NAMAHA
    Salutations to Lord Ganesha who is the bestower of boons to lineage

536. OM GOTRABHIDPOOJITA PADAAYA NAMAHA
    Salutations to Lord Ganesha whose lotus feet are worshipped by lineage

537. OM GOTRABHICHHATRUSUDANAAYA NAMAHA
    Salutations to Lord Ganesha who is the destroyer of the enemies of lineage

538. OM GOTRABHITPREETIDAAYA NAMAHA
    Salutations to Lord Ganesha who is the loving deity of lineage

539. OM GOTRABHIDROOPAAYA NAMAHA
    Salutations to Lord Ganesha who is the wisdom of lineage

540. OM GOTRAPAALAKAAYA NAMAHA
    Salutations to Lord Ganesha who is the guardian of lineage

541. OM GOTRABHIDGEETA CHARITAAYA NAMAHA
    Salutations to Lord Ganesha whose glories are sung by lineage

542. OM GOTRABHIDRAAJYA RAKSHAKAAYA NAMAHA
    Salutations to Lord Ganesha who is protector of the kingdom of lineage

543. OM GOTRABHIDVARADAAYINAE NAMAHA
    Salutations to Lord Ganesha who is the bestower of gifts to lineage

544. OM GOTRABHITPRANAYAAYA NAMAHA
    Salutations to Lord Ganesha who is the beautiful abode of lineage

545. OM GOTRABHIDBHAYASAMBHAETRAE NAMAHA
    Salutations to Lord Ganesha who is the destroyer of the fear of lineage

546. OM GOTRABHINMANADAAYAKAAYA NAMAHA
    Salutations to Lord Ganesha who brought honor to lineage

547. OM GOTRABHIDGOPANAPARAAYA NAMAHA
    Salutations to Lord Ganesha who brings safety to lineage

548. OM GOTRABHITSAINYA NAAYAKAAYA NAMAHA
    Salutations to Lord Ganesha who is commander-in-chief of lineage

LORD GANESHA

549. OM GOTRAADDHIPA PRIYAAYA NAMAHA
Salutations to Lord Ganesha who is very dear to the sages of lineage

550. OM GOTRAPUTREE PUTRAAYA NAMAHA
Salutations to Lord Ganesha who loves the children of lineage

551. OM GIRIPRIYAAYA NAMAHA
Salutations to Lord Ganesha who loves the mountain

552. OM GRANTHAJNAAYA NAMAHA
Salutations to Lord Ganesha who is the knower of scriptures

553. OM GRANTHA KRITAE NAMAHA
Salutations to Lord Ganesha who is the author of scripture

554. OM GRANTAAYA NAMAHA
Salutations to Lord Ganesha who is the essence of scripture

555. OM GRANTHIBHIDAE NAMAHA
Salutations to Lord Ganesha who is the remover of obstacles in writing scripture

556. OM GRANTHAVIGHNAGHNAE NAMAHA
Salutations to Lord Ganesha who is the origin of scripture

557. OM GRANTHAADAYAE NAMAHA
Salutations to Lord Ganesha who is the vibration of the holy scripture

558. OM GRANTHASANCHAARAAYA NAMAHA
Salutations to Lord Ganesha who is immersed in listening to scripture

559. OM GRANTHASHARVANALOLUPAAYA NAMAHA
Salutations to Lord Ganesha who carries out the injunctions of scripture

560. OM GRANTHAADHEENA KRIYAAYA NAMAHA
Salutations to Lord Ganesha who is the great lover of scripture

561. OM GRANTHAPRIYAAYA NAMAHA
Salutations to Lord Ganesha who knows the philosophy of scripture

562. OM GRANTHARTHA TATTVAVIDAE NAMAHA
Salutations to Lord Ganesha who is the dispeller of doubts of scripture

563. OM GRANTHA SAMSHAYA VICHHAEDINAE NAMAHA
Salutations to Lord Ganesha who is the eloquent speaker on scripture

564. OM GRANTHAVAKTRAE NAMAHA
Salutations to Lord Ganesha who is supreme among the Gods who know scripture

565. OM GRANTHAGRANYAE NAMAHA
Salutations to Lord Ganesha whose glory is sung by scripture

566. OM GRANTHA GEETAGUNAAYA NAMAHA
Salutations to Lord Ganesha who is the song on scripture

567. OM GRANTHA GEETAAYA NAMAHA
Salutations to Lord Ganesha who is worshipped by scripture

Sri Ganesha Sahasra Naamavali

568. OM GRANTHAADI POOJITAAYA NAMAHA
     Salutations to Lord Ganesha who is praised in the beginning of scripture

569. OM GRANTHAARAMBHA STUTAAYA NAMAHA
     Salutations to Lord Ganesha who is filled with the wisdom of scripture

570. OM GRANTHA GRAAHINAE NAMAHA
     Salutations to Lord Ganesha who knows the spirit of scripture

571. OM GRANTHAARTHA PAARADRUSHAE NAMAHA
     Salutations to Lord Ganesha who is revealed through scripture

572. OM GRANTHADRUSHAE NAMAHA
     Salutations to Lord Ganesha who is the knowledge of scripture

573. OM GRANTHAVIJNAANAAYA NAMAHA
     Salutations to Lord Ganesha who is the researcher on scripture

574. OM GRANTHA SANDARBHA SHODHAKAAYA NAMAHA
     Salutations to Lord Ganesha who blesses us by revealing the esoteric meaning of the scriptures

575. OM GRANTHAKRITPOOJITAAYA NAMAHA
     Salutations to Lord Ganesha who worshipped by the authors of scripture

576. OM GRANTHAKARAAYA NAMAHA
     Salutations to Lord Ganesha who produces scripture

577. OM GRANTHAPARAAYANAAYA NAMAHA
     Salutations to Lord Ganesha who is engaged in the study of scripture

578. OM GRANTHA PAARAAYANAPARAAYA NAMAHA
     Salutations to Lord Ganesha who is engrossed in scripture

579. OM GRANTHA SANDAEHA BHANJAKAAYA NAMAHA
     Salutations to Lord Ganesha who dispells the ignorance about scripture

580. OM GRANTHA KRIDVARADAATRAE NAMAHA
     Salutations to Lord Ganesha who is the bestower of boons to the author of scripture

581. OM GRANTHKRUDGRANTHA VANDITAAYA NAMAHA
     Salutations to Lord Ganesha who is the creative intelligence of scripture

582. OM GRANTHAANURAKTAAYA NAMAHA
     Salutations to Lord Ganesha who is saluted by scripture

583. OM GRANTHAGRAAYA NAMAHA
     Salutations to Lord Ganesha who is deeply attached to scripture

584. OM GRANTHAANUGRAHADAAYAKAAYA NAMAHA
     Salutations to Lord Ganesha who knows scripture

585. OM GRANTHAATMA RAATMANAE NAMAHA
     Salutations to Lord Ganesha who showers supreme grace from scripture

586. OM GRANTHAARTHA PANDITAAYA NAMAHA
     Salutations to Lord Ganesha who is the greatest scholar who knows the meaning of scripture

LORD GANESHA

587. OM GRANTHA SOUHRIDAAYA NAMAHA
Salutations to Lord Ganesha who is dear to scripture

588. OM GRANTHA PAARANGAMAAYA NAMAHA
Salutations to Lord Ganesha who is a regular reader of scripture

589. OM GRANTHA GUNAVIDAE NAMAHA
Salutations to Lord Ganesha who is the beauty of scripture

590. OM GRANTHA VIGRAHAAYA NAMAHA
Salutations to Lord Ganesha who is the embodiment of scripture

591. OM GRANTHA SAETAVAE NAMAHA
Salutations to Lord Ganesha who is the bridge to scripture

592. OM GRANTHA HAETAVAE NAMAHA
Salutations to Lord Ganesha who is the source of scripture

593. OM GRANTHA KAETAVAE NAMAHA
Salutations to Lord Ganesha who is the fame of scripture

594. OM GRAHAAGRAGAAYA NAMAHA
Salutations to Lord Ganesha who is supreme among those who know scripture

595. OM GRANTHA POOJYAAYA NAMAHA
Salutations to Lord Ganesha who is worshipped by scripture

596. OM GRANTHAGAEYAAYA NAMAHA
Salutations to Lord Ganesha who is the creator of scripture

597. OM GRANTHAGRATHANALAALASAAYA NAMAHA
Salutations to Lord Ganesha who loves to churn the ocean of scripture

598. OM GRANTHA BHOOMAYAE NAMAHA
Salutations to Lord Ganesha who is the ground of scripture

599. OM GRAHASHRAESHTAAYA NAMAHA
Salutations to Lord Ganesha who is supreme among the planets

600. OM GRAHAKAETAVAE NAMAHA
Salutations to Lord Ganesha who is the great banner of the planets

601. OM GRAHAASHRAYAAYA NAMAHA
Salutations to Lord Ganesha who is the refuge of the planets

602. OM GRANTHA KAARAAYA NAMAHA
Salutations to Lord Ganesha who is the scriptural authority

603. OM GRANTHA KAARA MAANYAAYA NAMAHA
Salutations to Lord Ganesha who honors the authors of scripture

604. OM GRANTHAPRASAADAKAAYA NAMAHA
Salutations to Lord Ganesha who is engaged in spreading scripture

605. OM GRANTHASHRAMAJNAAYA NAMAHA
Salutations to Lord Ganesha who is the knower of scripture

Sri Ganesha Sahasra Naamavali

606. OM GRANTHAANGAAYA NAMAHA
    Salutations to Lord Ganesha who is the limbs of scripture

607. OM GRANTHA BHRAMA NIVAARAKAAYA NAMAHA
    Salutations to Lord Ganesha who is the dispeller of dilusion through the knowledge of scripture

608. OM GRANTHA PRAVANA SARVAANGAAYA NAMAHA
    Salutations to Lord Ganesha who is perfect in scripture

609. OM GRANTHA PRANAYATATPARAAYA NAMAHA
    Salutations to Lord Ganesha who is the enjoyer of scripture

610. OM GEETAAYA NAMAHA
    Salutations to Lord Ganesha who is song

611. OM GEETAGUNAAYA NAMAHA
    Salutations to Lord Ganesha who is the virtue of song

612. OM GEETA KIRTAYAE NAMAHA
    Salutations to Lord Ganesha who is the singer of song

613. OM GEETA VISHAARADAAYA NAMAHA
    Salutations to Lord Ganesha who is an expert singer

614. OM GEETA SPEETAYAESHASAE NAMAHA
    Salutations to Lord Ganesha who is the essence of song

615. OM GEETA PRANAYINAE NAMAHA
    Salutations to Lord Ganesha who is the lover of song

616. OM GEETA CHANCHURAAYA NAMAHA
    Salutations to Lord Ganesha who is the inspirer of song

617. OM GEETA PRASANNAAYA NAMAHA
    Salutations to Lord Ganesha who is pleased with song

618. OM GEETATMANAE NAMAHA
    Salutations to Lord Ganesha who is the spirit of song

619. OM GEETALOLAAYA NAMAHA
    Salutations to Lord Ganesha who is immersed in song

620. OM GATASPRUHAAYA NAMAHA
    Salutations to Lord Ganesha who is the revealer of the knowledge of song

621. OM GEETAASHRAYAAYA NAMAHA
    Salutations to Lord Ganesha who is the beautiful abode of song

622. OM GEETA MAYAAYA NAMAHA
    Salutations to Lord Ganesha who is the embodiment of song

623. OM GEETA TATTVARTHAKOVIDAAYA NAMAHA
    Salutations to Lord Ganesha who is the exponent of song

624. OM GEETA SAMSHAYASANCHHAETRAE NAMAHA
    Salutations to Lord Ganesha who is the dispeller of doubts about the power of song

LORD GANESHA

625. OM GEETA SANGEETA SHAASANAAYA NAMAHA
Salutations to Lord Ganesha who is the discipline of song

626. OM GEETAARTHAJNAAYA NAMAHA
Salutations to Lord Ganesha who is the knower of the meaning of song

627. OM GEETATATTVAAYA NAMAHA
Salutations to Lord Ganesha who is the philosophy of music

628. OM GEETAATATTVAAYA NAMAHA
Salutations to Lord Ganesha who is the philosophy behind singing

629. OM GRANTHAASHRAYAAYA NAMAHA
Salutations to Lord Ganesha who is the beautiful shelter of music

630. OM GEETAASAARAAYA NAMAHA
Salutations to Lord Ganesha who is the essence of music

631. OM GEETAKRITAE NAMAHA
Salutations to Lord Ganesha who is the creator of music

632. OM GEETA VIGNAVINAASHANAAYA NAMAHA
Salutations to Lord Ganesha who is the destroyer of obstacles in practicing music

633. OM GEETASAKTAAYA NAMAHA
Salutations to Lord Ganesha who is very much interested in music

634. OM GEETALEENAAYA NAMAHA
Salutations to Lord Ganesha who becomes one with music

635. OM GEETAVIGATA SANJWARAAYA NAMAHA
Salutations to Lord Ganesha who feels sick without music

636. OM GEETAIKADRISHAE NAMAHA
Salutations to Lord Ganesha who is revealed through spiritual music

637. OM GEETABHOOTAYAE NAMAHA
Salutations to Lord Ganesha who is the presiding deity over music

638. OM GEETAPREETAAYA NAMAHA
Salutations to Lord Ganesha who is pleased with music

639. OM GATAALASAAYA NAMAHA
Salutations to Lord Ganesha who relaxes in music

640. OM GEETAVADYAPATAVAE NAMAHA
Salutations to Lord Ganesha who is expert in instrumental music

641. OM GEETAPRABHAVAE NAMAHA
Salutations to Lord Ganesha who is the splendor of music

642. OM GEETAARTHATATTVAVIDAE NAMAHA
Salutations to Lord Ganesha who knows the philosophy of music

643. OM GEETAAGEETAVIVAEKAJNAAYA NAMAHA
Salutations to Lord Ganesha who blesses with the knowledge of music

Sri Ganesha Sahasra Naamavali

644. OM GEETAPRAVANACHETANAAYA NAMAHA
Salutations to Lord Ganesha who is the inspiration of music

645. OM GATABHIYAE NAMAHA
Salutations to Lord Ganesha who is fearless

646. OM GATAVIDVAESHAAYA NAMAHA
Salutations to Lord Ganesha who is the conqueror of jealousy

647. OM GATSAMSAARA BANDHANAAYA NAMAHA
Salutations to Lord Ganesha who is free from all bondages

648. OM GATA MAYAAYA NAMAHA
Salutations to Lord Ganesha who is free from *maya*, the illusory power

649. OM GATATRAASAAYA NAMAHA
Salutations to Lord Ganesha who is free from fatigue

650. OM GATADUKHAAYA NAMAHA
Salutations to Lord Ganesha who is free from grief

651. OM GATAJVARAAYA NAMAHA
Salutations to Lord Ganesha who is free from sickness

652. OM GATAASUHRIDAE NAMAHA
Salutations to Lord Ganesha who is free from attachment

653. OM GATAAJNAANAAYA NAMAHA
Salutations to Lord Ganesha who is free from ignorance

654. OM GATADUSHTAASHAYAAYA NAMAHA
Salutations to Lord Ganesha who is free from enemies

655. OM GATAAYA NAMAHA
Salutations to Lord Ganesha who is free

656. OM GATAARTAYAE NAMAHA
Salutations to Lord Ganesha who is free from affliction

657. OM GATASANKALPAAYA NAMAHA
Salutations to Lord Ganesha who is free from lower decisions

658. OM GATADUKHAVICHHAESHTITAAYA NAMAHA
Salutations to Lord Ganesha who is free from the thought of old enemies

659. OM GATAHANKAARA SANCHAARAAYA NAMAHA
Salutations to Lord Ganesha who is free from ego

660. OM GATADARPAAYA NAMAHA
Salutations to Lord Ganesha who is free from arrogance

661. OM GATAAHITAAYA NAMAHA
Salutations to Lord Ganesha who is free from inauspicious things

662. OM GATAADHVANTAAYA NAMAHA
Salutations to Lord Ganesha who transcends all knowledge

LORD GANESHA

663. OM GATAAVIDYAAYA NAMAHA
Salutations to Lord Ganesha who transcends all fear

664. OM GATAAGATANIVAARAKAAYA NAMAHA
Salutations to Lord Ganesha who removes the fear of the past and the future

665. OM GATAAVYATHAAYA NAMAHA
Salutations to Lord Ganesha who is free from worries

666. OM GATAPAAYAAYA NAMAHA
Salutations to Lord Ganesha who is free from danger

667. OM GATADOSHAAYA NAMAHA
Salutations to Lord Ganesha who is free of faults

668. OM GATAEHEPARASMAI NAMAHA
Salutations to Lord Ganesha who is transcendental consciousness

669. OM GATASARVAVIKAARAAYA NAMAHA
Salutations to Lord Ganesha who transcends duality

670. OM GAJAGARJITA KUNJARAAYA NAMAHA
Salutations to Lord Ganesha who bellows like the elephant

671. OM GATA KAMPITABHOOPRUSHTHAAYA NAMAHA
Salutations to Lord Ganesha who removes the fear of earthquake

672. OM GATARUSHAE NAMAHA
Salutations to Lord Ganesha who is the timeless one

673. OM GATAKALPASHAAYA NAMAHA
Salutations to Lord Ganesha who is free from any blemish

674. OM GATADAINYAAYA NAMAHA
Salutations to Lord Ganesha who is free from self-pity

675. OM GATASTAINYAAYA NAMAHA
Salutations to Lord Ganesha who has conquered sloth and sleep

676. OM GATAMAANAAYA NAMAHA
Salutations to Lord Ganesha who is beyond all honors

677. OM GATASHRAMAAYA NAMAHA
Salutations to Lord Ganesha who is free from tiredness

678. OM GATAKRODHAAYA NAMAHA
Salutations to Lord Ganesha who is free from anger

679. OM GATAGLAANAYAE NAMAHA
Salutations to Lord Ganesha who never fades

680. OM GATAMLAANAYAE NAMAHA
Salutations to Lord Ganesha who is untainted

681. OM GATABRAMHAAYA NAMAHA
Salutations to Lord Ganesha who is free from delusion

Sri Ganesha Sahasra Naamavali

682. **OM GATABHAAVAAYA NAMAHA**
Salutations to Lord Ganesha who is free from lower emotions

683. **OM GATATATTVARTHA SAMSHAYAAYA NAMAHA**
Salutations to Lord Ganesha who is free from karma

684. **OM GAYASURASHIRASHCHAETRAE NAMAHA**
Salutations to Lord Ganesha who is free from doubt

685. **OM GAYASURAVARAPRADAAYA NAMAHA**
Salutations to Lord Ganesha who severed the head of demon Gajaasura

686. **OM GAYAAVAASAAYA NAMAHA**
Salutations to Lord Ganesha who dwells in the holy pilgrimage center known as Gaya

687. **OM GAYAANAATAAYA NAMAHA**
Salutations to Lord Ganesha who is the Lord of Gaya

688. **OM GAYAAVAISINAMASKRITAAYA NAMAHA**
Salutations to Lord Ganesha who is saluted by the devotees of Gaya

689. **OM GAYAATEERTHAPHALA DYAKSHAAYA NAMAHA**
Salutations to Lord Ganesha who is the presiding deity in distributing the fruits of the pilgrimage to Gaya

690. **OM GAYAAYAATRA PHALAPRADAAYA NAMAHA**
Salutations to Lord Ganesha who is the bestower of fruits to the pilgrims who visit Gaya

691. **OM GAYAAMAYAAYA NAMAHA**
Salutations to Lord Ganesha who is the spirit of Gaya

692. **OM GAYAAKSHETRAAYA NAMAHA**
Salutations to Lord Ganesha who is the pilgrimage center, Gaya

693. **OM GAYAKSHETRANIVASAKRUTAE NAMAHA**
Salutations to Lord Ganesha who is the dweller in Gaya

694. **OM GAYAAVAASISTUTAAYA NAMAHA**
Salutations to Lord Ganesha who is praised by the angels of Gaya

695. **OM GAAYANMADHUVRITALASATKATAAYA NAMAHA**
Salutations to Lord Ganesha who has taken the vow to sing spiritual music

696. **OM GAAYAKAAYA NAMAHA**
Salutations to Lord Ganesha who is the greatest musician

697. **OM GAAYAKAVARAAYA NAMAHA**
Salutations to Lord Ganesha who is supreme among the singers

698. **OM GAAYAKESHTA PHALAPRADAAYA NAMAHA**
Salutations to Lord Ganesha who is the fulfiller of desires of musicians

699. **OM GAAYAKA PRANAYINAE NAMAHA**
Salutations to Lord Ganesha who enjoys the company of musicians

LORD GANESHA

700. **OM GAATRAE NAMAHA**
Salutations to Lord Ganesha who is the protector of musicians

701. **OM GAAYAKAABHAYADAAYA KAAYA NAMAHA**
Salutations to Lord Ganesha who makes musicians fearless

702. **OM GAAYAKA PRAVANA SVAANTAAYA NAMAHA**
Salutations to Lord Ganesha who reveals Himslef to musicians who sing "OM"

703. **OM GAAYAKA PRATHAMAAYA NAMAHA**
Salutations to Lord Ganesha who is foremost among singers

704. **OM GAAYAKODGEETA SAMPREETAAYA NAMAHA**
Salutations to Lord Ganesha who is pleased with spiritual songs

705. **OM GAAYAKODGEETA VIGNAGNAE NAMAHA**
Salutations to Lord Ganesha who is the fire that consumes the difficulties of His devotees

706. **OM GAAYAKENAAYA NAMAHA**
Salutations to Lord Ganesha who is expert in music

707. **OM GAAYA KESHAAYA NAMAHA**
Salutations to Lord Ganesha who is Lord of musicians

708. **OM GAAYA KANTARA SANCHARAAYA NAMAHA**
Salutations to Lord Ganesha who is the spirit that inspires musicians

709. **OM GAAYAKAPRIYADAAYA NAMAHA**
Salutations to Lord Ganesha who bestows good things to musicians

710. **OM GAAYAKAADHEENAVIGRAHAAYA NAMAHA**
Salutations to Lord Ganesha who gives Himself to the saintly musicians

711. **OM GEYAAYA NAMAHA**
Salutations to Lord Ganesha who is music Himself

712. **OM GEYA GUNAAYA NAMAHA**
Salutations to Lord Ganesha who is the virtue of music

713. **OM GEYACHARITAAYA NAMAHA**
Salutations to Lord Ganesha who is the history of music

714. **OM GEYATATTVAVIDHAE NAMAHA**
Salutations to Lord Ganesha who is the philosophy of music

715. **OM GAAYAKATRAASAGNAE NAMAHA**
Salutations to Lord Ganesha who burns the fatigue of musicians

716. **OM GRANTHYAAYA NAMAHA**
Salutations to Lord Ganesha who is the scripture on music

717. **OM GRANTHATATTVAVIVAECHAKAAYA NAMAHA**
Salutations to Lord Ganesha who contemplates the philosophy of scripture

718. **OM GAADAANURAAGAAYA NAMAHA**
Salutations to Lord Ganesha who is a deep lover

Sri Ganesha Sahasra Naamavali

719. OM GAADAJNAAYA NAMAHA
Salutations to Lord Ganesha who is strong-bodied

720. OM GAADAANGAAJALODVAHAAYA NAMAHA
Salutations to Lord Ganesha who loves to bathe in the Ganges

721. OM GAADAVAGAADAJALADHAYAE NAMAHA
Salutations to Lord Ganesha who is the ocean of mercy

722. OM GAADAPRAJNAAYA NAMAHA
Salutations to Lord Ganesha who has great awareness

723. OM GATAAMAYAAYA NAMAHA
Salutations to Lord Ganesha who is free from the pairs of opposites

724. OM GAADAPRATYARTHI SAINYAAYA NAMAHA
Salutations to Lord Ganesha who has a large military of angels

725. OM GAADAANUGRAHA TATPARAAYA NAMAHA
Salutations to Lord Ganesha who wants to shower the supreme grace upon His devotees

726. OM GAADAAKLESHA RASAABHIJNAAYA NAMAHA
Salutations to Lord Ganesha who knows the essence of all the scriptures

727. OM GAADANIRVRITTI SAADHAKAAYA NAMAHA
Salutations to Lord Ganesha who constantly contemplates on Himself

728. OM GANGAADHARESHTA VARADAAYA NAMAHA
Salutations to Lord Ganesha who is very dear to Shiva who holds the Ganges on His matted locks

729. OM GANGAADHARA BHAYAAPAHAAYA NAMAHA
Salutations to Lord Ganesha who removes the obstacles and fear even from Shiva, the holder of the Ganges

730. OM GANGAADHARA GURAVAE NAMAHA
Salutations to Lord Ganesha who, in certain ways, is guru even to His father, Shiva, the holder of Ganga

731. OM GANGAADHARA DHYANAPARAAYA NAMAHA
Salutations to Lord Ganesha who meditates constantly on His father, Shiva, the holder of Ganga

732. OM GANGADHARASTUTAAYA NAMAHA
Salutations to Lord Ganesha who is praised by Shiva, the holder of Ganga

733. OM GANGAADHARAA RAADHYAAYA NAMAHA
Salutations to Lord Ganesha who is worshipped by Shiva, the holder of Ganga

734. OM GATASMAYAAYA NAMAHA
Salutations to Lord Ganesha who is beyond everything

735. OM GANGADHARA PRIYAAYA NAMAHA
Salutations to Lord Ganesha who is the darling of Shiva, the holder of Ganga

LORD GANESHA

736. **OM GANGAADHARAAYA NAMAHA**
Salutations to Lord Ganesha who Himself is Shiva, the holder of Ganga

737. **OM GANGAAMBU SUNDARAAYA NAMAHA**
Salutations to Lord Ganesha who is beautiful like the Ganges

738. **OM GANGAAJALA RASAA SWAADA CHATURAAYA NAMAHA**
Salutations to Lord Ganesha who loves to drink Ganges water

739. **OM GANGAANEERAPAAYA NAMAHA**
Salutations to Lord Ganesha who meditates on Ganga

740. **OM GANGAAJALA PRANAYAVATAE NAMAHA**
Salutations to Lord Ganesha who enjoys bathing in Ganga

741. **OM GANGAATEERA VIHAARAKRITAE NAMAHA**
Salutations to Lord Ganesha who wanders on the banks of the river Ganga

742. **OM GANGAAPRIYAATMAJAAYA NAMAHA**
Salutations to Lord Ganesha who is very dear to Ganga

743. **OM GANGAAVAGAAHANA PARAAYA NAMAHA**
Salutations to Lord Ganesha who is engaged in worshipping Ganga

744. **OM GANDHAMAADANA SAMVAASAAYA NAMAHA**
Salutations to Lord Ganesha who sometimes lives in Mount Gandhamadana in the Himalayas

745. **OM GANDHAMAADHANAKELIKRUTAE NAMAHA**
Salutations to Lord Ganesha who plays in Gandhamadana mountain

746. **OM GANDHANULIPTA SARVAJNAAYA NAMAHA**
Salutations to Lord Ganesha who smears sandalwood paste all over His body

747. **OM GANDHALUBHYANMADHUVRATAAYA NAMAHA**
Salutations to Lord Ganesha who has vowed to worship with sandalwood paste

748. **OM GANDHAAYA NAMAHA**
Salutations to Lord Ganesha who Himself is gandha, the sandalwood paste

749. **OM GANDHARVA RAAJAAYA NAMAHA**
Salutations to Lord Ganesha who is king among the celestial musicians known as *gandharvas*

750. **OM GANDHARVAPRIYAKRITAE NAMAHA**
Salutations to Lord Ganesha who loves the *gandharvas*

751. **OM GANDHARVAVIDYAA TATTWAJNAAYA NAMAHA**
Salutations to Lord Ganesha who is expert in the science of music known to the *gandharvas*

752. **OM GANDHARVAPREETIVARDHANAAYA NAMAHA**
Salutations to Lord Ganesha who loves the *gandharvas* more and more

753. **OM GANKAARABEEJANILAYAAYA NAMAHA**
Salutations to Lord Ganesha who has His abode in the seed syllable, "GAM"

Sri Ganesha Sahasra Naamavali

754. **OM GANKAARAAYA NAMAHA**
Salutations to Lord Ganesha who is the fragrance of truth

755. **OM GARVIGARVANUDAE NAMAHA**
Salutations to Lord Ganesha who humbles the ego of the arrogant

756. **OM GANDHARVAGANASAMSEVAAYA NAMAHA**
Salutations to Lord Ganesha who is constantly propitiated by *gandharvas*

757. **OM GANDHARVA VARADAAYAKAAYA NAMAHA**
Salutations to Lord Ganesha who is the bestower of boons to the *gandharvas*

758. **OM GANDHARVAAYA NAMAHA**
Salutations to Lord Ganesha who is the *gandharva* or the celestial musician Himself

759. **OM GANDHAMAATANGAAYA NAMAHA**
Salutations to Lord Ganesha who is the elephant that loves sandalwood paste

760. **OM GANDHARVAKULADAIVATAAYA NAMAHA**
Salutations to Lord Ganesha who is the presiding deity of the *gandharvas*

761. **OM GANDHARVAGARVASANCHHETRAE NAMAHA**
Salutations to Lord Ganesha who is the dispeller of doubts of the *gandharvas*

762. **OM GANDHARVAVARADARPAGNAE NAMAHA**
Salutations to Lord Ganesha who is the fire that consumes the arrogance of the *gandharvas*

763. **OM GANDHARVAPRAVANA SWAANTAAYA NAMAHA**
Salutations to Lord Ganesha who is the peace of the *gandharvas*

764. **OM GANDHARVAGANA SAMSTUTAAYA NAMAHA**
Salutations to Lord Ganesha who is praised by the celestial musicians

765. **OM GANDHARVAARCHITA PAADAABJAAYA NAMAHA**
Salutations to Lord Ganesha whose lotus feet are worshipped by the *gandharvas*

766. **OM GANDHARVA BHAYADAAYINAE NAMAHA**
Salutations to Lord Ganesha who is the remover of the fear of the *gandharvas*

767. **OM GANDHARVA BHAYA HAARAKAAYA NAMAHA**
Salutations to Lord Ganesha who confers the blessing of fearlessness to the *gandharvas*

768. **OM GANDHARVA PRATIPAALAKAAYA NAMAHA**
Salutations to Lord Ganesha who maintains the devotion of the *gandharvas*

769. **OM GANDHARVA GEETACHARITAAYA NAMAHA**
Salutations to Lord Ganesha whose stories the *gandharvas* sing constantly

770. **OM GANDHARVA PRANAYOTSUKAAYA NAMAHA**
Salutations to Lord Ganesha who is always interested in the loving music of the *gandharvas*

771. **OM GANDHARVAGAANA SHRAVANA PRANAYINAE NAMAHA**
Salutations to Lord Ganesha who deeply enjoys the *gandharvas'* music

LORD GANESHA

772. **OM GANDHARBHAAJANAAYA NAMAHA**
    Salutations to Lord Ganesha who is the refuge of the *gandharvas*

773. **OM GANDHARVA TRAANA SANNADDHAAYA NAMAHA**
    Salutations to Lord Ganesha who is the giver of strength to the *gandharvas*

774. **OM GANDHARVA SAMARAKSHAMAAYA NAMAHA**
    Salutations to Lord Ganesha who fights for the *gandharvas* in the battlefield

775. **OM GANDHARVA STREEBHIRAARAADHYAAYA NAMAHA**
    Salutations to Lord Ganesha who is worshipped by the wives of the *gandharvas*

776. **OM GANAAYA NAMAHA**
    Salutations to Lord Ganesha who is the glorious music Himself

777. **OM GAANAPATAVAE NAMAHA**
    Salutations to Lord Ganesha who is highly skilled in music

778. **OM GACHHAAYA NAMAHA**
    Salutations to Lord Ganesha who is the head of the celestials

779. **OM GACHHAPATAYAE NAMAHA**
    Salutations to Lord Ganesha who is Lord of the celestials

780. **OM GACHHAVAAYAKAAYA NAMAHA**
    Salutations to Lord Ganesha who is the leader of the celestials

781. **OM GACHHAGARVAGNAE NAMAHA**
    Salutations to Lord Ganesha who is the fire that consumes the ego of the celestials

782. **OM GACHHARAAJAAYA NAMAHA**
    Salutations to Lord Ganesha who is king of the celestials

783. **OM GACHHESHAAYA NAMAHA**
    Salutations to Lord Ganesha who is the supreme authority of the celestials

784. **OM GACHHARAJANAMASKRITAAYA NAMAHA**
    Salutations to Lord Ganesha who is saluted by the head of the celestials

785. **OM GACHHAPRIYAAYA NAMAHA**
    Salutations to Lord Ganesha who is dear to the celestials

786. **OM GACHHA GURAVAE NAMAHA**
    Salutations to Lord Ganesha who is the guru of the celestials

787. **OM GACHHATRAANAKRITODYAMAAYA NAMAHA**
    Salutations to Lord Ganesha who is the strength of the celestials

788. **OM GACHHAPRABHAVAE NAMAHA**
    Salutations to Lord Ganesha who is the splendor of the celestials

789. **OM GACHHA PARAAYA NAMAHA**
    Salutations to Lord Ganesha who moves among the celestials

790. **OM GACHHAPRIYAKRITODYAMAAYA NAMAHA**
    Salutations to Lord Ganesha who is the well-wisher of the celestials

Sri Ganesha Sahasra Naamavali

791. OM GACHHAATEETAGUNAAYA NAMAHA
 Salutations to Lord Ganesha whose virtues are beyond celestial

792. OM GACHHAMARYAADA PRATIPAALAKAAYA NAMAHA
 Salutations to Lord Ganesha who maintains celestial order

793. OM GACHHADAATRAE NAMAHA
 Salutations to Lord Ganesha who is the supporter of the celestials

794. OM GACHHABHARTRAE NAMAHA
 Salutations to Lord Ganesha who is the upholder of the celestials

795. OM GACHHAVANDYAAYA NAMAHA
 Salutations to Lord Ganesha who is saluted by the celestials

796. OM GURORGURAVAE NAMAHA
 Salutations to Lord Ganesha who is the guru of all the gurus

797. OM GRUTSAAYI NAMAHA
 Salutations to Lord Ganesha who has sagely wisdom

798. OM GRUTSAMADAAYA NAMAHA
 Salutations to Lord Ganesha who is the sage called Gritsamadaaya

799. OM GRUTSA MADAABHEESHTA VARAPRADAAYA NAMAHA
 Salutations to Lord Ganesha who is the bestower of boons to the sages

800. OM GEERVAANAGEETA CHARITAAYA NAMAHA
 Salutations to Lord Ganesha whose glories are sung in Sanskrit

801. OM GEERVAANA GANASEVITAAYA NAMAHA
 Salutations to Lord Ganesha whose glories are sung by the divine species in Sanskrit

802. OM GEERVAANAVARADAATRAE NAMAHA
 Salutations to Lord Ganesha who gives boons to the divine language Sanskrit

803. OM GEERVAANABHAYANAASHAKRITAE NAMAHA
 Salutations to Lord Ganesha who is the destroyer of the fear of the *devas*

804. OM GEERVAANAGANA SANGEETAAYA NAMAHA
 Salutations to Lord Ganesha whose music is that of the *devas*

805. OM GEERVAANARAATI SOODNANAAYA NAMAHA
 Salutations to Lord Ganesha who is the remover of the afflictions from the *devas*

806. OM GEERVAANADHAAMNAE NAMAHA
 Salutations to Lord Ganesha who is the beautiful abode of the *devas*

807. OM GEERVAANAGOPTRAE NAMAHA
 Salutations to Lord Ganesha who is the sacred wisdom of the *devas*

808. OM GEERVAANA GARVANUDAE NAMAHA
 Salutations to Lord Ganesha who is the destroyer of ego of the *devas*

809. OM GEERVAANAARTI HARAAYA NAMAHA
 Salutations to Lord Ganesha who is the destroyer of the troubles of the *devas*

LORD GANESHA

810. OM GEERVAANA VARADAAYAKAAYA NAMAHA
Salutations to Lord Ganesha who showers blessings upon the *devas*

811. OM GEERVAANA SHARANAAYA NAMAHA
Salutations to Lord Ganesha who is the refuge of the surrendered *devas*

812. OM GEETANAAMNAE NAMAHA
Salutations to Lord Ganesha who is the cosmic sound

813. OM GEERVAANA SUNDARAAYA NAMAHA
Salutations to Lord Ganesha who is most beautiful among the *devas*

814. OM GEERVAANA PRANADAAYAKAAYA NAMAHA
Salutations to Lord Ganesha who is the giver of life to the *devas*

815. OM GACCHHATAE NAMAHA
Salutations to Lord Ganesha who is the goal of the *devas*

816. OM GEERVAANAANIKARAKSHAKAAYA NAMAHA
Salutations to Lord Ganesha who is the protector of the *devas*

817. OM GUHEHAA POORAKAAYA NAMAHA
Salutations to Lord Ganesha who is the fulfiller of the wishes of the *devas*

818. OM GANDHAMATTAAYA NAMAHA
Salutations to Lord Ganesha who is intoxicated with fragrance

819. OM GEERVAANA PUSHTIDAAYA NAMAHA
Salutations to Lord Ganesha who showers prosperity on the *devas*

820. OM GEERVAANA PRAYUTATRAATRAE NAMAHA
Salutations to Lord Ganesha who fights for the cause of the *devas*

821. OM GEETA GOTRAAYA NAMAHA
Salutations to Lord Ganesha whose lineage is "OM"

822. OM GATAHITAAYA NAMAHA
Salutations to Lord Ganesha who is beyond good and bad

823. OM GEERVAANA SEVITAPADAAYA NAMAHA
Salutations to Lord Ganesha whose lotus feet are worshipped by the *devas*

824. OM GEERVAANA PRATHITAAYA NAMAHA
Salutations to Lord Ganesha who is the light of the *devas*

825. OM GALATAE NAMAHA
Salutations to Lord Ganesha who is the life of the *devas*

826. OM GEERVAANAGOTRA PRAVARAAYA NAMAHA
Salutations to Lord Ganesha who makes the lineage of the *devas* prosperous

827. OM GEERVAANAPHALADAAYAKAAYA NAMAHA
Salutations to Lord Ganesha who is the giver of strength to the *devas*

828. OM GEERVAANAPRIYAKARTRAE NAMAHA
Salutations to Lord Ganesha who does good to the *devas*

Sri Ganesha Sahasra Naamavali

829. OM GEERVAANAAGAMAASAARAVIDAE NAMAHA
    Salutations to Lord Ganesha who has complete knowledge of the *devas*

830. OM GEERVAANAAGAMAASAMPATTAYAE NAMAHA
    Salutations to Lord Ganesha who has the wealth of the knowledge of the *devas*

831. OM GEERVAANA VYASANAAPAGNAE NAMAHA
    Salutations to Lord Ganesha who sets fire to the worries of the *devas*

832. OM GEERVAANA PRANAYAAYA NAMAHA
    Salutations to Lord Ganesha who is the lover of the *devas*

833. OM GEETA GRAHANOTSUKAMAANASAAYA NAMAHA
    Salutations to Lord Ganesha whose mind is always on music

834. OM GEERVAANA MADASAMHARTRAE NAMAHA
    Salutations to Lord Ganesha who is the destroyer of the arrogance of the *devas*

835. OM GEERVAANAGANA PAALAKAAYA NAMAHA
    Salutations to Lord Ganesha who is the protector of the divine species

836. OM GRAHAPATAYE NAMAHA
    Salutations to Lord Ganesha who is the presiding deity over the planets

837. OM GRAHAAYA NAMAHA
    Salutations to Lord Ganesha who is the planet Himself

838. OM GRAHAPEEDAAPRANAASHANAAYA NAMAHA
    Salutations to Lord Ganesha who receives our worship

839. OM GRAHASTUTAAYA NAMAHA
    Salutations to Lord Ganesha who removes the afflictions coming from the planets

840. OM GRAHAADHYAKSHYAAYA NAMAHA
    Salutations to Lord Ganesha who is propitiated by the planets

841. OM GRAHESHAAYA NAMAHA
    Salutations to Lord Ganesha who is the supervisor of the planets

842. OM GRAHADAIVATAAYA NAMAHA
    Salutations to Lord Ganesha who is supreme among the planets

843. OM GRAHAKRITAE NAMAHA
    Salutations to Lord Ganesha who is God of the planets

844. OM GRAHABHARTRAE NAMAHA
    Salutations to Lord Ganesha who is the creator of the planets

845. OM GRAHESHAANAAYA NAMAHA
    Salutations to Lord Ganesha who is the supporter of the planets

846. OM GRAHESHVARAAYA NAMAHA
    Salutations to Lord Ganesha who is the leader of the planets

847. OM GRAHAARADHYAAYA NAMAHA
    Salutations to Lord Ganesha who is the authority on the planets

LORD GANESHA

848. OM GRAHATRAATAE NAMAHA
Salutations to Lord Ganesha who is worshipped by the planets

849. OM GRAHAGOPTRAE NAMAHA
Salutations to Lord Ganesha who is the uplifter of the planets

850. OM GRAHOTKATAAYA NAMAHA
Salutations to Lord Ganesha who is the spirit of the planets

851. OM GRAHAGEETAGUNAAYA NAMAHA
Salutations to Lord Ganesha who is the wealth of the planets

852. OM GRANTHAPRANETRAE NAMAHA
Salutations to Lord Ganesha who is praised by the planets

853. OM GRAHA VANDITAAYA NAMAHA
Salutations to Lord Ganesha who is the inspirer for all the scriptures

854. OM GARVINAE NAMAHA
Salutations to Lord Ganesha who is saluted by the planets

855. OM GARVEESHWARAAYA NAMAHA
Salutations to Lord Ganesha who is the cow of plenty

856. OM GARVAAYA NAMAHA
Salutations to Lord Ganesha who is Lord of the cattle

857. OM GARVISHTAAYA NAMAHA
Salutations to Lord Ganesha who is proud of His position

858. OM GARVA GARVIGHNAE NAMAHA
Salutations to Lord Ganesha who dramatizes His pride

859. OM GAVAAMPRIYAAYA NAMAHA
Salutations to Lord Ganesha who is the lover of His devotees

860. OM GAVAANAATHAAYA NAMAHA
Salutations to Lord Ganesha who is the chosen deity of His devotees

861. OM GAVEESHAANAAYA NAMAHA
Salutations to Lord Ganesha who is the destroyer of arrogance

862. OM GAVAMPATYAE NAMAHA
Salutations to Lord Ganesha who is the supreme Lord of devotees

863. OM GAVYA PRIYAAYA NAMAHA
Salutations to Lord Ganesha who is the life of His devotees

864. OM GAVAANGOPTRAE NAMAHA
Salutations to Lord Ganesha who loves the food offered with devotion

865. OM GAVEESAMPATTI SAADHAKAAYA NAMAHA
Salutations to Lord Ganesha who is the trustworthy deity of devotees

866. OM GAVEERAKSHANA SANNADDHAAYA NAMAHA
Salutations to Lord Ganesha who is wealth given to the devotees

Sri Ganesha Sahasra Naamavali

867. **OM GAVEEBHAYA HARAAYA NAMAHA**
Salutations to Lord Ganesha who is ready to protect His devotees

868. **OM GAVEEGARVADHARAAYA NAMAHA**
Salutations to Lord Ganesha who is the remover of the fear of devotees

869. **OM GODAAYA NAMAHA**
Salutations to Lord Ganesha who humbles the ego of His devotees

870. **OM GOPRADAAYA NAMAHA**
Salutations to Lord Ganesha who is the bestower of plenty

871. **OM GOJAYAPRADAAYA NAMAHA**
Salutations to Lord Ganesha who is the giver of cattle wealth

872. **OM GAJAYUTABALAAYA NAMAHA**
Salutations to Lord Ganesha who causes victory of the devotees

873. **OM GANDAGUNJAN MATTA MADHUVRATAAYA NAMAHA**
Salutations to Lord Ganesha who is the strength of the devotees

874. **OM GANDASTHALAGALADHANA MILAN MATTALI MANDITAAYA NAMAHA**
Salutations to Lord Ganesha who has taken the pledge of protecting the *dharma*

875. **OM GUDAAYA NAMAHA**
Salutations to Lord Ganesha who is sweet

876. **OM GUDAPRIYAAYA NAMAHA**
Salutations to Lord Ganesha who loves sweets

877. **OM GANDAGALADDANAAYA NAMAHA**
Salutations to Lord Ganesha who blesses with His trunk

878. **OM GUDAASHANAAYA NAMAHA**
Salutations to Lord Ganesha who enjoys the divine porridge

879. **OM GUDAAKESHAAYA NAMAHA**
Salutations to Lord Ganesha who has no lassitude

880. **OM GUDAAKESHASAHAYAAYA NAMAHA**
Salutations to Lord Ganesha who is the supporter of those who have conquered laziness

881. **OM GUDALADHUBHUJAE NAMAHA**
Salutations to Lord Ganesha who loves to eat *ladhu* (the sweet balls)

882. **OM GUDABHUJAE NAMAHA**
Salutations to Lord Ganesha who is a sweet-eater

883. **OM GUDABUGGUNYAAYA NAMAHA**
Salutations to Lord Ganesha who is the great eater

884. **OM GUDAKESHAVARAPRADAAYA NAMAHA**
Salutations to Lord Ganesha who gives boons to the alert yogis

LORD GANESHA

885. OM GUDAAKESHAARCHITA PRADAAYA NAMAHA
Salutations to Lord Ganesha who is worshipped by the great yogis

886. OM GUDAAKESHA SAKHAAYA NAMAHA
Salutations to Lord Ganesha who is a friend of the yogis

887. OM GADAADHARAARCHITA PADAAYA NAMAHA
Salutations to Lord Ganesha whose feet are worshipped even by Vishnu

888. OM GADAADHARA JAYAPRADAAYA NAMAHA
Salutations to Lord Ganesha who brings victory to Vishnu

889. OM GADAAYUDHAAYA NAMAHA
Salutations to Lord Ganesha who is the wielder of the mace

890. OM GADAAPAANAYAE NAMAHA
Salutations to Lord Ganesha who is the holder of the club

891. OM GADAAYUDDHA VISHAARADAAYA NAMAHA
Salutations to Lord Ganesha who is expert in fighting with the mace

892. OM GADAAGNAE NAMAHA
Salutations to Lord Ganesha who is supreme in the knowledge of wielding the mace

893. OM GADADARPAGNAAYA NAMAHA
Salutations to Lord Ganesha who is the destroyer of arrogance of the demon Gada

894. OM GADAGARVA PRANAASHANAAYA NAMAHA
Salutations to Lord Ganesha who is the dispeller of the ego of the demon Gada

895. OM GADAGRASTAPARITRAATRAE NAMAHA
Salutations to Lord Ganesha who protected the surrendered demon Gada

896. OM GADAADAMBARA KHANDAKAAYA NAMAHA
Salutations to Lord Ganesha who condemned the arrogant ways of the demon Gada

897. OM GUHAAYA NAMAHA
Salutations to Lord Ganesha who is the great secret

898. OM GUHAAGRAJAAYA NAMAHA
Salutations to Lord Ganesha who is the elder brother of Goha, who is Subrahmanya, the second son of Shiva

899. OM GUPTAAYA NAMAHA
Salutations to Lord Ganesha who has a hidden trunk

900. OM GUHAASHAAYINAE NAMAHA
Salutations to Lord Ganesha who rests in the holy cave (of our heart)

901. OM GUHAASHAYAAYA NAMAHA
Salutations to Lord Ganesha who dwells in our heart

902. OM GUHAPRITIKARAAYA NAMAHA
Salutations to Lord Ganesha who loves the devotees' hearts

903. OM GOODHAAYA NAMAHA
Salutations to Lord Ganesha who is a mystery

Sri Ganesha Sahasra Naamavali

904. OM GOODHAGULPHAAYA NAMAHA
    Salutations to Lord Ganesha who is a mysterious principle

905. OM GUNAEKADRISHAE NAMAHA
    Salutations to Lord Ganesha who is One without a second in virtue

906. OM GIRAE NAMAHA
    Salutations to Lord Ganesha who is the mountain of virtue

907. OM GEESHPATAYAE NAMAHA
    Salutations to Lord Ganesha who is the dweller in the mountain

908. OM GIREESHAANAAYA NAMAHA
    Salutations to Lord Ganesha who is Lord of the mountain

909. OM GEERDAEVIGEETA SADGUNAAYA NAMAHA
    Salutations to Lord Ganesha who is the source of vocabulary

910. OM GEERDEVAAYA NAMAHA
    Salutations to Lord Ganesha who is the source of eloquence

911. OM GEESHPRAYAAYA NAMAHA
    Salutations to Lord Ganesha who is the lover of words

912. OM GEERBHUVAE NAMAHA
    Salutations to Lord Ganesha who is the universe of knowledge

913. OM GEERAATMANAE NAMAHA
    Salutations to Lord Ganesha who is the spirit of knowledge

914. OM GEESHPRIYANKARAAYA NAMAHA
    Salutations to Lord Ganesha who is the lover of knowledge

915. OM GEERBHOOMAYAE NAMAHA
    Salutations to Lord Ganesha who is Lord to the ground of knowledge

916. OM GEERA SANJNAAYA NAMAHA
    Salutations to Lord Ganesha who is the essence of knowledge

917. OM GEEHI PRASANNAAYA NAMAHA
    Salutations to Lord Ganesha who is the bliss of knowledge

918. OM GIREESHWARAAYA NAMAHA
    Salutations to Lord Ganesha who is the Lord of mountains

919. OM GIREESHAJAAYA NAMAHA
    Salutations to Lord Ganesha who is the son of Shakti, the mountain daughter

920. OM GIROSHAYINAE NAMAHA
    Salutations to Lord Ganesha who rests in the mountains

921. OM GIRIRAAJA SUKHAVAHAAYA NAMAHA
    Salutations to Lord Ganesha who gives happiness to the mountain king

922. OM GIRIRAAJARCHITA PADAAYA NAMAHA
    Salutations to Lord Ganesha whose lotus feet are worshipped by the mountain king

LORD GANESHA

923. **OM GIRIRAAJA NAMASKRITAAYA NAMAHA**
Salutations to Lord Ganesha who is saluted by the mountain king

924. **OM GIRIRAAJA GUHAAVISHTAAYA NAMAHA**
Salutations to Lord Ganesha who meditates in the caves of the mountain king

925. **OM GIRIRAAJA ABHAYA PRADAAYA NAMAHA**
Salutations to Lord Ganesha who makes the mountain king fearless

926. **OM GIRIRAJESHTA VARADAAYA NAMAHA**
Salutations to Lord Ganesha who is the fulfiller of wishes of the mountain king

927. **OM GIRIRAAJA PRAPAALAKAAYA NAMAHA**
Salutations to Lord Ganesha who is the protector of the mountain king

928. **OM GIRIRAAJA SUTAASOONAVAE NAMAHA**
Salutations to Lord Ganesha who is the son of the daughter of the mountain king

929. **OM GIRIRAAJA JAYAPRADAAYA NAMAHA**
Salutations to Lord Ganesha who brings victory to the mountain king

930. **OM GIRIVRAJA VANASTAAYINAE NAMAHA**
Salutations to Lord Ganesha who stays with the mountain people

931. **OM GIRIVRAJA CHARAAYA NAMAHA**
Salutations to Lord Ganesha who moves with the mountain people

932. **OM GARGAAYA NAMAHA**
Salutations to Lord Ganesha who is wisdom embodied

933. **OM GARGAPRIYAAYA NAMAHA**
Salutations to Lord Ganesha who is dear to Sage Garga

934. **OM GARGADEVAAYA NAMAHA**
Salutations to Lord Ganesha who is the God of Sage Garga

935. **OM GARGANAMASKRUTAAYA NAMAHA**
Salutations to Lord Ganesha who is saluted by Sage Garga

936. **OM GARGA BHEETI HARAAYA NAMAHA**
Salutations to Lord Ganesha who removed the fear of Sage Garga

937. **OM GARGAVARADAAYA NAMAHA**
Salutations to Lord Ganesha who brought the highest blessing to Sage Garga

938. **OM GARGASAMSTUTAAYA NAMAHA**
Salutations to Lord Ganesha who is praised by Sage Garga

939. **OM GARGAGEETA PRASANNATMANAE NAMAHA**
Salutations to Lord Ganesha who is pleased with the prayer of Sage Garga

940. **OM GARGANANDA KARAAYA NAMAHA**
Salutations to Lord Ganesha who gave bliss to Sage Garga

941. **OM GARGAPRIYAAYA NAMAHA**
Salutations to Lord Ganesha who is dear to Sage Garga

Sri Ganesha Sahasra Naamavali

942. OM GARGAMAANA PRADAAYA NAMAHA
    Salutations to Lord Ganesha who brought honor to Sage Garga

943. OM GARGAARI BHANJAKAAYA NAMAHA
    Salutations to Lord Ganesha who conquered the enemies of Sage Garga

944. OM GARGAVARGA PARITRAATRAE NAMAHA
    Salutations to Lord Ganesha who protected Sage Garga's family

945. OM GARGASIDDHI PRADAAYAKAAYA NAMAHA
    Salutations to Lord Ganesha who blessed Sage Garga with *siddhi* or supernatural powers

946. OM GARGAGLANIHARAAYA NAMAHA
    Salutations to Lord Ganesha who removed the afflictions of Sage Garga

947. OM GARGASHRAMANUDAE NAMAHA
    Salutations to Lord Ganesha who healed the sickness of Sage Garga

948. OM GARGASANGATAAYA NAMAHA
    Salutations to Lord Ganesha who is the friend of Sage Garga

949. OM GARGACHAARYAAYA NAMAHA
    Salutations to Lord Ganesha who channelled through Sage Garga

950. OM GARGARISHAYAE NAMAHA
    Salutations to Lord Ganesha who appeared as Sage Garga

951. OM GARGASANMANABHAAJANAAYA NAMAHA
    Salutations to Lord Ganesha who celebrated the honoring ceremony for Sage Garga

952. OM GAMBHEERAAYA NAMAHA
    Salutations to Lord Ganesha who is sublime

953. OM GANITAPRAJNAAYA NAMAHA
    Salutations to Lord Ganesha who is the master of mathematics

954. OM GANITAAGAMA SAARAVIDAE NAMAHA
    Salutations to Lord Ganesha who knows the essence of Vedic mathematics

955. OM GANAKAAYA NAMAHA
    Salutations to Lord Ganesha who is Lord of the *ganas*

956. OM GANAKASHLAGHYAAYA NAMAHA
    Salutations to Lord Ganesha who is praised by the *ganas*

957. OM GANAKA PRANAYOTSUKAAYA NAMAHA
    Salutations to Lord Ganesha who is loved by the *ganas*

958. OM GANAKA PRAVANA SVAANTAAYA NAMAHA
    Salutations to Lord Ganesha who brings peace to the *ganas*

959. OM GANITAAYA NAMAHA
    Salutations to Lord Ganesha who is the science of mathematics

960. OM GANITAAGAMAAYA NAMAHA
    Salutations to Lord Ganesha who is the knowledge of mathematics

LORD GANESHA

961. OM GADYAAYA NAMAHA
    Salutations to Lord Ganesha who is knowledge Himself

962. OM GADYAMAYAAYA NAMAHA
    Salutations to Lord Ganesha who is knowledge embodied

963. OM GADYAPADYA VIDYA VIVECHAKAAYA NAMAHA
    Salutations to Lord Ganesha who has thorough wisdom of prose and poetry

964. OM GALALAGNAMAHAANAAGAAYA NAMAHA
    Salutations to Lord Ganesha who is cosmic energy

965. OM GALADARCHISHAE NAMAHA
    Salutations to Lord Ganesha who is worshipped by the universal energy

966. OM GALANMADAAYA NAMAHA
    Salutations to Lord Ganesha who is intoxicated with energy

967. OM GALATKUSHTA VYATHAA HANTRAE NAMAHA
    Salutations to Lord Ganesha who is filled with energy that destroys any obstacles

968. OM GALATKUSHTI SUKHA PRADAAYA NAMAHA
    Salutations to Lord Ganesha who is the great energy that brings happiness to all

969. OM GAMBHEERA NAABHAYAE NAMAHA
    Salutations to Lord Ganesha who is the sublime-bodied one

970. OM GAMBHEERA SVARAAYA NAMAHA
    Salutations to Lord Ganesha who has a sublime voice

971. OM GAMBHEERA LOCHANAAYA NAMAHA
    Salutations to Lord Ganesha who has beautiful eyes

972. OM GAMBHEERA GUNASAMPANNAAYA NAMAHA
    Salutations to Lord Ganesha who is filled with sublime virtues

973. OM GAMBHEERAGATI SHOBHANAAYA NAMAHA
    Salutations to Lord Ganesha who walks with majestic steps

974. OM GARBHA PRADAAYA NAMAHA
    Salutations to Lord Ganesha who blesses with progeny

975. OM GARBHAROOPAAYA NAMAHA
    Salutations to Lord Ganesha who is the life of the embryo

976. OM GARBHAAPADA NIVAARAKAAYA NAMAHA
    Salutations to Lord Ganesha who removes the danger to the embryo

977. OM GARBHAGAMANA SAMBHUTAYAE NAMAHA
    Salutations to Lord Ganesha who dwells as the spirit of the baby in the embryo

978. OM GARBHADAAYA NAMAHA
    Salutations to Lord Ganesha who envelops the embryo to protect the child

979. OM GARBHASHOKANUDAE NAMAHA
    Salutations to Lord Ganesha who removes the grief of the baby

Sri Ganesha Sahasra Naamavali

980. OM GARBHATRAATRAE NAMAHA
    Salutations to Lord Ganesha who is the protector of the womb

981. OM GARBHAGOPTRAE NAMAHA
    Salutations to Lord Ganesha who is the hidden power of the womb

982. OM GARBHAPUSHTIKARAAYA NAMAHA
    Salutations to Lord Ganesha who strengthens the embryonic child

983. OM GARBHAGOURAVA SANDHANA SADHANAAYA NAMAHA
    Salutations to Lord Ganesha who brings honor to the baby

984. OM GARBHAGARVA NUDAE NAMAHA
    Salutations to Lord Ganesha who removes the ego of the pregnant woman

985. OM GARBHASHRAYAAYA NAMAHA
    Salutations to Lord Ganesha who is the greatest of all

986. OM GARBHAMAYAAYA NAMAHA
    Salutations to Lord Ganesha who is highly dignified

987. OM GARBHAA MAYANIVAARAKAAYA NAMAHA
    Salutations to Lord Ganesha who is the destroyer of ego

988. OM GARBHAA DHARAAYA NAMAHA
    Salutations to Lord Ganesha who is the destroyer of hatred

989. OM GARBHASANTOSHA SAADHAKAAYA NAMAHA
    Salutations to Lord Ganesha who is the solace of the afflicted

990. OM GAREEYASAE NAMAHA
    Salutations to Lord Ganesha who is the supreme truth

991. OM GARVANUDAE NAMAHA
    Salutations to Lord Ganesha who is the supreme principle

992. OM GARVAMARDINAE NAMAHA
    Salutations to Lord Ganesha who is the destroyer of ego

993. OM GARASANTAAPASHAMANAAYA NAMAHA
    Salutations to Lord Ganesha who is the healer of all grief

994. OM GURURAAJA SUKHAPRADAAYA NAMAHA
    Salutations to Lord Ganesha who is the king of the gurus who bring happiness

995. OM GANAJNAANA PARAAYANAAYA NAMAHA
    Salutations to Lord Ganesha who is who is absorbed in the knowledge of the creation of the *ganas*

996. OM GANAAGAMAJNAAYA NAMAHA
    Salutations to Lord Ganesha who is the knower of all the *ganas*

997. OM GANAANGAAYA NAMAHA
    Salutations to Lord Ganesha who is the limbs and the strength of the *ganas*

998. OM GAANA PRAVANACHETANAAYA NAMAHA
    Salutations to Lord Ganesha who is the spirit of the heavenly music

LORD GANESHA

999. OM GAANADHYAEYAAYA NAMAHA
Salutations to Lord Ganesha who is the goal of the music

1000. OM GAANAGAMYAAYA NAMAHA
Salutations to Lord Ganesha who is realized through spiritual music

ITI SRI GANAPATI SAHASRANAAMAVALIHI SAMPURNAM

Here ends the thousand names of and thousand salutations to Lord Ganesha in full

OM SHANTIHI SHANTIHI SHANTIHI